NEWS FOR THE 99%

NEWS FOR THE 99%

VOLUME 1

TIM WHEELER

Tim Wheeler
Sequim, WA
July 6, 2023

Published by International Publishers.

First Edition 2019

ISBN-10 0-7178-0755-X   ISBN-13 978-0-7178-0755-0
Typeset by Amnet Systems, Chennai, India

Dedication

For George A. Meyers, son of an Appalachian coal miner. Fearless union organizer, he was first to feel 'fresh winds' of class struggle blowing in the ranks of the working class. Witch hunters put him in prison for four years on false charges that he 'advocated force and violence.' He was the gentlest man in creation. They hated him because he organized the unorganized, African American, Latino, and white, women and men, Gay and straight, to fight for living wage jobs, equality, a safe and healthy environment, world peace, and socialism. We loved him. We will fight for what he fought for.

Table of Contents

Foreword

I first met Tim Wheeler nearly forty years ago and took an immediate liking to him. His warmth and joyful manner were infectious. I felt like I'd known him for years.

In retrospect, these qualities and his boundless energy, empathy, dogged determinism, inquisitiveness, and broad knowledge made Tim, a great journalist, and editor. I imagine practically anyone, except for a corporate boss, would feel immediately at ease sharing their story with him, knowing it was reaching sympathetic and understanding ears.

I'm not sure Tim ever intended to be a journalist. More likely journalism discovered him. Either way, he took to it like a fish to water, becoming a master storyteller, penning some 10,000 articles over nearly six decades. That's a lot of writing and a lot of getting to know people.

Tim freely acknowledges none of this would have been possible without the support and collaboration of his life's partner, lover and comrade, Joyce, herself a teacher, union and community activist, and mother of the couple's three rambunctious children. The stresses and strains, joys and heartaches of the Wheeler family are woven through his work.

Tim's journalism is motivated by a profound sense of optimism, humanism and working-class solidarity. Here is a refutation of the figment that journalism must be non-partisan to be objective. The veil is ripped from the corporate mass media, dominated by a few global conglomerates who shape the thinking of billions with their own class and social bias.

Tim's journalism spans the transition from print to the early days of digital media. In many respects, he anticipated the grassroots people's journalism of the internet age. His approach is brimming with anger over injustice and hypocrisy, partisan to the working class, and always challenging anti-working-class, racist, and other stereotypes. His writing voice is authentic, the same passionate voice you hear when he speaks or belts out a song.

And Tim is no sideline spectator either. He is immersed in many of the struggles he reports on. This gives him a deep understanding of the issues and the people. It explains his desire to give voice to those ignored and misrepresented by the corporate media. In the halls of Congress and at the White House, Tim told the truth to power. "My job as Washington correspondent was to expose, expose, expose, and expose again," he writes.

I became an avid reader of Tim's stories in the Daily World and People's World when I was in my 20s. His were often the first articles I was drawn to when opening the publication. Each story became my personal connection to some important event, many of which had national and global implications.

I invariably gained more profound insight into some class, racist or sexist outrage, or someone or some group of workers, or some community that courageously took a stand against seemingly insurmountable odds. Each story was told in the person's voice whether a coal miner, farmer, grieving parent, or protester. What we get are real stories of real people in real life in their living rooms, communities, workplaces and picket lines.

Tim's stories are a Marxist, working-class interpretation of crucial political events from the 1960s to the present. They chronicle the struggle of the American people to defend and expand democracy, for social justice, peace, and environmental protection.

They include anti-Vietnam war and Civil Rights protests, the Newark rebellion, anti-nuclear demonstrations, Watergate and Iran Contra scandals, 2000 election coup, Hurricane Katrina and other natural and industrial disasters, Democratic and Republican conventions, strikes, the collapse of socialism in the USSR and Eastern Europe, and rise of the modern extreme right and today's massive social justice movements.

Many of these gems are collected in this delightful two-volume set. They help us understand the events that have shaped our lives and the roots of the present political juncture pregnant with potential and danger. They are a gift to today's young activists who draw strength from what came before.

In reading the manuscript, I discovered articles of events I vividly recall from my youth. Tim bathes them in a new light. One is an interview with Jock Yablonski, the courageous leader of the rank and file movement to reform the United Mine Workers Union. I was a teenager living in Pittsburgh in 1969 when Yablonski, his wife, and daughter were brutally murdered by coal bosses and the corrupt Tony Boyle union leadership. The gruesome slayings, the last of the political assassinations of the 1960s, riveting the nation's attention for days. I remember being utterly horrified and sickened.

But here you'll find Tim's telling of the story, his interactions with Yablonski, moving coverage of the funeral overflowing with mourners, the grief and anger of the coal miners who bore the coffin of their martyred leader, and how the murders spurred on the reform movement.

Tim learned from some of the best Marxist journalists the U.S. working class has produced including Art Shields, Si Gerson, Carl Winters, James Jackson, and Billy Allen. In turn, he became one of the best working-class journalists of his era.

Tim acknowledges his debt to Shields, perhaps the greatest of U.S. labor reporters. Shields told Tim that every story naturally had villains and heroes. Shields was also acutely aware the rise of television presented unique challenges to print journalism. He insisted that writing had to reflect reality in all its complexity and visualized as if one were watching tv.

Among the most touching stories are the portraits of people Tim befriended and worked alongside. They include iconic journalists I.F. Stone and Helen Thomas, the Communist Party USA (CPUSA) labor secretary George A. Meyers, and steelworker rank and file leaders

Joe Henderson and Charlie Parrish, Civil Rights leader C.T. Vivian, leader of anti-war veterans David Cline, Jessica Lynch and Veterans of the Abraham Lincoln Brigade leader Moe Fishman.

One of my favorite portraits is of Frank Novich, a mutual friend and comrade. Frank was a coal miner in his youth, a merchant marine, and seafarer. Blacklisted for his union activity and CPUSA membership, Frank fought a long but ultimately victorious battle along with other blacklisted seafarers to return to work. But here we have the story of Frank and the mine mule he named Hannah. The story is told with such tenderness, affection, and humor it will have you laughing and crying.

Enjoy each gem. You're in for a treat.

John Bachtell
Chicago, 2019

Preface

Why I Wrote This Book

I estimate that in over half century as a journalist I have written about 10,000 articles, all of them "hunt and peck" with my two index fingers, starting with an old Underwood manual, graduating to a Tandy 200 laptop and finally to the battered, second hand MacBook I am typing on right now.

This book is a compilation of the best of those stories. It is not a memoir. Yes, I am in this book from start to finish. But I am not the subject of the book. I am the reporter. The subject is whatever arena of struggle I was assigned to cover. The heroes are the women and men locked in struggle to defend themselves and their families against natural or man-made disasters. I have tried to put "blood, sweat, and tears" into my stories. There was also plenty of laughter and joy along the way. Art Shields, the greatest labor reporter of all time told me often "make your stories sing."

This book is a record of more than half a century of the history of our nation and the world as I observed it. Since it consists mostly of breaking stories I wrote as the events were happening, they are a "primary source" not a reflection on those events written years or even months later. I tried to keep the stories more or less in chronological order but I often put two or three stories together if they had a common theme.

Virtually all the stories I wrote were assignments from the *Worker, Daily World, People's Weekly World* and the online *People's World*, publications sustained and circulated by the Communist Party USA (CPUSA). It gives me joy that my book is being published in 2019, centennial year of the founding of the CPUSA in Chicago in 1919. I joined the CPUSA in 1959—sixty years ago. Seven years

later, in 1966, I joined the staff of *The Worker*. I learned
to write from masters of the trade: Art Shields, Joe North,
Carl Winter, Si Gerson, John and Margrit Pittman, Ted
Bassett, George Morris, Mike Davidow, Erik Bert, Detroit
Bureau Chief, Billy Allen, many others. Today, the staff
of the online *People's World* keeps the banners flying of
class-struggle journalism. I salute them.

Another thought as I read over these stories. So many
of the crimes and foul deeds of our government, the
banks and corporations, are committed, reported in the
media for a few weeks or months and then forgotten.
The criminals get away even when they swindle millions
of people of billions, maybe even trillions of dollars in life
savings, homeowner equity, wages. An example is the
Savings and Loan scandal of the early 1990s. People's
life savings were wiped out. Hundreds of millions were
lost and stolen. Few, in any, went to jail and after some
months of headline coverage, the story vanished.

The same with the sub-prime mortgage crisis during
the administration of George W. Bush. Millions of home
buyers were duped into buying homes they could not
afford, paying ruinous mortgage rates, sometimes over
half their income. The bubble burst and the nation was
plunged into the worst economic crisis since the Great
Depression. Not a single one of the ringleaders of this
crisis was tried or convicted. And virtually no financial
reforms were enacted to prevent a recurrence of this
disaster which cost the people trillions in lost equity
and wages. Now the Republican-majority House and
Senate, and Donald Trump, are moving ruthlessly to
repeal Dodd-Frank and the meager few other safeguards
enacted to prevent a recurrence of the Bush-Cheney economic disaster. It is just a matter of time before another
economic collapse engulfs our nation.

I wrote many stories covering this crisis. One case
of grand larceny in particular exposes the capitalist
media's role in concealing the criminals. It is the series
of articles written by Pete Brewton in the *Houston Post*
exposing the role of the CIA in looting the Savings and

Loan banks to help pay for Ronald Reagan's criminal wars in Central America. The *Houston Post* expected this story to go viral. They sent out an alert that the series would appear and that reporters could come to their Washington bureau and pick up the series. I went to the *Houston Post* bureau. A long line of journalists was waiting to pick up the series. Yet none of the major dailies like the *New York Times* or the *Washington Post* picked up on this blockbuster expose. The People's Weekly World reported it. A year or so after Brewton's exposes, the *Houston Post* declared bankruptcy.

In 1996, the San Jose *Mercury News* ran a series of articles titled "Dark Alliance" by investigative reporter, Gary Webb, exposing CIA links to a drug smuggling ring in San Francisco that was bringing vast quantities of crack cocaine into California sold in the Black community, feeding the crisis of crack addiction, death from drug overdose, gun violence and mass incarceration in the Black community.

This narcotics racket generated ample loot for the CIA to bankroll its illegal, unconstitutional, and immoral wars in Central America. That story, too, was erased from the front pages by the ruling circles. Gary Webb was found dead with two gunshot wounds. It was ruled suicide although skeptics asked: How does a person who shoots himself to death shoot himself twice?

Did the CIA exact the ultimate revenge? I found one of the stories I wrote based on Webb's groundbreaking exposes. It is included in this book.

I too was bitten by a news reporter's lust for covering "breaking news." If a mine exploded, I went to the mine to interview the families of the trapped miners. If a factory caught fire and the exit doors were locked, I was on my way to North Carolina to cover the tragedy. If "high crimes" were committed, I was on my way to the Watergate to expose the perpetrator. If 19,000 votes were stolen in Florida's presidential election, I flew to West Palm to cover this "very American coup."

Being there, covering a story, was the essential first step. Writing in a style that conveyed respect and love for the people is also essential. Our effort at the *Worker, Daily World,* and continuing with the online *People's World* today is always to take the side of the people in their struggles both for living wage jobs and for decent living conditions. We see in these immediate struggles a longer range goal that will end in full political and economic democracy. Bernie Sanders calls it socialism. We agree with him.

In preparing to write this book, I re-read most of the stories, exposes, commentaries, and editorials I have written. Sarah Paul, who served as librarian of the *Daily World* and its successors, clipped and saved thousands of my articles and stashed them in several cardboard boxes. I found them in the morgue on the 4th Floor of our headquarters in New York City. I absconded with them. Those boxes are stored safely under my desk in our bedroom.

To retrieve the balance of the articles, I traveled to Frostburg University in Maryland and New York University's Tamiment-Robert F. Wagner Labor Archives to retrieve my articles from their microfilm collections of the *Worker,* the *Daily World, People's Daily World,* and *People's Weekly World.* I scanned hundreds more articles.

After traveling all that distance, I discovered that the University of Washington Library also has the *Worker/ Daily World/ People's World* on microfilm. I spent blissful hours retrieving more of my articles at the UW.

I also Googled myself with surprising results. One story I forgot I had written I found in the CIA's library, "sanitized" before it was released in 2010, a mere 30 years after I wrote it in 1980.. It is a story that exposes the CIA's covert intervention in Afghanistan, at least a year before the Soviet's sent in troops at the desperate request of the Afghan government reeling from terrorist attacks orchestrated by the CIA.

I was a one-person news bureau compared to the legions of reporters in the *New York Times* Washington Bureau. Yet I was sometimes the only reporter to show up. I remember one case. Three congress-members, Don

Edwards of California, Robert Kastenmeier of Wisconsin, and John Conyers of Michigan announced a joint news conference in one of their offices. I can't remember the topic but I was the only reporter to show up. A press secretary came to tell me. "We're going to delay the opening of this news conference for about ten minutes."

Then he got on the phone to the House Press Gallery, pleading that AP or UPI send over one of their reporters quick. Sure enough, the newswire reporter showed up, out of breath, and the news conference began. It happened more than once.

The most obvious omission from their coverage is labor news. In days gone by, many if not most of the major daily newspapers had a staff reporter assigned to cover labor news. One newspaper after another has eliminated the activities of labor unions from their daily coverage. Workers can be marching on the picket line in the freezing cold, on strike against one or another corporate giant. It is not a story worthy of coverage for the big city dailies.

In assembling this book, I decided it was too long. So I divided it in two. The other volume, *News from Rain Shadow Country*, is a collection of the stories I wrote about my youth growing up in Clallam County, Washington, and the news stories I have written about Washington State since we returned to our family farm near Sequim, Washington. I invite you to read both books.

NEWS FOR THE 99%

Chapter *1*

Working for the Movement

Out of the Grinders, into the Fire

I earned my Bachelor's Degree at Amherst College in 1964. Joyce and I and our son, Morgan, moved to Portland, Oregon, where my sister, Susan lived. I had been accepted in the Master of Arts in Teaching program at Reed College.

I took courses at Reed and taught at a Portland high school half a day. I was enthused about the teaching and devoted myself to preparing lessons and teaching English literature, incorporating readings from English and American authors.

The war in Vietnam was escalating. I used Henry David Thoreau's essay *Civil Disobedience* in my classes. There were frank discussions in my classroom about the injustice of this war and the necessity to stand up and oppose it.

The students seemed to enjoy the readings and participated enthusiastically in class discussions. The principal, too, seemed pleased when he observed my classes. Classes at Reed, however, were a different story. I missed many classes, many of them evening sessions. I preferred going to meetings of the anti-war and civil rights movement or spending time with Joyce and Morgan.

So at the end of the year I got failing grades at Reed. I didn't dispute that. What did anger me was the failing grade I also received from the mentor teacher at the high school where I taught. I had worked hard at doing the best job I could at teaching all three of my classes.

The principal called me in to express amazement at the grade one of his teachers had given me. "I have observed your classes. You have done an excellent job. You will be a good teacher," he said.

For a time, with the advice of Joyce, my parents, family and friends, I considered fighting the "flunkout" from Reed's MAT program. Yet I finally decided against that path. The struggle would be costly in time and dollars with an uncertain outcome. Already, I was moving in another direction, toward fulltime work in the movement.

In the meantime, I needed a job. I answered an ad in the *Oregonian* to become a hired hand on a farm about twenty miles east of Portland toward Mount Hood. We drove out to this lovely dairy farm one day and the owner hired me on the spot. I was an experienced cow milker.

So began a year of rising at 4 a.m. Joyce fixed me a flapjack breakfast and at 4:30 a.m. I was on the road to milk the fifty or so cows. I would clean the barn, distribute hay and at 10:00 a.m. drive home and fall into bed. Then, at 4:30 p.m., I was on the road out to the farm again for the evening milking. It was an exhausting schedule for the minimum wage, then $1.25 an hour.

Soon after I got that job, I put in job applications seeking work in the paper mills in the Portland region. We celebrated with wild abandon when I was telephoned in the spring of 1965, telling me to report to the Publishers Paper Company paper mill in Oregon City. I was hired at the mill owned by the *Los Angeles Times*, which produced the newsprint used in that newspaper along with other paper products. I toiled at that job for nearly two years.

I joined the union. The workers at the mill were represented by the Association of Western Pulp & Paper Workers (AWPPW). It was a newly organized breakaway from the International Association of Pulp, Sulfite, and Papermill Workers. It had just won recognition in a National Labor Relations Board election in October 1964. Also, the workers at paper mills up and down the west coast had just won a new contract after a solid strike so the workers were earning a base wage of $3.49 an hour—equivalent to $27 an hour today.

It meant my pay was nearly three times higher than I had earned at milking cows. AWPPW was a progressive union, in the midst of a militant fight to win equal pay for women, allied with the left-led International Longshoremen & Warehousemen Union (ILWU), and the Brotherhood of Teamsters. They had defended one of their staunchest members, Will Parry, a box factory worker in Seattle, a member of the Communist Party of Washington State, when he was hauled before HUAC and other witch hunt committees. He was later elected by AWPPW to serve as their lobbyist in Olympia, a job he carried out with great distinction. I had known Will, his wife Louise, and their two children since my childhood on the Olympic peninsula. So I could have made a good life as a union paper mill worker.

But the job itself was a killer. I worked a rotating shift—days one week, swing shift the next, graveyard the third, then back to day shift the fourth week. My life was in constant turmoil and I was perpetually tired. I read later that rotating shifts are so bad for the health they can actually shorten the life of a worker.

I was working on the grinders, one of the most brutal, deafening jobs in the mill. My partner and I straddled a gleaming, spinning shaft, perhaps twenty inches in diameter, with the grinder and it's four "pockets" mounted on it. We pulled seventy pound chunks of green wood from a flume behind us, filled with the frigid waters of the Willamette River. We turned, and shoved the wood into the "pocket." Then we pulled a lever that activated a hydraulic press that closed down, pressing the wood against the huge rotating grinder. The stones of the grinders ground the wood into pulp that cascaded down flowing in a river under the grinders. Then we raced on to fill the pockets on the neighboring grinder.

Each shaft had two grinders mounted on it. I loaded one grinder, my partner the other. The filled pockets, under full pressure from the hydraulic presses, acted

like a brake, slowing down the shaft, slowing the grinding process. If either of us failed to keep our pockets
filled, the shaft would speed up. Then the grinding on
the second grinder also sped up. Thus, I was pitted
against my partner with a built in motive for wanting
him to keep his pockets full. I know grindermen coming
nearly to blows when one or the other did not keep up.
It wasn't only wood being ground. We were being ground
to pulp as well.

Rarely did we have breaks together with our fellow
grindermen. But one night, the foreman was "jigging"
the grinders, running a cutting blade back and forth
across the stones to remove wood fiber that packed the
surface of the stones. During this twenty minute pause,
my partner and I did enjoy a few minutes to wolf down
our sandwiches and slurp coffee together.

"Where you from?" he shouted in my ear.

"Sequim, Washington, up on the Olympic Peninsula.
My mom and dad own a dairy farm up there."

A dreamy expression filled his face at the mention of
a dairy farm.

"God! I wish I was up there on that farm," he yelled.

I wasn't such a wild enthusiast for dairy farms. I had
given up work on a dairy farm to take the mill job. I
knew the endless toil seven days a week, month in and
month out, year after year, that dairy farmers endured
earning a few dollars more than a poverty income. Yet I
knew what he was thinking of. Milking parlors were so
quiet! Cows were such placid, gentle, creatures. Surely
farming was heaven compared to the sheer hell of the
grinders.

"Did you hear about the guy who died of hemlock poi-
soning here a few months ago?" my partner shouted.

"No. What happened?" I replied.

"He refused to wear his rubber gloves. He worked
that way several months and the hemlock slivers kept
poking his arms. He built up enough hemlock in his
system that it killed him. They hired you to take his
place. So wear your gloves if you want to stay alive." (A

botanist friend read this chapter and snorted. "That's bogus. Hemlock wood is not poisonous." So something else in the environment of that paper mill killed the guy I replaced. But I did wear those very heavy rubber gloves that reached all the way to my elbows).

Sometimes they asked us to do a double-shift, sixteen hours of toil on those grinders. Once, I left work and drove home so tired I could hardly stay awake behind the wheel. When I arrived at the front door, Joyce told me, "The mill just called. They want you to come back for another shift."

The worst of all was the midnight shift. The human brain has a built-in sense of time, a "circadian rhythm." The hours from midnight to 8 a.m. seemed to last forever. I thought I would die on my feet. I had nightmares of toppling into the river of pulp that flowed beneath the grinders, pulling me up into the giant digesters, boiling with sulfuric acid. A brimstone cloud engulfed that paper mill, hell on earth.

I have never forgotten working in that mill and the lessons it taught me: Workers, everywhere, but especially those doing hard manual labor in mass production face intolerable working conditions and must have a union to protect them. The only strength that workers have is their labor power. Their only protection from the greed of their corporate employers is their unity, brothers and sisters standing against a common enemy.

Mass Struggle in the City of Roses

Sometime in the spring of 1964, Mike Zagarell, the Youth Director of the Communist Party USA, visited Portland. He met with our Party club and argued passionately that we should join in working to defeat Barry Goldwater's bid for President. I argued vehemently against it. How could we support LBJ?

Yet Mike persisted, citing the provocative pro-war threats spewed by Goldwater, his open hatred of unions, his stated opposition to civil rights laws that the Democrats on Capitol Hill had promised to enact into law. Furthermore, Mike stressed that we were not endorsing LBJ any more than we had endorsed his slain predecessor, John F. Kennedy. Rather, we were joining in the broad labor-led coalition of progressive forces working to defeat the ultra-right danger, the gravest threat to democracy in our nation.

That meeting was a turning point in my thinking. Zagarell clarified a Marxist strategy for fighting against the extreme right that has guided me ever since. During the discussion, Mike had quoted from *United Front Against Fascism,* a report delivered by the great Bulgarian Communist leader Georgi Dimitroff, during a meeting of the Communist International in Moscow in 1937.

I got hold of Dimitroff's booklet and read it avidly. Later developed into the Popular Front, Dimitroff's strategy was the key to creating a broad, world-wide coalition that defeated Hitler fascism. I understood immediately the application of the United Front strategy here in the United States. I underlined to myself the warning by Dimitroff that "those who fail to struggle against fascism in its preparatory stages will never be able to defeat fascism when it is full-blown." What were we facing here in the U.S. if not the "preparatory stages" of fascism?

My deeper understanding of the class struggle was not shaken even in the years ahead when LBJ betrayed the people and escalated the war in Vietnam. The people had spoken decisively in the 1964 election, swamping Goldwater with their votes against him. It was, above all, a vote against war. We simply shifted over and began the long, difficult task of mobilizing the people against the Vietnam War.

I remember a fierce debate on the Vietnam War, sponsored by students at Reed College, between Oregon Senator Wayne Morse versus Wisconsin Senator William Proxmire at the Civic Arena, the biggest meeting hall in Portland. The hall was packed and the rafters reverberated as the crowd cheered Morse. He and Alaska Senator Ernest Gruening were the only U.S. Senators with the courage to vote no on the Tonkin Gulf Resolution, the fraudulent measure rammed through August 7, 1964 by President Lyndon Johnson to justify escalation of the war in Vietnam. Morse had warned that this resolution violated the U.S. Constitution with Congress surrendering to the Executive Branch the power to wage war without a declaration of war. Morse warned that oceans of blood would flow because of this political cowardice. And he was right. The Vietnam War would rage on for a decade costing millions of Vietnamese lives and the lives of 56,000 GIs.

* * *

On March 7, 1965—"Bloody Sunday," Alabama State Troopers attacked and brutally beat peaceful voting rights marchers as they attempted to walk across the Edmund Pettus Bridge in Selma, Alabama. Clubbed almost to death was John Lewis, the youthful organizer of the Student Non-Violent Coordinating Committee (SNCC).

Dr. Martin Luther King, Jr. issued a nationwide call for solidarity actions to coincide with a March 21 march from Selma to Montgomery demanding enactment of the Voting Rights Act. We had been organizing a chapter of the W.E.B. DuBois Club in Albina, the African American neighborhood of Northeast Portland. We had worked hard to establish good working relations with the community, especially the youth.

We decided the best strategy was to organize a march from a park in Albina, down across one of the bridges that spanned the Willamette River and on through downtown Portland. The demands would be an end to the racist terror inflicted on peaceful marchers across Alabama and the South exercising their Constitutional rights of freedom of assembly. The second demand was immediate enactment of the Voting Rights Act.

We drafted and mimeographed thousands of leaflets and began distributing them throughout Albina and the greater Portland area. The idea caught hold. Soon, community organizations in Portland were sending their members to pick up leaflets.

Then, out of the blue, a DuBois Club leader got into a shouting match in his living room when he attempted to order another comrade to perform a task. The comrade said he wouldn't do it. Much shouting back and forth ensued. We were thunderstruck when this club leader suddenly shouted, "It's all off. Everything is cancelled." He stormed upstairs and slammed the door to his bedroom.

I was thunderstruck and so was my sister Susan. "We can't quit now," Susan protested. I looked at her and she added, "I guess it's you and me and the rest of the club. We've got to push on"

So Susan and I and other comrades toiled on, with a great deal of help from the Black community in Portland.

When we assembled that glorious, sunny morning March 21, 1964 in a small park in Albina, the crowd grew and grew until it numbered in the thousands. The turnout was so large that Portland Police decided on the spot to clear the streets and allow us to march down the avenue curb to curb. It was the largest civil rights march in Portland history. The Communist Party and the W.E.B. DuBois Club deserve credit for taking the initiative. But the credit for the huge turnout belongs to Portland's African American community.

Once again, we were part of a broad democratic upsurge sweeping the nation. LBJ had told Dr. King that enactment of the Voting Rights Act was not on his agenda for 1965. But it was at the top of the people's agenda. We put it on LBJ's agenda. A few months later, he signed the Voting Rights Act opening the way for the enormous gains in Black voter clout, the election of hundreds and now thousands of African American and Latino elected officials.

That huge democratic victory by itself proved the correctness of the Party's decision to work for Goldwater's defeat. We could never have pushed through the Voting Rights Act if Goldwater and the Republican right had won that election. To his credit, LBJ played a crucial role in jawboning the House and Senate to pass the Voting Rights Act without crippling amendments.

Joyce was enrolled at Portland State University, training to become a schoolteacher. I babysat our two-year old son, Morgan, while she went off to classes. I remember driving home from the paper mill, falling into bed and drifting off to sleep one morning. Joyce left for her classes at Portland State leaving Morgan in my care. He played happily. Once, he crawled into the kitchen, opened the refrigerator door and pulled out a carton of eggs. When I awoke, he was splashing happily in the midst of a dozen broken eggs, a giant raw omelet in the middle of our kitchen floor.

Other times he would pull himself up beside the bed where I was snoring. "Daa! Daa! Daa!" he said over and over while patting me rhythmically on the cheek. I would barely awake long enough to see that he was safe and happy and I would fall back asleep.

In the late autumn of 1965, Danny Rubin, an organizer for the Communist Party USA, came from CPUSA headquarters in New York to conduct a series of educational seminars for our Party club in Portland. Joyce and I, my sister Susan and her husband, and others participated in those seminars.

At the end, Danny took me aside. "Would you accept an assignment to go full time for the Party? There are a number of assignments open. One is being an organizer in Florida; another is helping out with Party youth work. Another is writing for the *Worker*."

I was stunned by the offer. I asked him for time to consult with Joyce and other comrades in Portland. He agreed but stressed that the Party needed an answer soon because the Party was then preparing for its 18th Convention in New York City. It was to be the second convention since the Party's victory, the Supreme Court ruling that in effect overturned the Cold War Smith Act and the McCarran Act. Party leaders, Gus Hall, Henry Winston, Carl Winter, George Meyers and many others were freed from prison. The 18th Convention would be a celebration of that victory and the beginning of the Party comeback.

I discussed Danny's offer with Joyce, my sister Susan, Ralph Nelson, then the Chair of the Party in Oregon, DuWayne and Billie Jo Rader, who were trusted comrades, and many others. The consensus was that I should accept the offer. Joyce and I agreed that she should stay in Portland with Morgan until the winter term ended at Portland State; I would fly in early January to New York.

I flew on a red-eye special from Portland sometime in mid-January 1966. It was the first time I had ever flown in an airplane. I sat in a window seat of the Boeing 707 as we flew eastward, staring down into the inky darkness. Scattered here and there were the lights of unknown cities and towns like heaps of glittering jewels on the black velvet below the plane's wing. I was flying into the unknown, into a future full of promise for myself, my family, and the people. I was going to spend my life writing the stories of their struggles, their victories, and bitter defeats.

I Learn From Movement Veterans

Danny Rubin picked me up at LaGuardia Airport at some impossible hour. I slept that night—or should I say morning—at Danny and Dot's apartment in the Park Slope neighborhood of Brooklyn. They had two lively children, Rosie and Joey.

The subway system was shut down by a transit strike led by the eloquent and very militant Mike Quill. A judge had ordered Quill to end the strike and instruct the workers to return to work. Quill snapped back, "Let the judge drop dead in his black robes!"

The strike continued and the workers' won substantial increases in wages and improved working conditions. But three days after the strike ended, it was Quill who tragically died from a heart attack. It was to be a harbinger of the sharp, relentless, unending struggles by the working class, and the people, that I would witness and write about in the years to come.

Danny had already left for work hours before I woke up that January morning. It had snowed and six or seven inches of snow had fallen. It was bitterly cold. Yet I decided to hike into the CPUSA headquarters in mid-Manhattan. I had no hat and twenty minutes after leaving the comfort of the Rubin home, my ears were frozen. I stopped in a shop and bought a cap with ear-flaps and managed to trudge the rest of the way across the Brooklyn Bridge and up Broadway to the Party's headquarters.

It was a handsome but soot-blackened old brick town-house on 26th Street, just off Broadway that had been given to the Party by Corliss Lamont, a wealthy member of the Party who was married to the granddaughter of John Jacob Astor, the 19th Century "robber baron" who built the house in 1881. Astor's son, Vincent, had willed it to his daughter. When Lamont died, he bequeathed the house to the CPUSA and the *Daily Worker*. It was to suffer several fire-bombing attacks by rightwing terror-ists in the years I worked there.

When I arrived, I was greeted by everyone at Party headquarters. I was one of a new generation of young comrades coming in to work for the Party just months after the leadership had been released from prison. They had served years in jail on trumped up charges under the infamous Smith Act and McCarran Act falsely accused of advocating the "violent" overthrow of the government.

I was introduced to men and women who were heroes to me: CPUSA General Secretary Gus Hall and National Chairman, Henry Winston, Betty Gannett, Dr. James Jackson, Gil Green, Carl Winter, editor of the *Worker*, and Helen Winter, then the International Affairs Secre-tary of the Party. Not present was Mike Zagarell who was on an extended trip somewhere. He may have been in the Soviet Union attending a Marxist-Leninist school.

Mike's absence was fortuitous for me. I was invited to move into his tiny, scruffy apartment on the Lower

East Side. In early February, Joyce and Morgan left Portland on the train to Vancouver B.C. They traveled on the Canadian National ($80 Canadian for a sleeper-roomette and three meals per day) to Montreal. My parents had moved to Franconia, NH where my father and my older brother, Steve, were professors. So my parents drove up to Montreal and picked Joyce and Morgan up.

I traveled up to the North Country and had a delightful reunion with the family in the old, handsome Franconia resort hotel that now housed Franconia College. My parents were elated at their new-found freedom from the endless toil of dairy farming. They had left our farm in the loving care of Ollie Hansen, a Norwegian-American farmer from Minnesota who was leasing our place. (Within a year or so, he had made our dairy herd one of the champion milk producers in the Sequim-Dungeness Valley).

A few days after arriving in Franconia, my folks drove us down to Boston and we took the train to New York. We settled into Mike's apartment for a few weeks until he returned.

We moved then to Yonkers to stay with Gus and Elizabeth Hall in their large, commodious old frame house. We enjoyed many wonderful evenings with Gus and Elizabeth, genial and hospitable hosts. Henry and Fern Winston were the next to leave town on a prolonged trip, I believe to the USSR where Winnie was to get treatment for the brain tumor that had caused such excruciating headaches for him when he was at Terre Haute Federal Penitentiary. Prison authorities arrogantly ignored his complaints, accusing him of malingering. But their vicious racist negligence led to his permanent blindness. On his release from jail, Winston proclaimed, "They have robbed me of my eyesight but not my vision."

We moved into the Winston's comfortable apartment, a modern high-rise in Spanish Harlem and enjoyed life there for about a month. We got a call from Alva Buxenbaum, one day. She lived in Brooklyn and had found a rent controlled apartment on Eastern Parkway in Brooklyn.

We visited it immediately. It was a fourth floor walkup, a spacious two bedroom apartment with worn but still beautiful parquet hardwood floors. Since we were on the top floor, the apartment had wonderful light through the large windows and a sweeping view out over the rooftops of Brooklyn toward the southeast.

Joyce was then pregnant with our second child. So we would have to lug two children, groceries, diapers, and every other necessity up those stairs. I believe we were the only gentiles in the building. The other tenants were Hassidic Jews who walked on the sidewalks on both sides of the parkway on the Sabbath in all their finery.

We became fast friends with our neighbors. We became the "shabbos goy" of the apartment building, turning on and off their kitchen stoves that they were forbidden to touch on the Sabbath. More important, the owner of the apartment was a skinflint who systematically allowed the heating oil to run empty during the winter months. The heat would periodically go off and our apartments would turn bitterly cold.

One elderly couple, Hassidim who had emigrated to the U.S. from Finland, suffered the most. She was afflicted with terrible arthritis and the cold was unendurable for her. On the other hand, Joyce and I had a young child—and another on the way. We could not stand the cold either.

When the heat went off, I walked down the stairs and knocked on the door of these neighbors. Together we were on the phone to the rent-control office demanding that they act to get the owner to order delivery of oil.

After we had won several of these victories, our neighbor said to me, "Are you sure you aren't a Jew?"

I laughed. "When the heat goes off, we all freeze." My mother's maiden name was Lukes, I told him. She thought maybe somewhere back in our distant past in Europe we were Jewish and had changed the spelling of the name to avoid anti-semitic persecution. But my paternal great grandfather was a Methodist preacher, a missionary to India.

In the months that followed, I attended many meetings of the top leadership, then called the Secretariat, of the Party. The Party was then preparing for its 18th Convention at Webster Hall on the Lower East Side of Manhattan. I was assigned to sit on the stage at Webster Hall along with several other young people to show the world that the CPUSA was alive and well, recruiting activists from the younger generation to replace elderly comrades who had given their lives to the struggle.

I immediately got into a rhythm of dividing my time— half youth work for the Party with Zagarell, half with the *Worker* serving as a general assignment reporter. I enjoyed both assignments but the *Worker* was pulling me steadily toward writing news copy, always ready to race at top speed to the scene of the action.

Troops Terrorize Ghetto As Police Take Over in Newark

Ghetto Rebellion, War Against the Poor

July 16, 1967
We gathered in the library where the *Worker* staff held its story conferences one sweltering morning in July 1967. Prominently featured in the *New York Times* that morning was a story about the angry explosion in Newark, New Jersey, over the arrest of John Smith, an African American cab driver.

Smith had been accused of "tailgating" a police vehicle and driving the wrong way on a one-way street. He was also accused of using "offensive language" and "assault" against the police officers as they arrested him.

The confrontation escalated and soon the headlines blazed about the "riot" in Newark.

What should we do? Carl Winter and the elders of the staff were discussing the options back and forth. I spoke up. "I'd like to take the train over to Newark and do some reporting."

It was agreed. Our staff photographer, Bill Andrews, and I took the subway up to the train station and boarded a train for Newark.

When we got off the train, Newark was like a war zone. National Guard jeeps and trucks were everywhere. We walked over to the offices of the Newark Community Development Corporation, (NCDC) the "war on poverty" agency in Newark.

I interviewed Timothy Still, Newark's director of the NCDC. He told me of NCDC's efforts to prevent violence. Yet the anger against police brutality, chronic unemployment and poverty could not be contained. That interview was published in the next edition of the *Worker*.

Andrews and I made daily trips to Newark covering the deadly "rebellion of the poor" in New Jersey's largest city.

More reckless than smart, Bill and I went to the police headquarters one day. We walked into their city room where plainclothes detectives were sitting at their desks. They were all white men.

"Can I help you?" demanded one of the detectives.

"I'm a reporter for the *Worker*," I blurted. "I want to examine the death certificates of the people who have died. Can you tell me where I can find those records?"

A dead silence fell over the city room, twenty or more detectives staring at me in disbelief.

The beefy officer pulled back his jacket and rested his hand on the butt of his Smith and Wesson.

"I'm sorry. I can't help. You and your buddy would be well advised to get on the next train back to New York City. This is a very, very dangerous place," he said menacingly.

As Bill and I were beating a hasty retreat, a telephone receptionist just inside the entrance leaned over and whispered to me, "Go to the hospital in the Central Ward. They have everything you need."

We headed there immediately. Sure enough, the Coroner's Office was located there. They had a report on every death inflicted by the police and National Guard during that uprising.

I sat for two hours copying word for word the reports of the gunshot wounds that ultimately killed twenty-six people in Newark. Most of them died from gunshot wounds in the back.

The *Worker* featured the article on the front page, quoting verbatim from the coroner's report.

A few days later, I returned to the hospital, this time by myself. When I walked in to the Emergency Room, I came upon an African American woman in tears being comforted by a surgeon in his white surgical gown. They were standing in the waiting room and the surgeon was speaking to her in a low voice.

I waited. The surgeon turned away. Girding myself, I stepped up and told her who I was. I asked her if I could interview her. She nodded.

The *Worker* carried that story too on the front page.

National Guardsmen shot ten-year-old Eddie Moss to death a few days later as he rode in the family car with his parents in Newark.

I tracked down the family in their Central Ward home. When I knocked at the door, a woman invited me in. Her eyes were red from weeping. She told me she was Eddie Moss' mother. I was just beginning to ask my first question when Eddie Moss' father intervened. "We don't want any interviews," he said, his voice shaking with grief and anger.

I apologized and got up to leave.

I wrote up the story of the child's death, the funeral, and the heartbroken parents. But that was an interview I was never able to complete.

Here is the first report I wrote from Newark and a second story based on the coroner's reports.

Newark Negroes Starved, Homeless
The Worker

July 1967
NEWARK, NEW JERSEY—The Negro people of Newark counted their dead and wounded last week as thousands wandered homeless, and hungry in the wake of a murderous five-day invasion of the Central Ward by cops and National Guardsmen.

Governor Richard Hughes reluctantly withdrew the National Guard after leaders of the Negro community warned him that only with the removal could the loss of life be stopped.

A committee of sixty business, religious, education and social work leaders met Tuesday at the Rutgers Law School in Newark to discuss an immediate program to deal with the crisis.

The committee condemned Governor Hughes for having described the situation as "open rebellion and criminal insurrection!" They rejected the Governor's recommendation that the police and National Guard investigate charges of brutality against themselves.

On critical list

At Newark City Hospital, six victims of police attacks remained on the critical list, with bullet wounds in back, chest and head, according to Louis Ginsberg, hospital administrator.

Mrs. Tina Copeland, 128 South Sixth St., pleaded with hospital officials for more information about her wounded nineteen-year-old son.

"I've been looking for him since Friday," she told me, her eyes brimming with tears. "I just found out today he has been here in the hospital since then. They shot him in the leg. Now they are getting ready to take off his leg because he has no feeling in it."

"When will they let me talk to him?"

"The hospital says 'no visitors,' and the only sure thing they will say is he is in 'fair condition.' "

She said she had last seen her son Friday evening when he left home to go to work at a Ford Motor Company assembly plant.

"I guess he got shot down the street at the bus stop. But the police won't tell how it happened. Everybody in the family has been looking for him since then," she said.

"I hope the Negro people get what they're fighting for. It's always the innocent people who suffer the worst."

A Negro woman at the hospital administration desk said many children had died as police opened fire on ghetto residents. "The youngest was a three-year-old girl," she said. "Quite a few of the children have been dead on arrival. The latest was a boy, eleven-years-old, who came in yesterday."

She estimated fifteen children were admitted to the hospital with bullet wounds in chest or back.

Mrs. Catherine Clark, South Orange Ave., told me about the food emergency in the neighborhood as she stood with several other women on the front steps of the Robert Treat School in the heart of the ghetto.

"If the government can declare an emergency other places why can't they declare one here right now?" she asked. "Our kids have got to eat. I haven't shopped since Saturday a week ago. I've got an eleven-month-old baby and no milk."

Mrs. Minola Smith said, "I have four children and no food. I had to borrow from my neighbor but now she's all out too."

Mrs. Jesse Mason said, "There should be a committee organized to deal with this situation."

Thousands of mothers waited in line at emergency distribution centers up to six hours to receive a loaf of bread, a few slices of bologna and a half head of cabbage. Tens of thousands went hungry because Mayor Addonizio and Governor Hughes have refused to ask President Johnson to declare Newark a disaster area. Johnson himself has had ample opportunity to take that step since he has been in touch with Governor Hughes.

Instead, city and state officials have done everything in their power to throw the blame for the human suffering onto the backs of the oppressed Negro citizens.

The newspapers have sought to justify the reign of terror by the police and National Guardsmen as "measures to deal with criminal insurrection."

The sixty-man citizens' committee organized to draw up a program for the crisis in Newark released a statement which said:

"The white people of Newark is in a minority and yet all effective power is in their hands."

This condition must be changed immediately, the statement says.

It adds, "A large segment of the Negro people is convinced that the single, continuously lawless element operating in the community is the police force itself, in its callous disregard for human rights."

Death Roll in Newark: Victims of Cops' Fire
The *Worker*

July 25, 1967
NEWARK, NEW JERSEY—Children, mothers, fathers, and grandmothers, were laid to rest in funerals last week, the victims of police gunfire during the vicious invasion of the Central Ward two weeks ago.

One hundred residents of the community gathered last Wednesday at the Whigham Funeral House, 580 High St. for the funeral of Edward Moss, ten, who fell under police bullets Friday, July 14, while riding with his parents in a car.

As friends and relatives of the Moss child mourned, the Reverend William E. Hedgebeth, pastor of Mt. Olives Church of Christ Disciples delivered a sermon.

He said the child's death symbolized "a sacrifice so that the poor might eat and have a decent place to live." He said, he was "serving notice on landlords and the city to fix up the houses in the area and keep them up."

The funeral did not record the fact that many were shot in the back by the police.

But the coroner's reports, uncovered by the *Worker*, revealed how they died.

The following is the listing of the deaths as recorded in the Essex County Medical Examiner's Office at Newark City Hospital.

1. "Unknown Adult Negro. Homicide by shooting. Shotgun wounds of the back, perforating the heart and left lung.
2. "Jessie Jones, 31. Homicide by shooting. Bullet wounds of abdomen, perforating liver, aorta.
3. "Rufus Council, 14. Homicide by shooting. Bullet wounds to the left side of head perforating the brain, hemorrhage."
4. "Robert Lee Martin, 24. Homicide by assault with blunt instrument. Fractured skull, hemorrhage of the brain. Bullet wounds to the arm, and back of left shoulder."
5. "Unknown Adult Negro No. 2. Homicide by shooting. Bullet wound in right chest perforating right lung."
6. "Richard Talliaferro, 25. Homicide by shooting. Bullet wound of back, perforating right lung."
7. "Leroy Boyd. Homicide by shooting. Bullet wound to left side of back, perforating diaphragm, stomach."
8. "Cornelius Murray. Homicide by shooting. Bullet wounds of left arm, left chest, perforating lung, diaphragm."
9. "Albert Mersier, 20. Homicide by shooting. Bullet wounds of back, perforating aorta, hemorrhage, asphyxiation by bleeding."
10. "Edward Moss, 10. Homicide by shooting. Bullet wounds of right side of head, fractured skull, hemorrhage of brain."
11. "William E. Furr, 24. Homicide by shooting. Shotgun wounds of the back, perforating both lungs."
12. "Hattie Gainer, 53. Homicide by shooting. Bullet wounds of chest, perforating the heart."
13. "Ralph Hawk, 24. Homicide by assault with blunt instrument. Laceration to scalp. Fractured skull, laceration of the brain. Cerebral hemorrhage."
14. "Rose Abraham, 42. Homicide by shooting. Bullet wounds of the abdomen."
15. "Eloise Spellman. Homicide by shooting. Shotgun wound of neck."

16. "Isaac Harrison, 73. Homicide by shooting. Shotgun wounds of chest, abdomen."
17. "Rebecca Brown, 29. Homicide by shooting. Bullet wound of the abdomen."
18. "James Rutledge, 20. Homicide by shooting. Shotgun wounds of back, perforating skull, heart, kidneys, lungs, liver and spleen."
19. "Raymond Gilman, 20. Homicide by shooting. Bullet wounds to the back of head."
20. "Michael Pugh, 12. Homicide by shooting. Bullet wounds of abdomen."
21. "Tedoc Bell, 28. Homicide by shooting."

Joyce and Her Anti-Draft Sisters are Arrested
Based on Dec. 7, 1967 story in The Worker

NEW YORK—We needed more income. I was earning $86 per week as a staff reporter for the *Worker*. Our rent was $86 monthly but we were still just scraping by. The

Photo by *WORKER staff reporter, Bill Andrews. The author's wife, Joyce Wheeler, is second from right holding the sign 'End The Draft NOW!'*

New York Party district hired Joyce to work part time. Frances Bordofsky, office manager, loved Joyce dearly because the minute she stepped into the office, she noticed that someone had left the mimeograph machine in an inky mess. Joyce took charge and cleaned up the mimeograph machine until it gleamed like new.

We were so active in our Brooklyn Party club that Joyce was soon elected club chair. The Club in turn was active with the New York chapter of the W.E.B. DuBois Clubs. Together with the anti-Vietnam war movement, the Dubois Clubs organized the Student Mobilization Committee Against the Vietnam War called the "Mobe."

The most burning issue was the military draft, in fact so hot that thousands of youthful protesters were burning their draft cards and announcing loudly, "Hell No, We Won't Go!"

The anti-war movement decided to stage a nationwide "Stop the Draft Week" in December of 1967. The "Mobe" in New York City picked the Whitehall Induction Center in lower Manhattan as its target with the aim of shutting down or at least disrupting the conscription of young men for the escalating war in Vietnam. The strategy for December 5 was for women to sit down in the street in front of the Induction Center.

The event was immortalized in a photo snapped by *Worker* staff photographer, Bill Andrews, which illustrates this story. We framed and display the photo proudly on our walls. Joyce is sitting on the pavement holding a sign, "END THE DRAFT NOW!" Beside Joyce is her close friend and DuBois Club comrade, Carmen Ristorucci who is looking over her shoulder. I also recognize Lenore Weiss sitting at the far left and another DuBois Club activist, Naomi Chessman, sitting with an "END THE DRAFT NOW!" sign in her lap. The others I needed help in identifying. (See postscript at the end of this story.)

Police barricades were up and police officers stood grim-faced in a row watching the crowd that formed in front of the Induction Center.

Soon paddy wagons arrived and the police moved in, arresting the women and hauling them roughly, like gunny sacks, to the paddy wagons for transport to jail.

I hurried back to the office, wrote up my story and raced to catch the subway to Brooklyn to retrieve our children from the day care center. When we arrived home, I made dinner for the kids, gave them baths and got them into bed.

At some point in the evening, I checked the refrigerator. There on one of the shelves was half a luscious cantaloupe. Just looking at it made my mouth water. I took it out and devoured it, the juice trickling from my chin.

Night fell. The hours ticked away. Finally, at about 2 a.m., I heard the door of our apartment unlock and soft foot treads in the hallway. I got out of bed and padded into the kitchen. Joyce turned and greeted me with a weary smile. Droplets of perspiration had formed on her brow. She was standing in front of the refrigerator, with the door open, bent over, rummaging through the shelves.

"Where is that cantaloupe?" she demanded. "All the time I was in jail sweltering away, all I could think of was that sweet, juicy cantaloupe. It was all I thought about riding the IRT out here to Brooklyn. Where is it?"

I stood with guilt written all over my face.

"The dog ate it," I mumbled. (We didn't have a dog.)

There are some transgressions, in a marriage that are never forgiven, never forgotten. That demonstration, too, was never forgotten. Women, mostly young women, continued to play a leading role in the anti-war movement.

The anti-war movement had been gathering strength for several months. Eight months earlier, April 4, 1967, Dr. Martin Luther King Jr. came to Riverside Church on New York's upper west side at the invitation of Clergy & Laity Concerned About the Vietnam War. He delivered his momentous speech denouncing the Vietnam War, accusing the U.S. of being "the world's greatest purveyor of violence."

The bombs dropped on Hanoi, he told the crowd, are "exploding in the ghettoes" of Detroit and every other American city sweltering with racist oppression. A nation that squanders billions on foreign wars while millions of its own people struggle to survive loses its "spiritual uplift."

The speech marked a turning point. It was a signal that the two greatest issues facing the nation, peace abroad and equality at home are inseparable. With one speech, King helped overcome a split that divided the greatest movements in the nation—the civil rights movement and the anti-war movement.

The speech was a hot topic of discussion in the Party. Dr. James Jackson, one of the CPUSA's leading theoreticians, hailed it as a long stride toward world peace and African American equality while also deepening the class consciousness of the American people.

Dr. King was defying the ruling class, refusing to be boxed into an assigned role as a "civil rights leader," Jackson added. King was growing as the logic of the struggle developed. He was moving leftward in both thought and action.

I was not assigned to cover King's speech. But one week later, April 15, 1967, Dr. King and Dr. Benjamin Spock led a huge march from the Sheep's Meadow in Central Park to the United Nations. Joyce and I and our children, Morgan and Donald Nicholas, joined that procession walking with the CPUSA and DuBois Clubs contingent. I was assigned to cover that march for the *Worker*.

I was elated by the immense size and diversity of the crowd that stretched from curb to curb on the city's widest avenues. Angry chants echoed in the canyons of the city, "Hell No We Won't Go!"

I was to hear Dr. King one last time. On February 23, 1968, *Freedomways Magazine* sponsored a celebration of Dr. W.E.B. Dubois' 100th birthday at Carnegie Hall.

King was the featured speaker. The hall was packed to capacity. I listened as raptly as everyone else:

"We cannot think of Dr. Dubois without recognizing that he was a radical all of his life," said Dr. King in his deep, resonant voice. He continued:

> Some people would like to ignore the fact that he was a Communist in his later years. It is worth noting that Abraham Lincoln warmly welcomed the support of Karl Marx during the Civil War and corresponded with him freely. In contemporary life, the English-speaking world has no difficulty with the fact that Sean O'Casey was a literary giant of the 20th Century and a Communist or that Pablo Neruda is generally considered the greatest living poet though he also served in the Chilean Senate as a Communist. It is time to cease muting the fact that Dr. DuBois was a genius and chose to be a communist. Our irrational, obsessive anti-communism has led us into too many quagmires to be retained as if it were a mode of scientific thinking . . . . Dr. DuBois' greatest virtue was his committed empathy with all the oppressed and his divine dissatisfaction with all forms of injustice.

Every time I hear a recording, today, of Dr. King speaking, chills run up and down my spine. I have no doubt that he was the greatest orator, ever, in U.S. history, perhaps ever in world history. He was the prophet of the poor and the oppressed and his voice was like thunder.

Yet this speech was different. His voice did not soar as it did in his "I Have a Dream" speech or his last great speech, "I Have Been to the Mountaintop." Instead, he spoke quietly, in a more conversational tone, as if he was reasoning with us. Yet his words were so eloquent, his meaning so profound, that once again I felt those chills running up and down my spine. He was rebutting Cold War anti-communism, the evil twin of racism, the two ideological pillars of U.S. imperialism. We all stood in a prolonged ovation.

Forty-one days later, April 4, 1968, while leading garbage workers on strike in Memphis, Tennessee, Dr. King died from an assassin's bullet. I was attending a Marxist-Leninist school on the Lower East Side with about two-dozen comrades from across the nation. King's murder hit us like a lightning bolt. In our class was Carolyn Black from Chicago who had worked with Dr. King in the Southern Christian Leadership Conference. We met and agreed that Carolyn should be released from the school so she could travel down to Atlanta to march behind the mule-drawn buckboard carrying Dr. King's coffin. Carolyn left immediately to join the funeral procession. She marched for herself but she was also representing us and her Party comrades all across the nation.

The entire nation was in mourning, once again reeling from the string of assassinations that included President John F. Kennedy, his younger brother, Robert Kennedy. Soon it would strike down Malcolm X. None of us at the school had any doubts that these political murders were the work of a profoundly racist, anti-labor conspiracy orchestrated at the top of our nation's political elite aimed at stopping our country from making a turn in a progressive direction.

Years later, Joyce and I and our three children settled in Baltimore. Joyce was an elementary class room teacher, elected repeatedly without opposition as the Secretary-Treasurer of the Baltimore Teachers Union, AFT Local 340. She was a fearless BTU Building Representative who led her school during a month-long teacher strike. President Nixon ordered the "incursion" of Cambodia accompanied by saturation bombing. Joyce went to a BTU meeting, stood, and read aloud her resolution denouncing the invasion of Cambodia as a dangerous escalation of the Vietnam War, a crime against humanity.

A faction in leadership of Local 340 supported the fanatical anti-communism of AFT President, Albert Shanker.

Shanker never spoke out against any war crime committed by the Nixon Administration. But Nixon's war crimes were so despicable and the public outrage so widespread, that these elements remained silent. Joyce's resolution was adopted without opposition.

Post Script

I put the photo of Joyce and her anti-war sisters on Facebook and asked friends, especially those who had been active in the DuBois Clubs, to help identify the women sitting to Joyce's left and right. (Joyce is the women to the right holding the sign with the message "END THE DRAFT NOW." Here are some of the responses:

Carmen Ristorucci: "Wish I could help you. I remember making so many phone calls asking everyone to join us and was pleasantly surprised at those who knowingly would spend an evening in jail with me..."

Matt Berkelhammer: "Left to right, to the best of my recollection (names at the time) Lenore Weiss, Elissa Krauss, Unknown, Naomi Chesman, Ruthie Portnoy, Gail Tobman, I'm going to take a guess Jenny Maida, Carmen Ristorucci, Joyce Wheeler, Unknown....."

Jack Radey: "Ruthie Portnoy in the white coat, head turned to the left..."

Jo-Ann Demas: "Next to Ruth Portnoy on her right is Gail Tobman...Is that me behind Gail Tobman? . . . "

Esther Moroze: "Naomi became Nomi Smith...."

Michael Scott: Tim, that woman with her hair braided on the top of her head is Alice Gorman. She lived in Brighton Beach in the Amalgamated houses on Ocean Parkway in Brooklyn."

Jeanne H. Ross: "Unfortunately I wasn't there. However, I did lead a group which stopped traffic on the West Side Highway and caused considerable chaos. Alas, some beatings but no arrests...."

One friend tagged a photo of Phyllis Kalb sitting in the second row.

We may not remember everyone's name but their deeds will never be forgotten.

Chapter 2

25 Years Covering the Capital

In the spring of 1968 Joyce and I moved with our children to the Washington D.C. area where I took up my duties covering the nation's capital for the *Daily World*. It was my assignment for twenty-five years. I covered a vast range of stories. Among the most dramatic were the struggles of workers in the cities and towns of rural areas within driving distance of Washington D.C., especially the coal miners of Appalachia.

Dark as a Dungeon: the Mannington Mine Disaster

I was in my office in the National Press Building on the afternoon of November 20, 1968, cleaning up in preparation for Thanksgiving. It had been a year of hard struggle settling in to my new job as Washington correspondent of the *Daily World*.

My editors insisted that I call myself "Bureau Chief" but I looked around and it was only me, a chief with no one else to give orders to. So I was on the run to cover all three branches of the Federal Government, all the mass organizations of the people with offices in the District of Columbia, and plenty of stories outside Washington as well.

I was looking forward to Thanksgiving, a time to be with Joyce and our two sons, Morgan and Donald. Joyce was due to deliver our third child within a few days so that too required plenty of preparations.

Smoke billows from the portal of Consol Mine # 9 near Mannington, W. Va. Photo courtesy of U.S. Dept. of Mine Safety and Health Enforcement

Her delicate condition did not spare her domestic duties. In the sweltering heat of a Washington summer, she rode the D.C. bus with little Morgan and Nick, crisscrossing D.C. and the suburbs searching for an apartment. She found one in Arlington, Virginia. I was too busy covering the news and writing up my stories to be concerned with finding a place to live.

The phone rang. It was Si Gerson, managing editor of the *DW*. "Tim," he said. "Are you listening to the news? A coal mine has exploded just outside Mannington, West

Virginia. About eighty miners are trapped underground. Any chance you could get over there and cover it?"

I hesitated. What if Joyce went into labor while I was gone? But I thought again: eighty miners trapped! How could I stay home and enjoy a Thanksgiving feast knowing what the coal miners and their families were enduring?

"Yes," I said. "I'll leave immediately."

I took the bus to our home in Arlington, Virginia, and kissed Joyce and the children goodbye. I climbed into my parent's Chevy II. (We had just become caretakers of "Old Blue," my parent's Chevy II, while my folks were in England where my father was studying for his doctorate at Oxford University). I took off, driving due west toward the West Virginia line. It was cold. The sun was sinking in the west. I had hours of driving, time to think about coal miners.

I had come of age, politically, in a household that revered coal miners as the "shock troops" of the labor movement. Just a month or so earlier, Tom Myerscough, a veteran coal miner and a lifelong Communist Party member, had come to my office for a visit. He regaled me with stories of his years of struggle to win living wages and decent working conditions for miners.

He had been a leader of the National Miners Union (NMU), a short-lived but epic struggle to unionize coal miners, at a time when John L. Lewis was collaborating with the mine owners and betraying the interests of the coal miner rank and file.

Myerscough told me that he had been assigned as an organizer in Harlan County, Kentucky in 1931, when coal miners across the nation were waging a bitter strike battle against outright starvation. Myerscough had been arrested for engaging in organizing the strike in Harlan, the county immortalized by Kentucky's Florence Reece in her song, "Which Side Are You On?"

The sheriff turned Myerscough over to company gun thugs who drove him high up a twisting mountain road across the border into Virginia. Tom knew their plan was to murder him as they had murdered many other union organizers in that coal-rich region of Appalachia. They stopped by the side of the mountain road, dragged Myer-scough from the car and began to beat him mercilessly. Myerscough saw a chance and took it. He charged away toward the side of the road and leaped out into space. He came crashing through the branches of the trees, tumbling over the rocks on the mountainside. The enraged gun thugs unleashed a fusillade of bullets that zinged around him as he rolled hundreds of feet down the mountainside. But he escaped, living to fight another day.

About 10 p.m. that night, I arrived at the Champion Company Store in Little Laurel Run, West Virginia, about 100-yards from the portal of the Mountaineer Number Nine Mine owned by Consolidation Coal Company, a wholly owned Rockefeller property. Powerful floodlights were focused on the mine portal where clouds of thick black smoke were belching.

The store was crowded with surviving miners and the families of the miners trapped underground.

Rescue crews had come from neighboring mines equipped with oxygen cylinders and underground breathing devices in hopes they could enter the mine and bring the miners out alive. Reporters and TV camera crews were also there. It was a grim-faced crowd.

Here are stories I filed over the two days I was on assignment covering that tragedy. I filed those stories by reading them aloud from a yellow legal pad over a pay phone outside the Champion Company store. On the other end of the line was Madeleine Provinzano, an excellent typist who once served as a secretary for the editor of the *New York Times.*

Ghosts of Dead Haunt the Mines
Special to the Daily World

November 23, 1968
MANNINGTON, WEST VIRGINIA—The ghosts of sixteen dead miners are rising to haunt the mine owners, here, as hopes wane for the seventy-eight miners trapped in "Consol Mine Number Nine."

Fourteen years ago, November 13, 1954, sixteen men died in this same mine. Charles Priester Jr., a miner who has come to join in the rescue attempt here, told this reporter the grisly tale of this disaster. "When the mine exploded the Company sealed it up quick." Priester said. "They stopped pumping the air in. Then when they went to open it up five months later they found the bodies of the miners. They were all decomposed.

"But three of the miners they found were down under the Continuous Miner. And on the ribs of the heading right next to them they found a long chalk mark. It stretched for about 500-feet marking the path those miners had walked. They were looking for fresh air, so they went back deeper into the mine but they marked the ribs so the rescue team would be able to find them.

"They were alive when the company sealed it up. They found them down under the Continuous Miner wrapped in burlap. They wrapped themselves up in burlap for protection against the heat. They were wearing their gas masks. They were just waiting there for the rescue team.

"The company knows we remember the last time. That's why they are so hesitant to seal it up this time.

"What does the company care," He said bitterly. "If we die they tell us they can always find someone to replace us. They pretend like they care now because all the newspapers are here. They know everybody in the country is watching them.

"This is a big Company here. They care about one thing and that is to get that coal out of there. If we don't get 10,000 tons of coal out of there in a day the superintendent he comes out and chews our asses out. With that kind of production you have to figure that Continuous Miner is moving fast."

Cutting Corners

"I'll give you an example of the way this company cuts corners. When they cut a new heading, they cut a full 120-feet stretch before they go back and rock-dust it to damp down the coal dust. But everybody knows that the heading should be rock dusted as the heading is being cut. They should cut a few feet and then damp it down. That takes time. It's quicker to cut the whole stretch. That's how gas accumulates, and coal dust.

Damping down the coal face and the walls of the heading, he said, is essential to safe mining practices but these rules are violated constantly in the drive to maximize production.

Charles Armstrong, a Negro miner with twenty-one years' experience in the Consol Number 9 mine broke in, "All the crews are shorthanded. We used to have sixteen men on a section. Now we have four and we are putting out more coal with four than we did with sixteen.

"When you work shorthanded you begin to make slips trying to keep up with the machines. That's how accidents happen.

"The Company is always trying to cut corners, cut down the crews, speed up production, cut the costs.

"Don't listen to these white collars in there," he said angrily pointing toward the room where officials of the Consolidation Coal Company were offering explanations for this disaster. "They don't know nothing. They do everything by telephone.

"Why is Boyle, president of the United Mine Workers, so all-fired anxious to tell everybody that the mine was safe? What does he know about it? He wasn't in that mine. We know about the conditions in that mine. We work there."

The rate of speed up in this mine is indicated by the following facts:

The 340 miners employed here extracted 9,400 tons of coal from Consol Mine Number 9 each day. Each miner extracted twenty-eight tons of coal in an eight-hour shift. The price of coal at the tip is $5.73 per ton.

The families who live near the Maude's Run portal have been evacuated. All roads to the two burning portals have been closed.

On the hill above the Champion Company Store is the Little Laurel Run elementary school. In the playground, today, the children dash and play, the sons and daughters of the miners.

"See the little boy with the green sweater on. He's in kindergarten," said a youthful bystander. "His father is one of the trapped miners. He doesn't know it yet. He thinks his dad is working in another mine."

No Fire Drills in Death Mine
Special to the Daily World

November 22, 1968
LITTLE LAUREL RUN, West Virginia—An official of the Consolidation Coal Company admitted that miners at the mine face of Consol Number 9 here had no fire drill practice to enable them to deal with an explosion like those that continue to rock this mine.

"There were no fire drills in the mine," John Roberts, public relations official of the coal company, admitted when pressed by reporters.

"Many of the seventy-eight miners trapped in the methane gas explosion miles underground are young and inexperienced," he added.

Rescue squads composed of miners from every mine in the State are streaming into this tiny, unincorporated mountain village. Nathanial Walker, forty-two years in the mine, said, "Negligence caused these accidents. The company puts on the pressure to produce. They push the Continuous Miner past the safety limit. This causes pockets of gas to accumulate, and that is how explosions occur."

He said the exhaust tubes with their giant exhaust fans should never be more than six feet from the face of the coal vein.

Past the safety margin

"But they push past this six foot safety margin all the time," he said. "It takes time to carry that exhaust tube up to the coal face. So the foreman will say, 'Well, let's go five minutes more.'

"Federal inspectors inspect these mines only once monthly. They should inspect these mines two or three times a week. Consol Number 9 is seven miles long."

Chesley Burns, a miner, said, "There are rescue squads waiting at the union hall to go in and build a fire wall. That's the only thing they can do to smother the fire. It's still burning somewhere in the shaft between Llewelyn and Maude's Run."

They can't send anybody in until they know it's safe.

The mine, one of the richest soft coal mines in the country, runs three or four miles deep. It stretches for seven miles from Farmington to Mannington.

The people of the towns have turned out in mass to aid the rescue effort.

Neighbors throw their arms around the bereaved, crowding into the cheerless store.

Monitoring devices have been installed at all the portals to the mine to detect any signs of life. Red Cross trucks are stationed everywhere, as the long night hours of waiting drag on.

Can be tomb

The company continued to deny that it would block off the mine with concrete blocks to smother the fire. This would turn the mine into a tomb for the seventy-eight men. If this were done, as it has been in the past, the mine would be abandoned for as much as a year to allow the fire to burn itself out. A test hole has been driven into the mountainside to test the gas content, the temperature, and to detect signs of life in the shaft.

Another explosion rocked the Llewellyn portal this morning. A fire there is raging out of control. Smoke billows out of the portal, and casts a black pall over the lovely mountain valley.

Reporters have been demanding in a chorus to be allowed to visit the local union, which has jurisdiction over this mine, but the company has blocked this so far.

A Grandmother Asks, "Is there a List?"

Special to the *Daily World*

November 22, 1968

FARMINGTON, WEST VIRGINIA, NOVEMBER 22—"Is there a list?" asked an aged woman, pushing through the huddled crowd of women at Number 9 portal. She reached the bulletin board and ran her finger down the paper. "Yes," she said tearfully, "here it is—Lester." She read her grandson's name out loud.

Lester Willard and other miners are trapped three miles underground, while the mothers, the wives, the children stand in the long, lonely vigil waiting word of their fate. Almost all hope is gone.

Katherine Jenkins, sitting with scores of relatives in the Champion Company Store across the road from Portal Number Nine of the Consolidation Coal Company mine, told me, "We just wait. All anybody can do is wait. He went to work on Tuesday night. It happened Wednesday. We have one son. He's in Vietnam."

Beverly West, eighteen, is sitting in the Champion Company Store, as she has since Wednesday when she heard of the disaster. Her father, forty-nine, a machine operator, is one of the trapped miners.

"I haven't given up hope," she said. "My mother is over at my aunt's house. My uncle is in the mine, too. Mama was sleeping when I left. I have two cousins in the mine too. My uncle was killed in an explosion fourteen years ago. My daddy is a supply man, so he's all over the mine."

A pregnant mother wiped her eyes with a crumpled paper towel. "Someone should start a babysitting pool," she said, shifting the two-year-old child she held in her weary arms.

'Our Only Thought is Saving Those Men'

Daily World Staff Correspondent

November 23, 1968

LITTLE LAUREL RUN, West Virginia—Nathaniel Stephens, coalminer, father of ten children, is one of

Photo courtesy of West Virginia Office of Miners' Health, Safety, and Training

twenty-one miners who escaped from Number 9 Mine last Wednesday when methane gas exploded trapping seventy-eight of his fellow workers.

Stephens, a Negro, lives in a neat white frame house on Echo Hill. Through his living room window can be seen the giant conveyor belt, the silos, and the railroad sidings of the Consolidation Coal Company "Consol Mine Number 9" where he has labored for twenty-nine years. The mine has had forty-four citations against it in the past three months for "repeated violations" of the Federal Safety Code.

Stephens stood in his kitchen and recounted to this reporter the story of his brush with death.

"I was on the slope, down at the bottom. It's 1,400 feet from the portal. I'm a main line motorman. My job is to transfer the coal from the coal face to the rotary dump. Then the coal is dumped onto the conveyor belt and it runs up out of the mine to the tip.

"I had just placed a tip on the bottom of my car at the face and I was getting ready to run it back. I got a call from Ray Parker on the radio. He operates the dump. He told me to tell my buddy on the face that we better get out of the mine. I switched off my motor and brought it to a complete stop. I got off and anchored it and then we walked up the slope to the portal. I didn't hear the explosion. When I got out they told me what had happened and they advised me to go home.

"There were only four of us who reached the top in my crew. The others came out after we did.

"The Lord works in mysterious ways. I just want the rest of my fellow workers to be rescued. I have worked twenty-nine years in Number 9. I have lived twenty-two years in this same house. Every miner is thinking about just one thing right now: getting down to those workers. We aren't thinking about anything else.

"I thank God I got out. I pray that my fellow workers will get out."

Mr. Stephens sat at the dining table listening and stroking their young daughter's head. Stephens said the local union has not yet called a meeting to decide what action they should take. "The ministers in the churches have been down at the company store holding some prayer meetings. The people are giving aid to the families of the men."

Now the mine owners are considering sealing the mine as a last resort to smother the fires that rage in the miles of twisting corridors that honeycomb this mountain. If this is done the fate of the seventy-eight miners is sealed.

The families continue to sit stoically in the smoky, cheerless Champion Company Store. They recall that officials were quick to abandon hope in the case of the mining disaster earlier this year when miners were trapped for ten days in May without food and water in the Hominy Falls incident. These miners were ultimately rescued.

Jimmie Ross, a high school sophomore, is cutting classes to join the round-the-clock vigil. "My dad works in this mine, but he wasn't down there. If they seal the mine, Dad will be out of work for at least a year. They could seal it for five years."

The mine employs 340 workers. At one time more than 900 worked here but that was before mechanization. From the tip at Little Laurel Run, 9,400 tons of soft coal are extracted daily. The price at the tip is $5.73 per ton.

Above the door of the Company Store is a sign which states: "Through these portals pass the finest coal miners in the world."

Inside, turkeys are advertised at .49¢ a pound with the admonition, "Place your order now for Thanksgiving."

Chapter 3

Which Side are You On?

Jock Yablonski: Warrior for Coal Miners' Lives

I drove home from Mannington, West Virginia grieving for the trapped miners and their families, in no mood to celebrate Thanksgiving. A few days after that feast, Joyce gave birth December 8, 1968, to our third child, Susan Melissa Wheeler.

The Mannington mine disaster, the death of those seventy-eight miners entombed forever in Consol Mine Number 9, would trigger a struggle in the mine fields that would shake the entire nation.

I had witnessed the appearance of United Mine Worker President Tony Boyle at a news conference in the Champion Company Store standing beside John Corcoran, President of Consolidation Coal Company. Boyle had defended Consol's mining practices and safety record even as seventy-eight miners were still trapped underground.

It was a near unprecedented display of insensitivity, an outrageous case of collaboration with the company that every miner knew cared only for maximum profits, the lives and health of the miners be damned.

This crisis gave a huge boost to the struggle of miners for increased mine safety and health, especially the fight for compensation for the deadly Black Lung disease. Yet Tony Boyle was so determined to bow and scrape to the mine owners that he kept the UMW out of the fight for enactment of the Black Lung Compensation law.

Miners and their advocates, especially Dr. I.E. Buff, the Charleston physician who spearheaded the fight for the Black Lung bill, were forced to organize the Black Lung Association to fight for this legislation. Rank and file miners, UMW regional vice presidents like Jock Yablonski, Dr. Loren Kerr of the UMW Health & Welfare Fund, all flocked to the Black Lung Association. Members of Congress, notably Representative Ken Heckler (D-W.Va.) stepped forward, introducing the Black Lung bill and mustering support for it.

The Mannington disaster and Tony Boyle's shocking display of sympathy for Consol caused UMW leader, Jock Yablonski, to announce his candidacy for President of the union. Yablonski lost in an election so crudely rigged by Boyle and his henchmen that rank and file miners in the coalfields were outraged and determined to fight back.

Soon after the election results were announced, I walked up to K-Street, where the *UMW Journal* had its editorial offices, knowing that Yablonski had his office in D.C. in that building. I was seeking a comment from Yablonski on the struggle against Black Lung Disease.

I stepped into Yablonski's office. He was a gruff man with a gravel voice. He shook my hand but then said with an edge of irritation in his voice, "Why do you want to interview me? There are hundreds of miners in town today picketing UMW headquarters to protest the rigging of the election. Those miners will answer your questions."

I was stunned. I always consulted the AP and UPI "day book" in the National Press Club upstairs from my office to see what important events were happening in Washington. Somehow I had missed this momentous event.

I thanked Yablonski and rushed out of his office and headed across McPherson Square to cover the miners' protest outside UMW headquarters where Boyle was holed up. I got a good article on the protest.

In the meantime, President Nixon was engaged in open war against the Black Lung law, sabotaging the law by slashing funding for its enforcement by tinkering with the permissible levels of exposure to coal dust to deny benefits.

I was in my office during an especially dead time of the year for news with Christmas coming on. I got no answer as I made one phone call after another. Then on the spur of the moment I thought: Why not call Jock Yablonski? I telephoned information for Clarksville, Pennsylvania, the town in the coalfields of Appalachia where Yablonski lived with his wife and daughter. They had a listing.

I telephoned the number and after two or three rings, a voice answered. It was unmistakably Jock Yablonski's gravel voice.

I asked him for his reaction to Nixon's latest outrageous slur that the coal miners were gold-brickers seeking Black Lung benefits they did not deserve. I will never forget the combination of anger and sadness in his voice as he denounced Nixon's cruelty and blasted his warped priorities in squandering billions on the war in Vietnam while working class people in the U.S. went hungry and sick.

I thanked Yablonski for the interview and wrote up the story and sent it in to the *Daily World*.

Just a few days later, the news erupted across the nation: Murderers had broken into their Clarksville home and assassinated Yablonski, his wife and his daughter on New Year's Eve. I would have been in shock over this vicious triple murder in any case. But I was conscious that I was one of the last people to speak to Yablonski before he was murdered. I could hear his gravel voice still ringing in my ears.

I made immediate plans to travel to Western Pennsylvania to attend the funeral of the Yablonski family. Here are some of the stories I wrote about that tragedy, that crime against a family and the working class.

Miners Shut Pits for Yablonski Rites
By Tim Wheeler
Daily World Washington Bureau

January 10, 1970

WASHINGTON, PENNSYLVANIA, January 9—In sub-zero temperatures the coal miners buried here the martyred Yablonski family today—Joseph, his wife Marguerite, and their daughter, Charlotte.

Snow mantled the frozen coal-rich mountains surrounding this town and blanketed the Washington Cemetery, their final resting place, as hundreds of grief-stricken miners gathered at the gravesite.

From the funeral home in Clarksville this morning, the bodies were carried to the Immaculate Conception Church here for last rites.

The Vesta Mine, the Robena, the mines of Island Creek and Consolidation Coal Companies fell silent as scores of thousands of miners walked out of the pits in bitter mourning for their slain leader and his family. At least ninety-five percent of the miners were off their jobs.

"They'll have to kill us all before they stop us," choked one shattered miner to this reporter as he sat in a pew waiting for the service to begin. "I'll tell you what I think about the Labor Department's investigation—a day late and a dollar short."

Where were the Feds then?

"Now the place is swarming with the Feds," said another miner gripping his temples with trembling fingers. "Where were they on New Year's Eve?"

He was referring to the night Yablonski, his wife and daughter were gunned down in their home near here. The Labor Department announced yesterday that it was opening an investigation of the recent United Mine Workers election in which Yablonski opposed incumbent W.A. (Tony) Boyle for the presidency.

Leading the pallbearers with coffins to the altar were Yablonski's surviving sons, Kenneth and Joseph Jr.

Monsignor Charles Owen Rice of the Holy Rosary Catholic Church in Pittsburgh, a close friend of Yablonski, led the celebration of the high mass. Monsignor Rice, who married the Yablonskis thirty years earlier, said it was a mass of resurrection and hope.

The vestments were white, the altar was draped in white, and candles flickered in the brilliantly-lit gothic-style church.

Rice said the murders capped the decade of the "frightful Sixties" and shocked a nation battered by the ugly war" in Vietnam and by an "almost unbelievable progression of assassinations." He said "echoes of the assassination of the Kennedy brothers and Dr. Martin Luther King" could be heard in the Yablonski murders.

"He made friends, but like other strong men he made enemies," Rice went on. "He died with his work unfinished but with a ringing declaration that work had to go on."

'A deed of infamy'

The murder of the two women, he said, was "chilling, efficient, and premeditated. It was not a matter of chance," he said. "It was worked out . . . it was a deed of infamy . . . "

He said, "As we contemplate these caskets we ponder why and by whom? It is frightening to think what is abroad in the land."

Kenneth Yablonski said his father was murdered "because he was determined to give the miners a chance to change their union. He did more for the miners in the past year than he had done in all the previous thirty years. Jock Yablonski believed that "The heart of the union was in these miners who go into the pits. We entrust our father to the coal miners' who loved him so much."

He called on the miners to be pallbearers. The miners came forward and carried the coffin out of the church.

Children in scarlet choir gowns sang hymns as the simple oak caskets passed up the aisle and out of the church for burial.

Dr. Buff Charges Owners behind Yablonski Killing
Daily World Washington Bureau

Dr. I.E. Buff
Courtesy of University of Virginia

WASHINGTON, JANUARY 6— Dr. I.E. Buff, an ally of the coal miners' "Black Lung" movement, accused the mine owners today of ordering the execution of Joseph A. Yablonski, rank and file leader.

"I don't believe this was a union killing," Buff declared in a telephone interview with the Daily World from his office in Charleston, West Virginia. "We want the real murderers apprehended and punished. The 'interests' were behind this."

Asked what he meant by "interests," Buff declared: "That means the mine owners, the railroads, the oil interests, steel—the Mellons and the Rockefellers. I don't mean that they were directly involved. But it ends up with them. They are the gangsters in the well-pressed suits," he declared angrily.

Buff was also sharply critical of United Mine Workers president, W.A. (Tony) Boyle. "Boyle's statement on the murders was weak. Where is he? Why doesn't he speak out?" Buff declared.

Both lives in danger

"Jock Yablonski told me on several occasions that both of our lives were in danger. He asked me if I were scared. I said no. He said he wasn't either. I told him he was affecting not only the union but the coal interests themselves."

Buff said that the attempt to destroy the rank and file coal miners' movement would backfire and could lead to the "nationalization of the coal mines."

He told the *Daily World* the coal miners of Greene County in western Pennsylvania and the miners in West Virginia, enraged by the assassination of Yablonski, his wife and daughter, are spontaneously walking off their jobs. Tens of thousands, he said, are expected to attend the funerals.

He said he sent telegrams today to U.S. Attorney General John Mitchell, FBI director J. Edgar Hoover and Pennsylvania Attorney General William C. Bennett demanding the full disclosure of the assassins. The telegrams demand the apprehension and punishment of the "actual murderers, not only the one who pulled the trigger, but the one who ordered this done."

"Professional murder" charged

"This was a professional murder." He said. "The fact that they murdered his wife and daughter shows it was committed by gangsters who don't want any witnesses."

Buff said a clear motive exists for the political assassination. Yablonski had planned a new exposé of the coal industry in his suit against Tony Boyle, charging election frauds in his unsuccessful bid for UMW president.

"He had information on the mine interests that he was going to reveal in the suit," Buff charged. "He was going to expose the non-union contracts, the 'sweetheart' contracts. Many of the big companies are operating non-union and his charges would have exposed the coal companies for the gangsters they are."

Yablonski's election committee, he added, was being converted into a committee to continue the struggle for ousting the Boyle machine.

"It was going to continue to organize the revolt within the United Mine Workers to make the UMW into a democratic union," he said.

'Miners led safety drive'

The miners' struggle, he said, is the spearhead of the "safety struggle of all working men in the country. It is a movement to liberate the workers, not only in the coal industry." He pointed out that the movement for occupational safety has now spread to the textile workers who are decimated by the "white lung" disease.

"This touches the copper workers, the chemical workers, the steel workers. They all have this in common—it is going to cost money."

Labor in a state of shock

"This has shaken the entire labor movement," declared Russ Leach, director of the Alliance for Labor Action. "We want the murderer caught and those behind this exposed."

Yablonski's attorney, Joseph Rauh, left here with Yablonski's son, Joseph Jr., for Pittsburgh and was unavailable for comment today. Representative Ken Hechler (D-West Va) told reporters Yablonski was a "fearless man."

"He was not afraid of threats or beatings. Coal miners owe Yablonski a lasting debt for speaking out for the rights of the rank and file miners."

This reporter met Yablonski on two occasions and spoke with him by telephone at his home last December 18. He was a tough man with flinty blue eyes and a gravel voice. He was a man of the rank and file.

When miners left a shift in western Pennsylvania and travelled to Washington to picket the UMW headquarters, Yablonski went down to speak with them and shake their hands. His opponent, Tony Boyle, remained hidden in the tomblike offices of the UMW here.

He was undaunted by his defeat in the recent UMW elections. After President Nixon threatened to veto the Mine Safety bill, Yablonski told the *Daily World*, coal miners would stage a nationwide shutdown if necessary to force passage of the bill.

Stressed mine safety fight

"They have plenty of money for the war in Vietnam," he added. "They never have any money for the working people. It's rather tragic. We are disturbed by President Nixon's inconsistency on this—$136 per month is mighty little compensation for someone who is disabled."

Yablonski turned to all allies in his struggle for a democratic union.

Yablonski appreciated the extensive coverage by the *Daily World* to the mine safety struggle. And when asked by the *Daily World* for his opinions of the coverage he said he wished the *Daily World* would write more on the subject of coal mine safety.

A Visit to "Bloody Harlan"
Daily World

April 13, 1978
HARLAN, KENTUCKY—Along the spine of Cumberland Mountain, on Highway 421, I could see 100 miles

Company housing in Harlan County owned by Duke Power in Brookside, KY. House in foreground was the home of Jerry Rainey, a United Mine Worker. Duke Power threatened the family with eviction during the 1974 Brookside strike. Photo courtesy of Jack Corn, U.S. Environmental Administration

across the mountaintops, south into Tennessee, east into Virginia, and westward into the blue-green interior of eastern Kentucky. Spring had come to Appalachia. The road swerved and I drove down toward the valley of the Cumberland. From below came the roar of diesel engines and around the bend a giant Mack truck appeared. Snarling brutishly, hogging the road, spewing black clouds. Another and yet another truck came in a deafening convoy. Each was piled high with coal.

This was "Bloody Harlan" County, owned by Duke Power, U.S. Steel, Blue Diamond Coal and St. Joe Minerals. Here, seventy percent of the coal is mined by non-union labor.

On Martin's Fork of the Cumberland, the loaded coal hopper cars of the L&N Railroad seemed to flow down the valley like black blood from an open wound. Scattered beside the road are homes, ruined by past floods: their roofs caved in; their tarpaper siding torn; their porches collapsing. Litter is everywhere. Cars, upended and rusted, lie in front yards like mechanized cadavers. Children, sad-eyed, were standing by the roadside, watching silently as Duke Power's scab trucks roared by.

On the outskirts of the town of Harlan (County seat, population 3,318) is a hospital. It is crowded. According to the Vital Statistics of the U.S., the national mortality rate in 1970 was 9.5 per 1,000 population. In Harlan County it was thirteen per 1,000. The U.S. tuberculosis mortality rate is 2.6 per 100,000, but Harlan County, population 37,370, has lost from two to four citizens to TB every year over the past two decades, three to four times the national TB death rate. Pneumonia and influenza took thirty-three lives in Harlan in 1970, more than three times the national death rate for these diseases.

In every health index—infant mortality, cancer, heart disease, stroke, malnutrition—Harlan County's death rate is alarmingly higher than the nation's.

Thousands of Harlan-Countians, miners or former miners, are afflicted with Black Lung, silicosis, or other lung ailments. Harlan has had more than its share of the 5,255 miners killed in Kentucky mine disasters between 1920 and 1969.

From 1950 to 1970, Harlan County's population dropped from 71,751 to 37,370—one of the most precipitous population loss rates anywhere in the nation. The 1970 U.S. census also shows that the 9,456 families in Harlan County had a median annual income of $4,682. Less than half the nation's average median income of $9,590. The census counted 698 families with annual incomes of $1,000 or less. Those on public assistance totaled 1,351 and their average annual welfare income totaled $1,041 for that year. The county had only five residents who reported annual income of $50,000 or more.

The most elementary sanitary services, taken for granted elsewhere, are denied the people here. There is no public trash collection. According to the census, 59.8% of the dwellings lack "some or all plumbing." Bell Telephone has carved the county into five exchanges and long distance rates are charged for calls as short as three miles.

Even natural disasters in Harlan County are man-made. Clear-cutting of forests on the mountaintops by Georgia Pacific Corporation has denuded the ground. So has strip mining by U.S. Steel in the Lynch area of Harlan County. Last year, seven inches of rain fell on April 4 in a twelve-hour period. The bare mountainsides served as giant funnels gathering the waters into a rampaging flood that swept down the valleys carrying away the miner's cabins and mobile homes. It was the fourth major flood disaster since 1957.

Despite a letter writing campaign to Congress by the Harlan County "Volunteers for Flood Control," the U.S. Army Corps of Engineers has stubbornly refused to undertake flood control measures on grounds that the County cannot satisfy a "Cost/Benefit Ratio" requirement.

Duke Power, U.S. Steel and Georgia Pacific, incapable of shame, are not embarrassed by this appalling human misery. Yet eastern Kentucky has buried in its mountains an estimated 30 billion tons of high-grade bituminous coal. The contradiction between such colossal natural wealth and such human poverty is stark.

They favor the rational provided by the author Harry Caudill who wrote in *Night Comes to the Cumberland*, that the problem with the mountain people is "genetic." They are too "inbred" and the "IQ rate" in the county is declining. He proposed an Army base be situated in Harlan to bring new "genes." This slander against the people of eastern Kentucky is reminiscent of Nazi "master race" ideology.

The Harlan Countians I interviewed did not fit this stereotype. The Reverend Hugh Cowans, a blind disabled miner who lives with his wife in Evarts, showed me his pay slip for the week ending July 15, 1935. It read, "133 tons @ 9¢ per ton . . . $11.97."

"That was before the deductions," he said with a laugh. "We had to pay for our own blasting powder and caps, all our tools, our headlamp batteries. They paid us in scrip that we could only use at the company store. After we paid our bills, we ended up owing the company."

His wife interjected, "If they bust up the UMW they'll go right back to that."

Reverend Cowans, well over six-feet tall, held out his hand less than a yard from the floor. "We were mining twenty-eight-inch coal—I worked on all fours twelve, fourteen, sixteen hours a day. I was secretly organizing for the UMW in 1936. I had to crawl up to other miners in the mine and get them to sign the UMW checkoff slip."

Reverend Cowans, who is Black, recounted an incident in which company gun thugs, enraged by his union activities, forced him and his brother-in-law from the mine at gunpoint, forced his brother-in-law to strip naked, and they beat him with their gun belts until blood ran down his back. "It would have been suicide for me to move; they would have shot me down," Cowans said.

Jobs for Black miners were plentiful during the pick-and-shovel days, but the mine owners viciously discriminated against Blacks now that the mines are mechanized, he said. "It is a conspiracy to drive the Black miner out, to starve him and his family," he said. "It is rough for a Black man here in America."

Cowans said the Ku Klux Klan is extremely active, these days, spearheading the mine owners' drive to destroy the UMW from outside as well as from within. Of President Carter's Taft-Hartley strikebreaking injunction, Cowans said, "Men are not supposed to live under slave labor. Our right to strike is the only weapon we have. You can't pay a miner enough. You can't give him enough fringe benefits. Under this contract, the companies aren't going to give us retirees anything but a twenty-five dollar a month raise."

Mrs. Cowans broke in angrily," They are the ones who sweat blood to build the UMW. Is there any fairness when miners who retire after 1974 get $400 or $500 a month and those who retired before get only $275?

Later I drove back through Evarts. On May 5, 1931, striking coalminers in this village defended themselves against an invasion of company gun thugs. Two thugs and one miner were killed. Troops were sent in and forty-three strike leaders were arrested. Strike leaders W.B. Jones and William Hightower were framed on "conspiracy to commit murder," charged and sentenced to life prison terms. They were not released until ten years later, Christmas Eve, 1941.

A reign of terror was unleashed. In 1933 alone, gun thugs murdered fifty-six men, women and children to preserve Harlan County's union-free environment. It was during this period (November 1931) that author Theodore Dreiser led a citizen delegation here to probe the terrorism against miners. In this delegation was a Union Theological Seminarian named Arnold Johnson, who later became an outstanding leader of the Communist Party USA. It was this investigation that gave Harlan its name, "Bloody." Among the victims was Harry Simms, an organizer for the Young Communist League, murdered while leading strike relief efforts in Harlan.

It was also in this period that Florence Reece penned her immortal song about Harlan, Which Side Are You On? with its verse, "Don't scab for the bosses, don't listen to their lies. Us poor folks haven't got a chance unless we organize."

Forty-three years after the "Battle of Evarts," a Duke Power foreman armed with a shotgun murdered Lawrence Jones, a young miner on strike for a UMW contract at the Brookside Mine.

The Brookside Miners told me they were prepared to stay out 101 days longer, if necessary, to win a just contract. They angrily rejected President Carter's strike-breaking Taft-Hartley injunction and debunked his call

for workers to "exercise voluntary restraint" and "sacrifices" in the name of "fighting inflation."

"Where are the Duke Power's sacrifices?" they asked.
Jerry Rainy, a veteran of the Brookside Strike, said, "I
personally would not vote for a contract if I had to pay
a single dollar for hospital care that the company paid
before." The Brookside miners' victory in winning their
1974 strike against Duke was the opening shot of the
flight to organize all the non-union or company union
(Southern Labor Union) miners in eastern Kentucky.
That battle has now shifted to Stearns, Kentucky west
of here, where miners are fighting a bitter strike battle
for a UMW contract.

Talking to these miners in the Deaton Grocery Store
a few yards from the Brookside mine portal, you see
clearly the enormity of President Carter's crime in siding
with the coal operators against these miners and their
families

A young miner, Jerry Humfleet, said, "When they
brought that Taft-Hartley down on us, they were taking
away our human rights right there."

Striking Pittston miners in their camouflage fatigues and supporters at
Camp Solidarity in Southwest Virginia.

Buses Roll in to Camp Solidarity
People's Daily World

Oct. 18, 1989

CAMP SOLIDARITY, Virginia—The foliage on the mountainsides around Camp Solidarity has turned golden, red and russet. A hint of frost is in the air on a brilliant October morning. The miners' strike against Pittston Coal Group that began April 5 has lasted 155 days, but the outpouring of solidarity with the 1,900 strikers continues to increase.

The miners are now building a bunkhouse at the camp to accommodate visitors in bad weather. "Cold weather is coming on," said James "Buz" Hicks, president of United Mine Workers of America Local 1259. "We want the company to know they won't freeze us out or starve us out. If it takes the whole winter we're going to last one day longer than Pittston."

As he spoke, three pickup trucks arrived from White Pines, Tenn., overloaded with two tons of canned goods. They were a gift from 180 truck drivers, members of Local 519 of the United Brotherhood of Teamsters, employees of Roadway Express. "We've got to help these miners and their families," declared teamster Earl Bare. "They've been out a long time and they need it. They'd do the same for us."

Hugh Lesner and Cliff Chandler, officers of United Steelworkers Local 1299 in Detroit, were at the camp discussing with Hicks the logistics for a caravan of 150 vehicles that will arrive here October 27 bringing steelworkers and teamsters from Michigan and Western Ohio. "We've already raised $52,000 to bring with us and our goal is $125,000," said Lesner. "We've had gate collections and we have a dance and a dog and suds party planned. People have just been outstanding. I think this is the birth of the labor movement all over again."

Hicks said he estimates 40,000 people have come to Camp Solidarity or to the rallies in nearby St. Paul, Virginia, in the past seven and a half months. "The Oil, Chemical and Atomic Workers was here this week," he said. "I talked to a lot of rank and file people about a merger of OCAW and the UMWA and they are behind it 100 percent. What better than to have all energy workers under one roof?"

October 14 was "Pennsylvania Day" and a fleet of buses, pickups and cars had brought 500 trade unionists from Philadelphia, Harrisburg and Pittsburgh. They were preparing to push on to a strike rally in Hardy, Kentucky, where non-Pittston miners recently walked out when they learned that coal they were mining was being used to fill Pittston's orders.

Hardy is a three-hour drive over steep, twisting roads. We joined the mile-long caravan led by a pickup with UMWA banners fluttering and a fleet of chartered Greyhounds. Along the way, residents, some with "We Support UMWA" signs in their yards, waved from their porches. Drivers of oncoming vehicles gave thumbs up victory salutes.

The strikers are wary of predicting victory but the signs are unmistakable that the tide is beginning to turn in their favor. The UMWA last week re-affiliated with the AFL-CIO. The miners' ranks are so solid and the nationwide support for the strike so impressive that even Labor Secretary Elizabeth Dole traveled here October 12. She talked with strikers on the picket line at Pittston's Moss 3 prep plant where most of the 3,000 sit-down protesters have been arrested. Dole arranged a meeting in her office last Saturday between UMWA President Richard Trumka and Pittston chief executive Paul Douglas. Afterward she announced she will appoint a "super-mediator" to help settle the strike.

When the convoy arrived at the municipal park in Hardy, a tiny mining town, hundreds of camouflage-clad miners and their families were on hand to greet the Pennsylvanians and serve them lunch.

Shirley Watson and Nyoka Stanley, wives of two striking miners in Eastern Kentucky, were serving from a table laden with homemade cakes and pies. "We found out Thursday that we had a lot of people coming in for this rally," said Watson. "We called up every union family we knew and told them to bake, bake, bake. 'Bring it in! If you can't bring it in, we'll go and pick it up.'"

Stanley interjected, "It's just inspiring to see people coming in to give us their support. We need all the help we can get. It's one big fight."

Leonard Fleming, co-administrator to UMWA District 19 in Eastern Kentucky and Tennessee, told the *PWD*, "To see these buses roll in here from Pennsylvania, filled with people who have traveled all night, it just gives us a tremendous boost." He said UMWA picket lines in Eastern Kentucky are solid. "The three mines we struck here in the selective strike are no longer filling orders for Pittston. There are a lot of threats from the companies that they are going to close the mines. It is intimidation. The miners here are standing strong."

Waiting in line for a chilidog was Al Smith, an organizer for Hospital and Health Care Employees, Local 1199P, in Pittsburgh, Pennsylvania. "This is a critical fight that will set the stage for the labor movement in the next decade," he said. "I see unity. The support for these miners has not petered out at all. It's growing stronger every day. The labor movement is making a comeback."

Tom Bennington, a striking Eastern Airlines pilot from Miami said he came "to take lessons from the miners on how to conduct a good strike. We're supporting the miners and they are supporting us. I think the labor movement has been asleep for a long time, shrinking and shrinking. We woke up and now we're starting to grow."

Eastern's boss, Frank Lorenzo, has invited pilots to cross the picket line and help "rebuild" a non-union Eastern. "You can cross the picketline," said Bennington, "but a year from now when Eastern is gone, you'd be unemployable. I would never even think of crossing the picketline."

Julius Uehlein, president of the Pennsylvania AFL-CIO, told the crowd he has been a member of the United

Steelworkers for fifty-three years. Coming to the rally in Hardy was his way of returning a favor by former UMWA president John L. Lewis, who launched the drive to organize the Steelworkers in 1937 with a $1 million contribution from the UMWA.

Uehlein introduced Judy Hayes, Pennsylvania AFL-CIO secretary-treasurer. The Pennsylvanians came with food, clothing and money to help the strikers, Hayes said. "But we give so little and take so much."

"We take back your strength, your warmth, your friendship, your commitment to a struggle you must win! You must win not only for yourselves but for the union movement in the United States. We look to you to lead a struggle that thousands upon thousands of trade unionists will follow."

The crowd chanted, 'We will win!"

"Welcome to Class Warfare in Southwest Virginia"
People's Daily World

August 24, 1989
LEBANON, VIRGINIA—"Welcome to class warfare in Southwest Virginia," UMWA Vice President Cecil Roberts greeted AFL-CIO President Lane Kirkland and a delegation of top leaders of the AFL-CIO as they arrived here Wednesday afternoon in the pouring rain. "We have a message for all those corporate union busters out there. We won't go back."

A huge crowd of striking Pittston coal miners and their families cheered as Roberts greeted the AFL-CIO leaders. The crowd picked up the chant, "We won't go back!"

Minutes later, Kirkland and the other members of the delegation, all clad in the camouflage fatigues, which have become the symbol of the striking Pittston miners, were arrested as they sat down outside the Russell County Courthouse to protest more than $8 million in fines levied against the United Mine Workers of America.

UMWA President Richard Trumka thanked the labor movement for coming to the defense of the miners.

Kirkland responded by quoting the famous song "Which side are you on?" by Florence Reece. "'In a fight like this," said Kirkland, "there are no neutrals there.'" The question, he said, is, "which side are you on?" Kirkland told the crowd he was proud to be there, and introduced members of the delegation.

The group included AFL-CIO Secretary Treasurer Thomas Donahue and presidents of a number of national unions: Gerald McEntee, American Federation of State, County and Municipal Employees; John Sweeny, Service Employees International Union; George Kapantais, Machinists; William Bywater, Electronics Workers; Henry Duffy, Air Line Pilots Association, and Lenore Miller, Retail, Warehouse & Department Store Union, as well as Steelworkers Vice President Leon Lynch and AFL-CIO Executive Board Member Barbara Hutchinson.

More than 1,000 miners and their families stood under umbrellas, drenched to the skin, after waiting in a pounding rain for hours for them to arrive. They filled both sides of the street in this beautiful mountain town, framed by peaks of the nearby mountains.

Despite the downpour, people's spirits kept getting higher. They waved picket signs that read, "We want a contract!" and chanted "UMWA all the way!" A state trooper was greeted by a roar as he drove past in his car.

A group of ministers, bluegrass musicians playing the banjo, guitar and mandolin, led the crowd in singing, "We shall not be moved." When I asked what the name of the group was, they looked at each other inquiringly. "We're the Picketline Pickers," one said.

Earlier today, the AFL-CIO leaders spoke at a rally at the Bell Tower on the grounds of the State Capitol in Richmond, Virginia. An AFL-CIO spokesperson told PWD that the rally was in solidarity with striking Bell Telephone workers, Eastern Airlines strikers and the Pittston miners.

A major purpose of the rally, she said, was to pressure Governor Gerald Baliles to stop using Virginia state troopers as strikebreakers in Southwest Virginia. The troopers are escorting Pittston coal trucks and strike-breakers and have arrested more than 2,000 strikers.

James "Buz" Hicks, president of UMWA Local 1259, told the *PDW*, "You couldn't ask for a bigger morale booster than this demonstration of solidarity. This is one of our biggest days so far. You can see the gleam in the eye of these mineworkers who have been on strike since April 5."

Hicks said the strikers deeply appreciate that the highest-ranking labor leaders in the nation would travel to Southwest Virginia to be arrested alongside the striking coal miners. "But we also appreciate the rank-and-file people who are coming in here to help us. That's where it's at," Hicks said. "It shows that the whole country is concerned and does not want us to lose this fight. Pittston has done organized labor a favor. They woke everybody up and everybody is getting on the bandwagon."

Peter Michalzik, general secretary of the Brussels-based International Federation of Miners, arrived here Tuesday, touring the picket lines at each of Pittston's twelve mines in this region. If Pittston Coal Group succeeds in breaking the UMWA, he told the miners, it would encourage similar union-busting tactics around the world. "I don't think we would sit down and quietly watch that happen," he said.

Decker Miners Win Four Year Strike
People's Weekly World

Aug. 10, 1991

SHERIDAN, Wyo.—Embattled coal miners voted 153 to 44 to ratify a new contract with Decker Coal Co. on July 30, clearing the way to settlement of their four-year strike in Wyoming's coal-rich Powder River Basin.

Larry Deeds, president of United Mine Workers of America Local 1972, told the *World* that workers will return to their jobs as soon as Decker meets all the conditions in the tentative agreement. That includes reinstating fired strikers and removing from the payroll the permanent replacements Decker hired eleven days after 243 miners walked out of the mine on October 1, 1987.

The deal hangs on acceptance of a job buyout agreement by fifteen former strikers and an early retirement package by at least fifty others.

"The Decker strike will be recorded as one of the most monumental labor struggles in recent times," Deeds said. "There are very few cases where the labor movement has been able to maintain its solidarity for four years and come out with a significant victory."

Like the UMWA's strike against Pittston Coal and the Daily News strike in New York City, "it shows us that when workers are in trouble other workers have to come to their support," Deeds said. "That's the meaning of labor solidarity. That is what coal miners, steelworkers and other trade unionists will be marching for in Washington, D.C. on August 31."

He said that a number of Local 1972 members plan to fly to D.C. to join the Solidarity Day '91 demonstration.

Despite the relatively small number of workers involved and their remote location, the Decker strike became a celebrated labor struggle. The UMWA poured in financial and organizational support. President Richard Trumka and Vice President Cecil Roberts travelled here repeatedly to assist. The local also organized its own members and their community supporters in Sheridan. Solidarity marches were staged through downtown Sheridan, and rallies at the center of town.

A publicity campaign was launched to popularize the struggle. Decker Coal fires the power plants of Chicago and Detroit. The labor movement in those cities responded with a vigorous campaign demanding that the utility companies buy coal elsewhere.

"We were supported by a tremendous outpouring of generosity from other unions across the country and Canada," Deeds said. "But it was the courage, stamina and determination of our own members and their families that enabled us to hold out."

The Rocky Mountain region, birthplace of the Western Federation of Miners and the Mine, Mill, and Smelter Workers, has a century-long history, he said. "When General Custer was being defeated at the battle of the Little Big Horn, copper miners in Butte, Montana, were organizing their first union. The Ludlow Massacre of striking coal miners took place a few hundred miles east of here in Colorado."

Deeds said about 3,000 miners, mostly non-union, are employed in strip mines owned by Exxon, Gulf, ARCO, Peabody Coal, Consolidation Coal, Shell and Mobil Oil in the Powder River Basin, a region with trillions of tons of coal in seams as thick as twenty-five feet. Peter Kiewit and Sons of Omaha, Neb., and Pacificorp, a Portland, Ore., holding company, joint owners of the Decker mine, raked off $100 million annually in profits at the mine, an estimated $400,000 in profits yearly from each miner.

"In the 1960s and 1970s, workers could go it alone and win," said Deeds. "But today we are dealing with multinational corporations, massive concentrations of economic power. We've had to reach out to other unions, churches and community groups to form alliances to win. This is not just a labor struggle. It is a class struggle."

As partial restitution for its unfair labor practices, Decker has been ordered to reinstate each striker with $35,000 in back pay. The tentative agreement also pushes wages to $18.50 per hour for the day shift with an 80¢ hourly difference for swing shift and $1 per hour for midnight shift. The deal also includes a 3 percent increase in the second year of the three-and-a-half year contract.

Deeds said the package also includes improvements in job security, health and welfare benefits, job bidding and work rules.

Decker was trying to force the miners to shoulder most of the costs of the family health care plan. All Decker miners will enjoy benefits in the new contract, including the handful who crossed the UMWA picketlines to continue working after the strike began. But replacement workers hired after the strike began will be fired.

One possible sticking point is Decker's proposal to "buy out" fifteen strikers, offering them early retirement on full pension and lump sum payments as high as $100,000 to keep them from returning to the payroll. Deeds said he does not know why the company singled them out, but during the strike, miners and their supporters sat down in front of scab coal trucks. Obviously, Decker would like to rid itself of these militants. "Decker planned from the beginning to break this strike and bust our union," he told me.

As workers voted overwhelmingly to ratify the contract July 30, he told the *Associated Press*, "In the age of Reagan and Bush unionbusting, it is an overwhelming victory on behalf of the union people of the United States. It is a victory in a long overdue class struggle. It gives the UMWA a firm base to proceed with organizing miners in the Powder River Basin."

Mine Union Leader on Massey CEO: "Handcuff him...Jail Him!"

People's World

April 16, 2010
CHARLESTON, W.Va.—Coal miners stopped production April 16 to mourn the twenty-nine miners killed in the explosion at Massey Energy's non-union Upper Big Branch mine, April 5, the worst mine disaster in forty years. The day was dedicated to reviewing safety procedures even as President Barack Obama, during a Rose Garden news conference, ordered a top-to-bottom review of mine safety enforcement.

United Mine Workers President Cecil Roberts, speaking to the Pennsylvania State AFL-CIO Convention in Pittsburgh, called for the arrest of Massey Energy CEO Don Blankenship for sacrificing miners' lives to squeeze out maximum profits. "U.S. marshals' should go to where he lives," Roberts thundered. "Handcuff him, put him in chains, take him to jail, set his fine at $40 million." The crowd roared.

Later, Roberts hailed President Obama's statement on mine safety. "His commitment to miners' health and safety is, in my experience, unmatched by any previous president," Roberts said, adding, "I especially applaud President Obama's determination that miners must have the right to refuse to work in unsafe conditions. UMWA members . . . have that right written into their contracts, but non-union miners do not have the protection of a contract and are at risk of being fired if they refuse to work in conditions that threaten their lives or their health."

Roberts pointed out that twenty-five-year-old Josh Napper had written a letter to his family just before he went to work, voicing fears for his life due to the gassy, dusty conditions in the mine, so bad the mine had been evacuated several times in recent weeks. Napper was one of the twenty-nine miners killed in the blast.

"There is something wrong with this picture," Roberts said. "When young men go off to war, they write these kinds of letters . . . you're not supposed to write that letter when you're going off to work."

Obama called for stiffer inspection and enforcement. Flanked by Labor Secretary Hilda Solis, Assistant Secretary of Labor for Mine Safety and Health Joe Main, and Mine Safety and Health Administrator Kevin Stricklin, the president told reporters, "There's still a lot that we don't know but we do know that this tragedy was triggered by a failure at the Upper Big Branch mine—a failure first and foremost of management, but also a failure of oversight and a failure of laws so riddled with loopholes that they allow unsafe conditions to continue."

Stronger mine safety laws were passed in 2006 after the Sago Mine disaster, Obama continued, "but safety violators like Massey have still been able to find ways to put their bottom line before the safety of their workers, filing endless appeals instead of paying fines and fixing safety problems.

"I refuse to accept any number of miner deaths as simply a cost of doing business," Obama said.

The president added, "For a long time, the mine safety agency (MSHA) was stacked with former mine executives and industry players." Obama said he is proud that MSHA is now headed by "former miners and health safety experts," Joe Main, former UMW director of safety and health, and mining engineer Kevin Stricklin, a lifelong advocate of miner safety.

Massey Energy "should be held accountable for decisions they made and preventive measures they failed to take," Obama continued. "But this isn't just about a single mine. It's about all our mines. The safety record at the Massey Upper Big Branch mine was troubling [and] far too many mines aren't doing enough to protect their workers' safety."

"In addition," Obama added, "we need to make sure that miners themselves, and not just the government or mine operators, are empowered to report any safety violations."

Representative George Miller, D-Calif., chairman of the House Education and Labor Committee, announced his committee will hold hearings on the disaster.

An Apple for Hannah
(A Christmas Story From the Coal Fields)
People's World

Dec. 27, 2017

NEW YORK—Frank Novich was enrolled in the 5th grade at the Catholic school in Shamokin, Pennsylvania and was instructed by his teacher, a priest, to memorize and recite the catechism all other children were assigned to memorize. Frank, already rebellious at eleven years of age, refused. The priest smacked Frank across the knuckles with a ruler. Frank stood up, picked up his books and walked out of the school.

That was the end of Frank's formal education but the beginning of his learning in the "university of hard knocks."

I heard Frank tell this story when I was commuting to New York from Baltimore to edit the People's Weekly World in the 1990s. He was the elevator operator in the building that houses the PWW and overheard me say while I was riding up to my office that I needed a place to sleep the four nights each week while I was in New York.

Frank invited me to sleep on a narrow monk-like bed in his living room. His apartment was in the Penn South co-op about four blocks from my office in the Chelsea district of Manhattan. The co-op had been constructed by the International Ladies Garment Workers Union to provide affordable housing in one of the most over-priced housing markets in the nation. Frank's offer was a godsend for me. His place was my rent-free "home-away-from-home" for eleven years and it gave Frank many hours to tell me his life story.

His father was an anthracite coal miner and his mother worked as a spinner in the local silk mill in Shamokin.

Photo courtesy Library of Congress

This took place sometime before 1920. The Novich family had emigrated from Poland in the distant past. Since they had been coal miners, they moved to central Pennsylvania seeking work in the anthracite mines. They settled in the town of Shamokin, inhabited by many other Polish immigrants. They were staunch members of the United Mine Workers, followers of union president, John Mitchell, who led them in the Great Anthracite Strike of 1902 broken by President Teddy Roosevelt.

Frank was still too young to work in the coal mines, even in those days when child labor was still legal and children would toil in the mines and mills while the owners played on the golf links.

His mother took her son to work one day and succeeded in getting him a job twelve hours each day in the silk mill. He was a "go-fer," running errands to help keep the mill humming. He toiled at that job for a couple of years but he hated it. He was big for his age, and mature. He pleaded with his father to get him a job in the mines. Finally, his father relented and again, Frank tagged along behind his father to the mine portal one morning.

They walked up to the mine boss. Frank's dad asked the boss if there was a job Frank could do.

"How old are you, son?" the mine boss asked. Frank turned red in the face.

But he and his father had anticipated this question and had practiced Frank's answer.

"I just turned fifteen," he lied.

"How would you like a job as a mule skinner? All you have to do is drive a mule with loaded coal cars up out of the mine."

Frank was hired. He was sent deep into the anthracite mine before dawn each morning together with a mule so anonymous she did not even have a name. No other job he ever worked in his sixty years as a worker would ever equal the fear that gripped him in the first few days, putting on his miner's helmet with the lamp that cast a feeble beam of light into the pitch darkness. A cold damp chilled him to the bone as he trudged down the narrow gauge tracks into the mine. He was grateful that the jenny mule was plodding beside him seemingly indifferent to the fear that gripped him. From that first day he talked to the mule as if she understood every word he spoke. Just hearing the sound of his own voice and the occasional purring sound she made with her lips, or her snort, a shake of her head, reassured him that all was well a half mile underground.

His job was to retrieve the mule from the stable at the mine surface, harness her, and lead her down to the mine portal and on into the mine, walking down the narrow tracks to the chute where the coal was loaded into the coal shuttle car. Frank was shown how to open the chute to let the coal rumble down and fill the car, how to hook the tugs to the single-tree, clear the reins up over the mule's back.

He would flick the reins against her rump and say "giddy-yap" and the mule would lean into the harness. The wheels would slowly turn and the loaded coal car, all sixteen tons, would roll up the slope toward the surface.

When they emerged from the mine, the tracks reached out over a trestle. Frank drove the mule—and the coal car—out that trestle. He pulled a lever and the coal car emptied the load, with a loud rumble into a mountain of anthracite below. Then he drove the mule in a circular roundabout back down into the mine to get another load.

He unhooked the mule and led her around to the other end of the coal car and hooked her up to the single-tree. They repeated this routine nine, ten, sometimes eleven times per shift, tiring for Frank but exhausting for the mule.

Frank was attracted to this jenny from the start and over their years together, it deepened into an abiding love. She was gentle with long ears and sad eyes, painfully thin but also strong. There is a reason they call a powerful woman or man "strong as a mule."

Said Frank to the jenny one day. "Well, It's time you had a name. I like the name 'Hannah.' Do you like it?"

Hannah pressed her muzzle against Frank's chest and rubbed her velvet lips up and down against his jacket as if to nod yes.

"O.K., 'Hannah' it is then."

Half way through each shift, he would sit on the loading dock and eat the lunch his mother had packed him. She often packed an apple or pear into the lard bucket along with the sandwich made from her delectable homemade bread. Hannah strained herself around and reached out with her muzzle, showing her teeth, begging for the apple.

"So you're hungry, are you?" Frank pulled out his pocket knife and cut the apple in two. Hannah crunched and munched the apple greedily.

From then on Frank filled half his lunch bucket with apples, pears, carrots, and other fruits and vegetables.

"Hannah, you are my best friend," Frank told her. And it was true. His assignment in the mine did not put him in close contact with the other miners. Hannah was his closest companion and Frank felt an almost human bond to the mule.

One morning Frank arrived at the stable to harness Hannah. Her stall was empty and she was not in the corral. Where the devil is she?

He hastily donned his work clothes, put on his helmet, turned on the lamp as he hastened down the slope into the mine. He was out of breath when he neared the coal loading dock a half mile into the mine. There standing in the darkness was Hannah.

"They want her to work a double shift," said the muleskinner that Frank was replacing. "They are cruel bastards." He left without saying goodbye.

Frank rushed up to Hannah and put his arms around her neck. She was trembling with weariness and she was lathered with sweat.

As Frank drove her up the slope with the loaded coal car he could hear her snort, blowing, and blowing trying to catch her breath. Frank threw his shoulder against the back of the coal car to help Hannah. He did the same for the second and third load. Finally on the fifth load, Hannah balked. She would not, could not, take another step. Her shoulders and rump were lathered into a thick foam of sweat. She stood panting. Frank snapped the reins against her rump and yelled, "Gid dap, Gid dap, Hannah."

He even tried to bribe her with a carrot. She was so exhausted she turned away from the carrot. Frank wrapped his arms around her neck.

"O.K., Hannah. I get it. One-and-a-half shifts is enough."

He bent down and uncoupled the tugs from the singletree. He led Hannah up out of the mine, into the sunshine. It was still early morning. The foliage on the oak trees that grew on the mountainsides had turned brown and rustled in the breeze. He walked the mule to her stall, lifted the harness from her back and hung it on pegs on the opposite wall. Then he pitched hay into her manger. He found an old worn out blanket and rubbed Hannah down, wiping away the sweat. She was shivering. He walked out of the stable, down the steep hill into Shamokin.

The next morning, when he walked back up the hill to the mine, the boss was waiting for him. He was in a fine rage and snarled at Frank for shirking his duty. When Frank attempted to open his mouth and defend Hannah, the boss's face turned purple with rage. "Hannah? Who in hell is Hannah? You're fired!"

Frank, who by now had turned sixteen, was once again unemployed. By coincidence, a few weeks after he was terminated, conditions for the humans in the mine became just as intolerable as it was for the mules. Speed up. Wage cuts. Cave-ins that buried the miners under tons of rock. Short fuses and lethal dynamite explosions. It was a nonstop bloodbath. The miners reached the breaking point and went out on strike. A deep stillness fell over Shamokin as the mine operations came to a standstill.

One morning, Frank took a notion to walk up the hill and visit Hannah. He took a small gunnysack from the toolshed and filled it with a dozen apples and an equal number of carrots. Christmas was coming and fresh snow had fallen on the little coal mining town. Frank waded through the snow, up the hill, turned left just inside the mine gates and walked over to the corral. There were all the mules standing close together for warmth. Frank stepped up on the bottom rail of the fence. He spotted her standing half asleep among the jennies and the jacks.

"Hannah," Frank called out. She opened her eyes, turned her head. She broke away from the herd and ambled over toward Frank. He pulled an apple from the gunnysack and she bit into it and crunched the fruit contentedly. Frank saw that she had put on weight, her coat sleek. She looked well rested.

"Well, old girl, the walkout has been good for you. You are getting the rest you deserve. I brought you this bag of apples and carrots. Merry Christmas, dear Hannah!" Her lips purred in gratitude and she nudged him with her muzzle, begging for another apple. "I'm going away, Hannah, and don't know when I'll be back. Goodbye, my dear friend."

He turned and headed back down the hill. "What am I going to do now?" he said to himself as he walked through the snow. There was that recruiting poster in the Post Office. "Uncle Sam Wants You!"

"I guess I'll join the Cavalry. Dad will need to lie just one more time about my age."

Two weeks after Christmas, around the epiphany, Frank Novich and his dad walked down to the recruiting station and Frank joined the Army. After basic training at Fort Dix, New Jersey, he was shipped to El Paso where he became a cavalryman, riding with his regiment in regular, illegal, forays across the Rio Grande into Mexico. "Just about as illegal as I am," the underage cavalryman muttered to himself. But that is another chapter in the life of Frank Novich.

Frank Novich outside his Penn South coop apartment building in the Chelsea neighborhood of Manhattan. A former coal miner and NMU seaman, he let me sleep on the studio couch in his living room for 11 years while I was editor of the People's Weekly World.

Chapter *4*

Give Peace a Chance

Anti-War Movement Speaks for the Majority

The Vietnam War had been escalating steadily for over two years when I first arrived in Washington D.C. in the summer of 1968 to take up my duties as *Daily World* correspondent. The body bags were returning in a steady stream, the death count of Vietnamese people and American G.I.s was climbing.

The anti-war movement was also surging and Washington was the destination for protest rallies large and small. Covering these protests, attending news conferences of the People's Coalition for Peace and Justice, the Student Mobilization Committee, Clergy & Laity Concerned, the Vietnam Moratorium, Vietnam Veterans Against the War, the Gold Star Mothers Against the War, and dozens of other anti-war movements became a major part of my assignment.

In the years I covered these protests, the peace movement grew from a minority movement to a majority movement reflecting overwhelming mass opposition to the war.

Initially spearheaded by students and youth, it soon included people of faith and the clergy. Dr. Martin Luther King signaled the unity of the civil rights movement and the anti-war movement with his Riverside Church speech. More and more African Americans, Latinos, and other people of color joined the anti-war outpouring.

The veteran's movement became an enormous factor, led by Vietnam Veterans Against the War (VVAW.) Organized labor played an ever larger role, forming Labor for Peace. Local 1199 Drug and Hospital Workers, the Retail, Wholesale, and Department Store Workers, led by Cleveland Robinson, chartered Amtrak trains to bring thousands of workers, a majority African American, to join the protests against the Vietnam War. There was also the Meatcutters and Butcher Workmen, led by Pat Gorman and Abe Feinglass, who swelled the ranks of labor and anti-war rallies.

I was one of many writers for the *Daily World* assigned to cover this powerful people's movement. Our newspaper fairly bulged with stories from every corner of the nation covering this mass upsurge.

That commitment to cover the anti-war movement continued in the decades that followed. We have carried stories about the struggle for peace whether it was the Soviet Union's struggle for peaceful coexistence, Cuba's gallant defense of their revolution from U.S. overt and covert warfare, the struggle by the people of Angola against South African intervention, the South African people's struggle to end apartheid, the Palestinian people's struggle for nationhood or the Iraqi people's struggle against invasions of Iraq.

Covering the anti-war movement remains a bedrock of the online *People's World* today.

DuBois Clubs Convention Cheers Soldiers 'Hell No, I Won't Go'

The Worker

September 12, 1967
NEW YORK, NEW YORK—"HELL, NO, I WON'T GO TO VIETNAM," declared Ronald Lockman, a Negro G.I. from Philadelphia last week at the opening of the W. E. B. DuBois Club's third annual convention at the Columbia University Campus.

Lockman told the cheering delegates Friday night at Schermerhorn Hall, he was under orders to report for embarkation to Vietnam this September but he would refuse to go.

"At first I felt alone but I soon found out that many Americans who oppose the war in Vietnam also support me," he said.

"I would like to see follow-the-leader in the army. I followed the lead of the Fort Hood Three in refusing to go. Who is going to follow me?" he asked.

The delegates and observers rose to their feet cheering, clapping and chanting. "Hell no, we won't go."

Mrs. Grace Mora Newman, sister of Denis Mora, one of the Fort Hood Three, now imprisoned at Fort Leavenworth, said, "Exactly one year ago the U.S. Army started court-martial proceedings against the Fort Hood Three. No doubt they are getting ready now to court-martial Ronald Lockman. One thing is sure; the DuBois Club will be well represented at Fort Leavenworth."

The audience erupted in laughter and applause.

Mrs. Newman read a letter from Mora, a DuBois Club member, which said, "I know that I have done right because I have behaved according to my working class roots."

The hall was packed with 400 delegates and observers. A massive portrait of W. E. B. DuBois the Negro historian and revolutionary was draped behind the podium. Banners read, "End Racism," and "Radical Action for Socialism."

In the main report of the evening, Jarvis Tyner, a Negro furniture worker from Philadelphia and a founding member of the DuBois Clubs, said the greatest obstacle to the unity of the movements for progress in the U.S. is racism. He said Johnson's answer to the rebellions in America's cities was genocide just as that is his policy in Vietnam.

He said many sat back, while Black people were being mowed down by the National Guard, excusing their

inaction by saying to themselves, "I guess it was necessary, after all, things did get out of hand."

Tyner declared, "For those who sat back, let me say
to you, you cannot isolate what happened in Detroit
and Newark from the general climate in this country. If
they get away with that kind of fascist oppression in the
ghetto they will use it elsewhere."

"Peace movement beware. The ruling class makes little distinction between mass peace demonstrations and
riots."

He said students were a target for stepped-up police
suppression, and added, "Labor movement, you are a
target too. The ruling class fears strikes and mass picket
lines. The climate has been set with the attack on the
Black community. They will use the National Guard
against you also."

Tyner said the people in the U.S. have no real power.
This exposes the sham of U.S. democracy. "Politicians
in the U.S. are chosen in smoke-filled rooms by the
wealthy, powerful monopolies."

Monopoly domination, he continued, is the root of all
the evils that confront the American people.

"America is no Democracy. We live in a capitalist society which is inherently warlike, racist, immoral and
exploitative," he declared.

The demand for power by the powerless is growing
in the U.S., Tyner said. He described the crisis for the
young generation as "dwindling job opportunity and
militarism."

But without the unity of African American and white
people this crisis will never be resolved, he said.

"The DuBois Clubs look on Black Power as a means
to break the racist stranglehold in America," Tyner
declared.

"Conscious whites must be constantly vigilant to
racism every day, every hour, every moment." He said
one aspect of Black Power is Black pride. He said, "Black
pride tells me, 'I am Black and I am strong. I am Black

and I am proud, I am Black and I am beautiful, I am Black and I will struggle.'

"To be Black in America and to hold your head high and to continue to fight is the mark of a hero. Jim Bevel is a hero, Stokely Carmichael is a hero, Ronald Lockman is a hero, and Henry Winston is a hero." The delegates burst into prolonged applause.

"Whites who commit racist acts consciously are oppressed too," Tyner continued, "for they must cleanse themselves of racism in order to be free."

The DuBois Club favored Negro-white unity, he said, not for moral reasons alone, "but because history has destined that our emancipation will be a common one."

"It is not enough to favor Black and white unity. We must implement it," he added.

The DuBois Club has a two-fold task in this period, he said. "First to prove that Black and white unity is possible by being the most effective fighter against racism," and second to prove itself "the best fighter for a new socialist society."

Jim Peake, chairman of the convention, dedicated the meeting to George Vizard, DuBois Club organizer who was shot to death in Austin, Texas, last July by an unknown gunman.

Peake said, "If George could speak to us now, he would say 'Don't mourn, organize.'"

The opening session reflected the great ideological ferment taking place in the movement as guest speakers voiced conflicting views on the path to progress for America.

Julius Lester, a leader of the Student Nonviolent Coordinating Committee, who recently returned from Vietnam, said radicals deluded themselves in thinking the war in Vietnam can be stopped.

"You can't stop the war, you have to change the system," he declared.

He said the test of a radical's commitment was his readiness to match the reactionary violence of the war-makers and racists with violence for social change.

He pointed to the ghetto uprisings as the true form of revolutionary struggle.

The Reverend James Bevel, Director of the Mobilization Committee to End the War in Vietnam, took issue with this approach. He said the young generation had the opportunity to make a revolution in the U.S. and said, "Revolution has nothing to do with burning villages or cities or killing babies."

He said some radicals must prove their "masculinity by stepping on people, killing folks." Karl Marx, he pointed out, was above all else a humanitarian "who understood that freeing people meant freeing them to love each other."

He said revolutionaries must have a clear objective on how they planned to change society and not replace one coercive system with another.

75,000 in Candlelight March to White House
Daily World—Washington Bureau

October 17, 1969
WASHINGTON, OCTOBER 15—Seventy thousand men, women and children bearing 50,000 lighted candles filed past the White House last night to protest the war in Vietnam. Eighteen abreast, the marchers came in a river of flickering light that lasted four hours.

The candles cast a glow on the faces of the marchers. Thousands of Washington's black citizens, youths, children, government workers, entire families with infants in their arms began the march in silence.

Silence broken

At 10 p.m., two-and-one-half hours after the first marcher passed 1600 Pennsylvania Avenue, the silence was broken. A voice in front of the Treasury building cried out in the chill autumn darkness, "What do we want?" and the answering roar, "Peace" resounded on the avenue.

The chant swept down the line, "Peace Now." Then the crowd burst into song. They sang, "We Shall Overcome," and thousands sang. "All we are saying is give peace a chance."

"How many would you say are marching?" the excited reporters kept asking the harried Head Marshall. "Who knows?" he replied, as the marchers tramped past. "They keep revising the estimate upward. The last I heard was 60,000. All we know is that we bought 50,000 candles, and they were gone in ten minutes."

Tim Foster, a ten-year-old fourth-grader from Prince George's County, held his candle close to his chest as he walked past the White House. His cheeks glowed orange from the flame and from the cold, and he said, "I think this is so nice, to be all together like this with the candles. I'm going to bring my mom and dad to the November 15 demonstration."

The march began in the Sylvan Theater. As the sun set westward over the Potomac, the Amphitheater filled with humanity. In an unending stream the government workers, students and housewives poured across the Mall toward the base of the Washington Monument, the cherry trees were tinged yellow, red and burnt umber, and a cold sliver of moon appeared overhead.

Mrs. Coretta Scott King, who led the march, told the people, "Your presence here tonight is deeply inspiring. It shows the marvelous reawakening in the hearts and minds of the American people as they are moved to speak out against this extremely destructive and immoral war. We have seen that the only solution is to bring the boys home and bring them home now."

The crowd burst into applause.

She said that her son, Martin Luther King, 3rd, "has decided he will not give his life on the sacrificial altar" of the Vietnam War.

The crowd turned and headed toward Constitution Avenue for the march to the White House. Darkness had fallen and the river of candlelight spilled around the base of the Washington Monument and down Constitution Avenue.

Washington's massive turnout was by no means the largest in the nation. The national Moratorium office here buzzed with reports arriving from the "provinces." Sam Brown and Marge Sklencar, Moratorium coordinators, read the telegrams aloud, and reporters burst into spontaneous applause.

Nationwide tide

New York City Hall, he said, offered a "modest estimate" that 250,000 New Yorkers protested the war.

In Boston, 100,000 attended one rally, he noted, with 20,000 in Philadelphia. 15,000 in New Haven, 30,000 in one Chicago rally, 10,000 in Milwaukie. 12,000 in Cleveland, 2,500 in Atlanta. 2,000 in New Orleans, 1,200 in Fayetteville, Arkansas. 15,000 in Baltimore.

In Casper, Wyoming 200, and in Los Alamos, New Mexico 700, and others in thousands of small communities across the nation observed the Moratorium.

Fort Kent, Maine, passed a referendum in which ninety-nine percent of the citizens voted for immediate and total U.S. withdrawal from Vietnam.

A cheer went up from the reporters when Miss Sklencar read a telegram from Company E. 4th Battalion, U.S. Army, Fort Sam Houston, Texas.

"We, the undersigned, support your efforts to bring about a speedy end to the war," the telegram said. It was signed by twenty-five GI's with the following postscript, "more of us would have signed it if we could have afforded a longer telegram."

The jubilation was also a time of stocktaking too. Reverend Channing Phillips, the first black man to have his name placed in nomination for U.S. President by one of the major parties, praised the Washington crowd for its splendid mobilization against genocide in Vietnam, but he pointed out that the peace movement has remained altogether too quiet about the genocidal treatment of black Americans. And Mrs. King echoed this theme when she said that the war in Vietnam was a war against "the poor and the black people of America."

Big task ahead

While the turnout of all sectors of the population here in Washington was immense, it is clear that the peace movement has tens of millions more working people it must mobilize. The masses marching here were still predominately youthful and predominately white despite the fact that Washington is more than half black.

The Moratorium leaders told reporters last night that above all they want to enrich the social composition of the movement "to build the majority coalition against the war."

"We talk to people on the basis of the way the war affects them, where it hits them," declared Marge Sklencar. "When we talk to trade unionists, we talk about the war and taxes."

Sam Brown told reporters "this is not an event; it is a process."

The process has just begun.

War Crimes Hearings Set by House Bloc, Group Blasts Nixon's Pro-Calley Moves
The Daily World

April 7, 1971
WASHINGTON, APRIL 6—Members of Congress: Black and white, accused President Nixon today of using convicted baby-killer William L. Calley to justify racist support for his collapsing Indochina war.

Representative Bella Abzug (D-NY) told an overflow news conference in the House Rayburn Building that Nixon's intervention in behalf of Lieutenant Calley, convicted of murdering twenty-two unarmed Vietnamese men, women and children is "unconscionable."

Mrs. Abzug, together with Representative Ronald Dellums (D-Cal), Representative John Conyers (D-Mich)

and Representative Parren Mitchell (D-Md), analyzed President Nixon's attempt to use conscience-stricken moral reactions to the Calley verdict to gain support for his war. In the course of the news conference, a dramatic debate unfolded over the meaning of the case. Mrs. Abzug said it is President Nixon's "last gasp attempt" to hold back the tide of massive abhorrence of the Indochina butchery.

Hearings announced

"The moral convulsion comes from the realization that we have been killing innocent people in Indochina and have made killers of innocent boys," Mrs. Abzug said.

"The convulsion comes from the realization that the war policy is totally wrong and is one big immoral hoax. The people realize that, in their name, murder has been committed."

Representative Dellums had called the press conference to announce that he and other antiwar Congressmen will continue with Congressional hearings on "criminals responsible" for U.S. atrocities in Indochina.

The hearings, April 26-29, will be held in the House Cannon Building caucus room despite bitter opposition from war hawk House members. Dellums said that the House Speaker, Carl Albert had granted permission for the hearing. Dellums said that he hopes to hear testimony from former Presidential advisor Walt Rostow, McGeorge Bundy and from Vietnam Commander General William Westmoreland.

Also present at the press conference were three antiwar Vietnam veterans who told of orders they were given to commit genocide in combat.

Expose generals

Representative Dellums said Calley is a "scapegoat" and the question is "for whom?" He said the war crimes hearings will expose the guilt of Pentagon generals for the atrocities.

He said of Calley, "Yesterday, yes, a killer, but today Calley . . . knows you can be exploited to be a scapegoat for someone higher up."

Dellums said that the Calley case may mean "the right and the left" can come together in opposition to the war.

Representative Conyers strongly differed with Dellums on this point. "This man (Calley) is guilty of premeditated murder," Conyers declared. "He is not a scapegoat for anyone. Now the President is intervening and is seriously intimidating the reviewing officers." Conyers said the Calley atrocity is a stain on President Nixon, who can "inspire Congress to pass a detention law under which people in the District of Columbia can be incarcerated for committing no crime whatever, but who now releases a convicted murderer of twenty-two men, women and children."

Ultimate responsibility

The Michigan lawmaker said Calley's crimes open the question of ultimate responsibility for the atrocities. He said the Nuremburg principles "should have the fullest application in the hearings and should apply to "the civilian authority" in the war.

Robert B. Johnson, a West Point graduate, a Vietnam veteran and coordinator of the Citizens' Commission of

Inquiry of U.S. War Crimes, disputed Representative Conyer's position. He said Calley was a "victim," a pawn of forces beyond his control. "I think the evidence will convince you that there are hundreds of thousands of Calleys in Vietnam and hundreds of Mylais," Johnson declared.

Representative Abzug then grasped Johnson's sleeve and retorted, "Yes, but there are those who did not choose to kill civilians. Calley had a choice and he chose to kill civilians."

Vets Set Up April 24 Advance Guard in D.C.

The Daily World

April 20, 1971

WASHINGTON, APRIL 19—More than 1,000 Vietnam veterans in battle dress surged through the nation's capital today roaring opposition to the Indochina war.

Some on crutches and in wheelchairs, their tunics emblazoned with battle ribbons and medals, the Black, Brown and white veterans marched in regimental strength from the West Potomac Park today, to lay a wreath to the Indochina war dead, at Arlington National Cemetery.

Representative Paul N. McCloskey (R-Cal), a decorated veteran of the Korean War, marched with them and a contingent of widows and mothers of dead GIs as well as kin of prisoners of war also joined the column.

At the gates of Arlington Cemetery, the men and women doffed their jungle fatigue hats and helmets as Reverend Jesse Jackson led them in prayer.

Cemetery gates shut

Then the vets attempted to enter the cemetery but the iron gates were clanged shut, chained and padlocked in their faces.

The Director of Special Events at Arlington refused admittance to a group of five mothers, widows and disabled veterans who attempted to take two wreaths into the cemetery, one for the Indochinese victims of Nixon's war, the other for the 50,000 U.S. dead.

Some, on the verge of tears, cried out, "Why can't we enter Arlington Cemetery?"

McCloskey later denounced the cemetery officials for denying entrance to the vets. He said that the police "could touch off a confrontation" by this callous treatment.

Mrs. Virginia Warner, mother of a prisoner of war, said, "I am here to appeal to the middle-aged, middle-class Americans to stand up with these veterans. They can't do it alone. Instead of destroying Vietnam, let's rebuild America."

15 demands

Jan Crumb, leader of Vietnam Veterans Against the War, read to the throng the first of fifteen demands. "Immediate, unilateral, unconditional withdrawal of all U.S. armed forces and Central Intelligence Agency personnel from Vietnam, Cambodia, Laos and Thailand."

The men and women veterans responded with a standing ovation, cheers of "Right On" and clenched-fist salutes.

They roared approval as Crumb read the demand for "full amnesty" to all war resisters in the U.S. prisons or exile.

Other demands included an end to the military draft, an end to intervention, and the withdrawal of all U.S. troops from Latin America, Africa, Asia and elsewhere in the world, withdrawal of U.S. support for the "corrupt, illegal" puppet military regime in Cambodia and Vietnam.

They also demanded full official Congressional hearings in all charges of war crimes which they charged are committed as a matter of policy in Indochina. They demanded that Congress recognize that the only way to secure the release of POWs is to "stop the U.S. aggression" in Indochina.

They demanded proper care for all patients in Veterans Administration hospitals and job training and placement of every returning veteran. They also demanded drug rehabilitation for returning veterans and urged Congress to slash the military budget and launch a program "to meet the needs of the people."

They demanded that Congress meet in joint session "to hear a member of this assembly."

John Kerry, a leader of the demonstrators and former boat skipper on the Mekong River, told reporters here; as the GIs met to plan strategy, that a mood of anger hangs over the veterans because they were denied access to Arlington Cemetery.

"To tell them they can't lay a wreath to the memory of guys they knew who were shipped back here in body bags is just criminal."

This, plus the refusal of the Administration to permit the veterans to camp on the Mall is stirring bitter and mounting anger among the veterans.

In smoldering anger, the vets then marched across Memorial Bridge to the White House. As they swung past 1600 Pennsylvania Avenue, President Nixon's helicopter was landing on the East Lawn. The defiant veterans chanted, "Peace Now!" and "One, Two, Three, Four—We Don't Want Your ——War."

The vets, with canteens clanking on their hips and lugging bedrolls and knapsacks on their backs, brandished dummy training M-16 rifles as they marched on Pennsylvania Avenue to the West steps of the Capitol.

The vets spilled down the West steps of the Capitol and overflowed the plaza below as Representative Bella Abzug (D-NY) declared: "You are living testimony that the American people do not want to provide the manpower for this ugly, criminal, inhuman war.

"Those who have battled on the battlefield will now do battle on the field of peace," she said. "We are going to make the power structure reflect the will of the GIs, the women, the working people and the poor.

"We are going to stop the war machine and go on to a prosperous future for all of us," Mrs. Abzug said, as hundreds of clenched fists and cheers saluted her.

Representative McCloskey said, "It was an honor to walk with you this morning. No one deserves more the right to assemble here for a redress of grievances."

Two-Coast Marches Top One Million
The Daily World

April 27, 1971
WASHINGTON, APRIL 26—Under crimson banners, almost three-quarters of a million citizens chanting PEACE NOW marched majestically up Pennsylvania Avenue Saturday, the vanguard of the Spring Offensive against President Nixon's Indochina war.

Tens of thousands of Black, brown and white trade unionists in paper caps and hard hats, swelled the marchers' ranks, eventually sweeping aside marshals who sought to hold them to one half of the eight-lane boulevard. The thoroughfare was clogged from curb to curb with surging humanity. Constitution Avenue was then opened and masses flowed onto the street in a solid mass from the Ellipse.

The march was to begin at noon. But restless, active-duty GIs and the Vietnam Veterans struck out at 11 a.m., the masses in a wall behind them. At 3:30 p.m. a speaker from the rally platform announced, "Pennsylvania Avenue is absolutely impassable," throughout its fifteen-block length.

Largest in history

This reporter, who observed the entire march, judged the numbers as at least twice that of November 1969, which lasted about two-and-a-half hours and took up half of Pennsylvania Avenue. This rally lasted four hours and covered the avenue from curb to curb. When added to the demonstrators who flooded San Francisco on the same day, estimated to number as many as 250,000 the total turnout topped one million, the largest demonstration in U.S. history.

Veterans' contingent

"All we are saying is give peace a chance," sang the marching veterans. Jim Dehlin, Flushing, Michigan, a double amputee war veteran in a wheelchair, led the contingent. Red, green, blue and golden flags floated in a pageant the length of the avenue behind them. As the veterans approached the Capitol, they met New York trade unionists marching toward the staging area in the Ellipse, and a roar of greeting went out to the labor reinforcements. The unionists carried picket signs identifying them as members of United Auto Workers, Local 250.

Youth marched in boundless numbers, in floppy hats, castoff army coats and rag-tag blue jeans. A chorus-line of teenage girls, their arms linked, danced their way down the avenue, singing "Take it from the greedy; give it to the needy."

Dozens of campuses were marked off with banners. Kites flew overhead and huge balloons. One youth with a knapsack on his back glided along on roller skates. A bearded man in a turban pushed his bicycle as he marched. Army surplus canteens, filled with lukewarm water, were passed along. Labor's proud banners mingled with those of the youth:

"Furriers Joint Council supports peace," declared one.

"Stop Nixon!" Madison, Wisconsin Hospital Local 150.

"U.E. Local 506, Erie, Pa. Demands: Peace, Jobs, End the War Now."

"Local 140, United Furniture Workers."

"District 65 for Peace."

"American Federation of Government Employees, Local 2677."

"OEO wants out NOW!"

"Cleaners & Dryers Joint Board, AFL-CIO."

A broad-shouldered man in an orange hard-hat carried the sign, "IBEW, Local 58; Hard Hats for Peace!"

For the first time labor contingents were of massive proportions. Thousands came from New York City and thousands more from the Midwest.

Black and brown ranks

It was in the ranks of labor that vast numbers of Black and brown peace fighters were to be seen. The contingent of union government workers stretched for two blocks; 40 abreast. Hospital workers, mostly Black women in blue paper caps, marched more than a thousand strong, singing "Amen, Amen."

The National Council of Distributive Workers; District 65, marched in a contingent of hundreds. Chicano workers marched under a banner, "UFWOC, AFL-CIO," the Farm Workers Union. Thousands of welfare recipients marched under a banner that read, "$6,500 or Fight."

Angela Davis banner

The New York Committee to free Angela Davis carried a mammoth banner demanding the release of the Black woman Communist.

A green banner proclaimed "Brattleboro, Vermont" and close behind came another. "Bloomington, Indiana." An avenue-wide banner said, "U.S. Navy Seabees for Peace." Professionals and business men marched and a contingent of high school students against the war. A contingent of women marched in separate lanes. Youth of the Young Workers Liberation League surged past chanting, "Angela Out; Nixon In."

Scarlet banners read, "New York State Communist Party" and "Communist Party of Illinois." A banner which read, "Tennessee Communist Party" created a sensation among spectators and fellow marchers. A YWLL sign said, "Convict brass and Nixon too," and another said, "Que Viva Puerto Rico Libre—Free Puerto Rico." The crowd listened to the rally speakers beneath blooming azaleas and dogwood trees.

Call to Congress

Speakers demanded Congress stand up against President Nixon and end the war. The chant "Out Now" boomed against the Capitol dome. The day began in sunshine but a wind arose as Peter, Paul and Mary sang, "It's blowing in the wind" and dark clouds gathered.

Representative Bella Abzug, (D-NY,) drew laughter and cheers when she said, "It looks like everybody is here today except Richard Nixon. He's in retreat in Camp David. He's in retreat from the American people." She lashed Nixon for prolonging the war while 90,000 New York City workers face layoffs, welfare recipients face expulsion from welfare rolls, and hospital and health costs soar.

Harold Gibbons, vice-president of the International Brotherhood of Teamsters said, "We must turn to the Congress for a final solution to the Vietnam War, not the White House." The masses roared approval of Gibbons' plea.

Representative John Conyers; (D-Mich.,) said, "Unless we translate this into political action this will be another march to an empty capital."

"Richard Nixon must go," he cried, as the crowd roared.

Mrs. Coretta Scott King accused Nixon of "strengthening the ultra-right, the anti-labor, anti-Negro forces" in the nation, by prolonging the war. She demanded the withdrawal of all U.S. troops from Indochina by August 28, the date on which, her martyred husband delivered his "I have a dream" speech.

Coast to Coast With Great Peace March
People's Daily World

September 25, 1986
BRADY'S RUN, Pennsylvania—Gerda Range, a retired journalist, union organizer, mother of seven and grandmother of three, has walked over 2,900 miles from Los Angeles to this park in Beaver County, Pennsylvania. She is a participant in the Great Peace March for Global Nuclear Disarmament.

"I did not join this march to get away from a dull life," Range said as we marched at a swift pace in Western Pennsylvania. "I have a wonderful life, a family, a house by the beach. I joined because I feel that everything I hold dear is threatened by this insanity of thinking nuclear weapons are a deterrent to war. These weapons are ticking away, and if we don't get smart, they're going off."

The march had taken its participants through the deserts of the West, across the Continental Divide at Loveland Pass, over the Great Plains and into the industrial Midwest. The marchers have joined locked out USX steelworkers, LTV pensioners picketing for their pension rights, and anti-nuclear protestors rallying against the Perry nuclear plant in Ohio. They arrived in Cleveland in time for the annual "Freeze Walk," which people from all over the state participated in.

The marchers have been enthusiastically welcomed in places as far flung as Salt Lake City, Utah, where a

Great Peace March enters Washington D.C. at end of cross-country trek.

big peace rally was held, all across Iowa, where farmers and other sympathizers greeted their passing, and Ohio, where town after town showered the marchers with gifts, baked goods, financial contributions and hospitality. In Gerard, Ohio, church bells rang. Residents poured out of restaurants, schools, churches and barber shops to greet the marchers.

"There has been such a growth in our understanding of the issues," observed Range. "And it has gone both ways—they learned from us and we learned from them. We've had an opportunity to go into communities. We have listened to some very intelligent people who have given us information we did not have before. I think there was a special quality about Ohio. The people have a lot of brightness about what's happening. They seem to have a certain feeling of empowerment—and smarts—that just exhilarated me.

Range said many of the marchers are keenly aware of the crucial 1986 congressional elections and that for the next month they will be marching through Pennsylvania, where Representative Bob Edgar, an outstanding pro-peace House member, is challenging Senator Arlen Specter, a Reaganite Republican who voted for the MX missile, for confirmation of Chief Justice William Rehnquist and for the Gramm-Rudman law.

"What happens in Congress is absolutely basic," she said. "We've seen the vote on funds for nuclear testing where we made some progress. We saw the votes against aid to the contras—and then all of a sudden they turned around and voted for it. The votes are fairly close. It shows that every race in this election counts."

She hailed the Soviets' nuclear test ban. "We're carrying a banner, 'The Soviets Stopped Testing. Why Don't We?' And the Soviets have extended their ban once more. I was at the Nevada Test Site three times. It is a place where I, as an American, stood in very deep sorrow. It seems to me we just flaunted our testing rather than answer the Soviets in a cooperative manner."

One of the first vivid impressions for any visitor entering "Peace City," population 760, at the end of a day's march is the awesome level of organization. The nitty gritty of daily organization is coordinated by the Operations Council (OC,) which consists of the heads of all the various departments of the city. At one typical meeting this week, the OC planned the logistics of the entry into Pittsburg—including meals, the location of the tent city, and all the scheduled activities, including marching on the USX picketlines at Homestead.

The marchers are supported by a convoy that includes five trucks that carry the field kitchen; an enormous water tanker truck; two double-tandem tractor trailers that carry tents, sleeping bags, and back packs; a dozen more school buses which house the school classrooms; the first-aid station; a radio station; a 4,000 volume bookmobile; a media bus; an information bus, etc. Another bus, the "Peace City for the Performing Arts," carries the equipment of two musical groups, Collective Vision and Wild Wimmen for Peace.

All labor is performed by the marchers themselves, who volunteer two days each week to work in the kitchen, preparing food or washing dishes, loading or unloading the trucks.

Reveille is at 6 a.m. A timekeeper walks among the tents tapping a bell and announcing the weather forecast, how many miles will be marched and the location of the next encampment. The marchers break down their tents and wash up in time for breakfast at 7 a.m. Then, without awaiting an order to move, they drift out onto the highway and begin their twenty mile daily trek.

South Africa "We're Still in a State of War"
People's Weekly World

April 27, 1991

They are receiving a heroes' welcome wherever they go. Chris Hani and Toni Yengeni, leaders of the fight for freedom in South Africa, received an honor guard in Detroit, their first stop on a coast-to-coast tour, a rally at a local church, greetings from Representative John Conyers, and a meeting with Mayor Coleman Young. City Council President Maryann Mahaffey presented them with a testimonial resolution from members of the council.

In Chicago, their next stop, Hani and Yengeni were honored at a luncheon attended by 230 guests. Then they attended a reception hosted by Harold Rogers, a leader of the Coalition of Black Trade Unionists. Hani appeared on three radio talk shows and was interviewed by the *Chicago Defender* and the *Sun-Times*.

Their third stop was Washington D.C., for meetings with policy-makers and interviews with national media.

Audiences at every stop have contributed generously to the support the *People's Weekly World*, sponsor of the tour, and the work of the South African Communist Party.

The tour will include eight more cities.

Students Cheer South African Leader

People's Weekly World

April 1991

WASHINGTON—South African freedom fighter Chris Hani accused the apartheid regime of instigating terrorist attacks on his people and urged that U.S. economic sanctions be kept in place. Speaking Monday to an enthusiastic crowd at Howard University Hani, a leader of the African National Congress and South African Communist Party, blasted twelve European nations for deciding to lift the embargo on economic relations with South Africa.

"Sanctions were imposed because apartheid is regarded as a crime against humanity," he said. "That government is still in power. What has changed to justify lifting the sanctions? The people, the victims of oppression, should decide when sanctions should be lifted. That is why we are appealing to you, brothers and sisters, not to allow President Bush to lift them."

He debunked claims that reforms by the de Klerk regime justify resuming trade and investments. ANC members are still on death row, he said. The police and the South African Defense Force stand by as Inkatha death squads, armed with automatic weapons, wound and kill ANC supporters. Already, 3,000 people have died. The media call it "black on black" violence when, in fact, it is secretly fomented by the de Klerk regime, he charged. "We believe the government wants to destabilize the Natal region as much as possible, the heart of the working-class movement, where the ANC's following is the strongest. They want the ANC to negotiate from a position of weakness . . . De Klerk wants to organize a coalition to govern with blacks he can manipulate and control."

A moment of truth is April 30, when indemnification, the regime's promise not to prosecute or imprison ANC leaders, expires. Hani said the ANC has warned de Klerk they will walk out of the negotiations if the indemnification is not renewed.

Hani, Chief of Staff of the ANC's armed wing, Spear of the Nation, had another warning for de Klerk. The ANC unilaterally suspended military action last year. But at that time, ANC told the regime, "We're still in a state of war with you, there is no way we will surrender any weapons to you." The crowd erupted with applause.

He said the ANC has demanded the regime take action to disarm the death squads and halt the bloodshed. "We cannot negotiate when they are killing our people."

Hani said the ANC is negotiating with Chief Buthelezi to end the Natal violence and with the Pan African Congress, with the aim of building "a broad united front against apartheid" and a democratic, non-racial, South Africa. Aubrey McCutcheon III, Director of the Washington Office on Africa, urged the crowd to start now to mobilize pressure on Congress to keep sanctions in place. Congress would have thirty days in which to reject Bush's certification that South Africa has made sufficient progress dismantling apartheid to warrant lifting sanctions.

James Leas announced from the floor that he is one of 550 IBM employees circulating a petition demanding that IBM halt delivery of computers to South Africa used in warfare against the people. As the crowd applauded, Hani signed Leas' petition.

350,000 March for Peace and Justice in New York

By Tim Wheeler and Dan Margolis

April 30, 2006

NEW YORK—It was like a stroll on a perfect spring day but the 350,000 people who flowed down Broadway, April 29, were marching to bring the troops home from Iraq, for health care and education, to rebuild a nation torn by war, hurricanes and Bush-Cheney lies.

It was also the kick-off for the 2006 elections with the marchers determined to end ultra-right Republican control of the House and Senate and elect lawmakers November 7 who are responsive to the people's needs. The marchers assembled in the side streets north of Union Square and walked south to Foley Square for a street festival. Marching near the front were Veterans for Peace, Gold Star Parents and Military Families Speak Out. The father of Lieutenant Seth J. Dvorin, killed in Iraq, told the World, "I do this for my son . . . for 2,400 others who lost their lives . . . I think this is a worthless,

senseless war based on lies and deceit. It's a great war if you want to make profits . . . It's all for them, not for us."

The National Organization for Women mobilized a huge contingent to march behind its banner. ""I don't know the estimate of the size of this march but an unprecedented coalition came together to organize it," Olga Vives, NOW executive vice president, told the *World*. "Women, the peace movement, labor, veterans, religious groups all came together with one thing in mind: to call for an end to this war, to restore democracy. Our goal is to mobilize people today for the November elections. We need to take back the House and Senate before these extremists destroy our country and the world."

At least 30,000 trade union members marched, the largest ever labor movement turnout for a peace demonstration. Wilfredo Larencuent, Manager of the Unite Here Laundry Workers Joint Board, said, "The children of our members are the ones fighting and dying in this war . . . There's a move afoot to try to defeat the working class movement in this country, to try to control the oil or the natural resources of other countries. Our members oppose this war."

Todd Johnson, an electrician, was marching with twenty-five other members of Chicago's IBEW Local 134, who rode a bus overnight to get to the march. "So much money and so many lives are being wasted in Iraq," he said. "And in the Gulf Coast, Bush is trying to get rid of the prevailing wage for construction workers. It's ridiculous. Our country is definitely headed in the wrong direction."

Leading a contingent of transit workers was Roger Toussaint, president of the Transport Workers Union, just released from jail for defying New York State's Taylor law that bars strikes by public employees. Andy Griggs, a member of United Teachers of Los Angeles held the banner of U.S. Labor Against the War "People are making the connections," he told the World. "They see the profiteering by companies like Halliburton and Exxon while we are stripped of our benefits."

An estimated 10,000 Healthcare workers Local 1199 marched in their purple and gold T-Shirts chanting, "We're going to beat back the Bush attack" and "We are the union, the mighty, mighty union." A majority African American and Latino, Local 1199 members came from D.C., Baltimore, Philadelphia, and New England and New York City.

Vast numbers marched in the contingents of Riverside Church, The Quakers, Unitarian Universalists, Pax Christi and Church of Saint Francis. "No Torture, No War," proclaimed a banner carried behind a cage on wheels with a detainee in an orange jumpsuit slumped inside. Mike Maguire of Baltimore, said, "This is a call to conscience to shut down Guantanamo." Many carried hand-lettered placards calling for impeachment of Bush and Cheney. Another message was "Hands off Iran!" and "Stop the Invasion of Iran before it Begins."

The Communist Party USA and Young Communist League marched behind a bright red banner, "U.S. Out of Iraq . . . Rebuild America. No Money for War." CPUSA National Chairperson, Sam Webb, said, "It's a beautiful day, a beautiful crowd. Its sending a message to Bush and the Republican controlled Congress, 'Get out of Iraq!" Marching nearby was Connecticut CP organizer, Joelle Fishman, who chairs the CPUSA Political Action Commission. "This turnout could be decisive for the 2006 elections," she said. "The issues are coming together, all the people's movements are mobilizing."

Vinie Burroughs, an acclaimed actress, marched with the Raging Grannies Peace Brigade that recently won a court decision upholding free speech. "We were arrested protesting the war," she said. "It's an illegal, unjust, and immoral war. This is making visible to the Bush Administration that we need to get out of Iraq."

Liz Rivera Goldstein, chairperson of the National Network Opposed to the Militarization of Youth, came from her home in Port Townsend, Washington. "The military recruiting pitch isn't working very well. The military is juggling the numbers to hide the fact that youth are saying no to war, no to militarism," she said. "A lot of people across this country want change."

Winter Games Athletes Stand For World Peace, So Should We

2018—From the moment North and South Korean athletes marched together into the stadium, February 9, 2018 a spirit of unity and peace has dominated the Pyeong Chang Winter Olympics. These games could not have been held in a place of greater world tension, menaced by storm clouds of thermonuclear war.

This reporter witnessed that tension first hand in 1983 when I was one of several hundred delegates to the International Organization of Journalists conference in Pyongyang, Democratic People's Republic of Korea (DPRK). Our hosts took us down to Panmunjom and a little further south to the armistice line.

I saw a U.S. Marine in full dress uniform standing at parade rest in a room that had the 38th Parallel running down the middle. Through the glass partition I reminded the Marine that the Armistice ending combat was signed in 1953. Thirty years of occupying Korea is long enough, I said. It is time to sign a peace agreement and bring all U.S. troops home. That was thirty-five years ago and the U.S. troops are still there and under Donald Trump it could become the flash point that incinerates Asia in a nuclear exchange.

The Republic of Korea and the DPRK are technically still in a state of war. Korea remains divided, a Cold War tragedy that has torn families apart, never to see each other again.

But floating above the unified Korean team at these winter games was a banner with a silhouette of Korea no longer divided, the deepest longing of the Korean people both north and south.

Two young women, Park Jong-an from South Korea and Chung Su Hyon from North Korea—both members of the unified Korean women's hockey team, jointly carried the torch that lit the flame for these games.

Watching the opening ceremonies from a VIP box was Kim Yo Jong, sister of North Korean leader Kim Jong Un. She shook hands with South Korean President, Moon Jae-in and invited him to visit DPRK's capital, Pyongyang. A grim-faced Vice President Mike Pence watched from the sidelines. In his first State of the Union, Trump denounced Kim Jong Un as "depraved." On arriving in Seoul, Pence vowed to clamp the "toughest and most aggressive" sanctions ever on North Korea.

It was completely at odds with the spirit of friendship that welled up from below at these winter games. U.S. Gold Medal skier, Lindsay Vonn, tweeted, "Walking in my last opening ceremonies with my teammates tonight was incredible. So honored to be a part of this team. Sports has the power to unite the world and watching North and South Korea walk together is what it is all about."

Adam Rippon, a champion figure skater, the first openly gay man on a U.S. winter Olympic team, soared on the ice, helping the U.S. figure skating team win a bronze medal. Moments after he skated, his team mate, Mirai Nagasu, a Japanese American from Arcadia, California, did a triple axel, the first American woman to perform this difficult spinning leap. Rippon and the rest of the American skating team were cheering from the sidelines. When Nagusu stepped from the ice, Rippon threw his arms around her in a fond embrace.

NBC news reporter, Mike Tirico, interviewed Rippon about his own performance and his teammates' prowess. Rippon spoke of growing up poor, one of six children in his family in Scranton, Pennsylvania, In his teenage years, he lived in a basement apartment, so strapped for money he could not buy groceries. And a few years later he was at the Olympic Winter Games. Tirico asked Rippon about his sharp criticism of Vice President Pence for his gay-bashing politics. One of the values his mother taught him, Rippon replied, is always to stand up and fight for your principles. He would not back down from his vow not to meet with Pence or to renounce his criticism of Pence for his gay-bashing.

Pence sent out a series of tweets claiming that he wishes the entire American team the best, including Rippon, and hoping for a U.S. victory in every event. Yet even this missed the spirit of these games.

Victory is secondary to joining with competitors from the nations of the world, groaning when they stumble and fall, cheering when they stand up and try again.

That generous spirit shined when Canadian figure skater, Patrick Chan, was on the ice. Chan fell twice as he attempted especially difficult axels. Yet he regained his feet and continued to skate. The Canadian team won the Gold Medal.

A fall on the ice is forgiven. What is unforgiveable is to give up.

The politics of hatred and division, of winner take all, were not welcome at these Olympics. The athletes seemed to be telling the world to embrace their way of seeing the world—of give and take, win and lose. Let South Korean President, Moon, accept that invitation and travel to Pyongyang! Mothball DPRK plans for nuclear missiles, and cancel Trump's drive for new, more dangerous nuclear weapons. That will mean a Gold Medal victory for all of humanity. *(Below: Diamond Mountain, beloved symbol of Korea. I brought this original silk embroidery painting back from the DPRK. The artist is unknown but I visited the studio and orbserved perhaps 100 women at work embroidering these magnificent works of art).*

On the Death of a Maine Schoolgirl

Let us walk through the dark
forest of Samantha's death and hear singing
in the tops of Androscoggin pines
her epitaph: 'We are meant
to live, not to fight and die.'

Her life raced down the cold
Atlantic, like an outbound
schooner running on
the Penobscot tide.
Hope sang in her taut heart like a
halyard in a Grand Banks gale.
'We are meant to live, not to fight and die.'

Listen, Grand Banks doryman,
to the song in Samantha's heart.
Listen, feller of Androscoggin pine.
Listen, Bath Iron builders of ships.

Listen, papermaker of the northwood.
Listen, potato grower in the valley
of the Kennebec.

Did you twine
in Samantha's heart this song
of life? Did you teach her
to frame the issue
Square as a clipper sail?
Bold common sense you bred
and the will to act
in a Maine schoolgirl.
To Andropov she wrote:
'We are meant to live, not to fight and die.'

The words sing
in the tops of the Androscoggin pines.
Sing in the soul of a
Brokenhearted widow-mother.
Sing across the rooftops of grieving
America. Samantha Smith
is the daughter of us all.

These words sing
in the Pripyat Marsh
where Soviet antifascist
Heroes lie.
Down the Volga shore,
across Siberia,
glowing in the midnight sun.

You in Washington
who will not hear,
listen to a down east
schoolgirl's' dying words:
We are meant to live,
not fight and die.

—Timothy Wheeler

Chapter 5

High Crimes

Watergate to George W. Bush's 2000 Election Coup

People's World

June 4, 2012

WASHINGTON—The Watergate Conspiracy was back in the headlines with the revelation that former FBI officer, W. Mark Felt, is the mysterious "Deep Throat" who fed *Washington Post* reporter Bob Woodward tips on the plot that gripped the nation in 1973-74.

From the day the break-in of the Democratic Party Watergate headquarters occurred, June 17, 1972, there has been a concerted effort to hide the real meaning of the conspiracy. Nominally, it was a bungled attempt to plant listening devices and rifle the files of the opposition party to insure President Richard Nixon's re-election in November of that year.

In truth, it was the tip of the iceberg of a multifaceted plot to destroy democracy and impose a police state in the U.S. It had its origins in the FBI's COINTELPRO spy and dirty tricks operation, initially aimed at the Communist Party USA but later expanded to encompass the Reverend Martin Luther King Jr. and thousands of other fighters for equality and world peace. There was the CIA's "Operation Chaos" aimed at sowing mayhem in the civil rights movement and the antiwar movement.

There was the Pentagon's CONUS Intelligence based at Fort Holabird, just outside Baltimore. Starting in

1969, U.S. Army intelligence established a computerized data-bank on millions of people, all engaged in constitutionally protected protest activities. The Pentagon assigned 1,500 agents to spy on peace groups, to infiltrate their meetings, and to instigate violence that could be used to confuse, discredit and isolate the antiwar movement.

I was there I covered these stories as Washington correspondent for the *Daily World*. When the Senate Watergate Committee convened, I was assigned a coveted seat in the Senate Caucus Room for the hearings chaired by Senator Sam Ervin (D-N.C.). I remember clearly the advice given me by my *DW* editors Carl Winter, John Pittman and Si Gerson. Avoid the "Who shot John" whodunit details of the Watergate conspiracy, they said. Focus on the underlying political meaning of the conspiracy, its fascist-like essence.

My front-page story in the May 18, 1973, edition was headlined, *Probe Stresses Peril to U.S. Constitution.*

Ervin opened the hearings with these words: "The burglars who broke into the Democratic Party's Watergate headquarters, June 17, 1972, were seeking to steal not the jewels, money, or other property of American citizens but something far more valuable: their most precious heritage, the right to vote in a free election. Those making this plan had the same mentality employed by the Gestapo in Nazi Germany."

I sat beside *Washington Star* correspondent Mary McGrory, a Pulitzer Prize winner, who muttered under her breath her profound loathing of Nixon and everything he stood for.

She took shorthand. During breaks, reporters would crowd around McGrory to make sure they had word-for-word the incriminating testimony of the infamous "White House plumbers" and their accomplices. A procession of Nixon hacks, thugs and goons paraded through the ornate chamber.

New York Red Squad cop Tony Ulasewicz, Nixon's bagman, told of handing out hush money from a $300,000 secret slush fund to buy off the burglars and all others with information that linked Nixon to the conspiracy. Nixon's counsel, John Dean, laid bare his orchestration, under Nixon's direct command, of a far-reaching cover-up after the burglars were arrested. Try as they might, Republican senators like Howard Baker (Tenn.) and Edward Gurney (Fla.) could not trip up the unflappable Dean.

There was Maurice Stans, Nixon's former commerce secretary who served as treasurer of the Committee to Re-Elect the President (CREEP). It played the main role in assuring Nixon's infamous "landslide" re-election. Stans calmly told of the shopping bags stuffed with corporate cash that flowed into Republican coffers to buy (or steal) the 1972 presidential election.

Some of the cash in crisp $100 bills was found in the pockets of the five Watergate burglars when they were arrested. Four of the five were Cuban émigrés, veterans of the CIA's Bay of Pigs invasion. (How quaint CREEP's fundraising methods seem compared to the hundreds of millions in corporate cash that bankroll the Republican machine today!)

The longer the Watergate hearings proceeded, the more we learned of Nixon's long-standing, secret efforts to impose a police state in the United States. Tom C. Huston, national chairman of Young Americans For Freedom, later a U.S. Army Intelligence officer, had been recruited by Nixon's Chief of Staff H.R. Haldeman to draft what later became known as the "Huston Plan."

It was a scheme to merge the intelligence agencies—the FBI, CIA, NSA, the various military intelligence agencies— into a Gestapo-like secret police under presidential command. Its task would be to engage in political espionage, mail surveillance, breaking and entering, illegal wiretapping, infiltration, dirty tricks and provocations.

The Watergate hearings proved that the Huston Plan was not merely a Nixon wish-list. There was, of course, Nixon's "Enemies List" of 30,000 or more progressive people targeted for repression. CREEP implemented many of the tactics outlined in the Huston Plan. Donald Segretti was the director of CREEP's dirty tricksters assigned to infiltrate and sow chaos in the ranks of Nixon's Democratic rivals. He told the hearings that his crew forged a letter on Maine Senator Ed Muskie's stationery accusing rivals Hubert Humphrey and Henry Jackson of sexual "offenses" including homosexuality.

The tricksters sent another forged letter to the ultra-right *Manchester Union Leader* in New Hampshire falsely reporting that Muskie had used the chauvinistic epithet "Canuck" to describe the many French Canadians in Maine and New Hampshire. They also planted a story in the *Union Leader* that Muskie's wife had told "dirty stories" on the campaign trail. At a news conference outside the editorial offices of the *Union Leader* to rebut these lies, Muskie burst into tears. It was the end of his presidential bid.

There was a surreal atmosphere in the capital as Nixon maneuvered desperately to avoid impeachment. One of his ploys was to pose as world statesman, too busy with shuttle diplomacy to be bothered with what his press secretary, Ron Zeigler, called a "third rate burglary."

A month after the Watergate hearings opened, I found myself on the White House press plane trailing Air Force One to the Western White House in San Clemente, California. There I covered Nixon's summit with Soviet Leader Leonid Brezhnev. What I remember most about that trip was actor Chuck Connor, star of *The Rifleman*, greeting Brezhnev when he stepped off the helicopter near Nixon's compound. Connor, a giant, lifted Brezhnev from the tarmac in a big bear hug and then presented the Soviet leader with a matching pair of Colt 45s. Brezhnev's face lit up with joy. It symbolized mankind's hopes for an end to the nuclear arms race. We gave front-page coverage to all the strategic arms negotiations in Moscow, Vienna and Washington even as outrage mounted against Nixon's escalation of the war in Vietnam and the Watergate scandal. We viewed Nixon's signature on the SALT and ABM treaties as a "forced retreat."

Within hours of filing my stories from San Clemente, I was back covering Watergate. The White House tapes, with the notorious "18-and-a-half-minute gap" were exposed. Nixon's attempts to suppress them were rejected by Judge John Sirica and the U.S. Supreme Court. The nation recoiled in outrage over the "Saturday Night Massacre" October 20, 1973, when Justice Department official Robert Bork fired Watergate Special Prosecutor Archibald Cox after Attorney General Elliot Richardson and his deputy were forced out for refusing to do so. Within hours, 430,000 angry telegrams hit lawmaker's offices. The people saw Cox's firing as nothing less than a coup d'état. The House Judiciary Committee began drafting articles of impeachment. His presidency in a state of collapse, Nixon resigned rather than go through impeachment.

Nixon was gone but a new ultra-right emerged. The conspiracy to undermine and destroy the Constitution and representative democracy did not end.

Many of the same tactics once again surfaced ten years later, with the exposure of President Ronald Reagan's Iran-Contra conspiracy. Once again, hearings were convened in the Senate Caucus Room, this time before a joint Senate-House committee.

I had a ringside seat as the strutting Lieutenant Colonel Oliver North in his drab olive service uniform bragged about his criminal enterprise under Reagan's command. He boasted of orchestrating the covert delivery of shiploads of Pentagon missiles to Iran, laundering the profits through numbered Swiss bank accounts to pay for weapons for the CIA's secret wars in Central America. This operation was in flagrant violation a congressional ban on arms for the Contras. Tens of thousands of innocent Nicaraguans and Salvadorans died in the Contra war.

As for Reagan arming Iran, he was also arming Saddam Hussein for the fratricidal war in which perhaps a million Iraqis and Iranians died. Representative Jack Brooks (D-Texas) asked North about a White House plan to declare martial law, round up 400,000 immigrants and imprison them in concentration camps in the event of a U.S. invasion of Central America.

The plan, codenamed Rex Alpha 84, also called for canceling the 1984 elections a "coup d'état."

Senator Daniel Inouye (D-Hawaii), chair of the joint House-Senate hearings, interrupted Brooks. "I want to remind you that we agreed not to get into that subject," Inouye said.

Donald Segretti died in Arlington, Virginia, a few years ago, run over by a car, mysteriously. But the Bush-Cheney campaign kept his sordid legacy alive in the stolen 2000 election. During the "Count-Every-Vote" struggle in Florida in that election, House Majority Leader Tom DeLay (R-Texas) recruited thugs who invaded the Board of Elections in Broward County, banging on doors and shouting for the workers inside to stop the vote count. The vote count was stopped and later a sharply divided Supreme Court handed the election to Bush.

I was in Florida that autumn covering what the *People's Weekly World* branded "A Very American Coup." It was an operation taken straight out of Segretti's book of dirty tricks. Representative John Conyers Jr. (D-Mich.) served on the Impeachment Committee in 1974, drafting the article indicting President Richard Nixon for war crimes in unleashing an illegal, unconstitutional war on Vietnam. Thirty-one years later, Conyers convened a Capitol Hill hearing on the so-called "Downing Street Memo."

The document contains minutes of a July 23, 2002, meeting of top British officials, including Prime Minister Tony Blair. It reveals that George W. Bush had decided to go to war in 2002 and intelligence was being "fixed" to justify that decision. Witnesses described the memo as a "smoking gun" proving that Bush tricked the nation with lies into an illegal and unconstitutional war, an impeachable offense. Later that afternoon, Conyers led a delegation of his colleagues to the White House to deliver petitions signed by 560,000 people demanding that Bush answer the allegations of the Downing Street memo.

Again this reporter was there. "Let Conyers in! Let Conyers in!" antiwar demonstrators chanted as White House guards blocked Conyers' way. Finally, the guards opened the gate so the petitions could be passed through. At a rally across the street, an exultant Conyers hailed the rising antiwar protests. "Keep it coming. We need a million signatures, 5 million, 20 million," he said. "The people are rising once more against the specter of Watergate, determined to stop an illegal war, stop Bush from shredding the Constitution, to stop another coup before it happens."

A "Third-rate Burglary"
World Magazine

July 15, 1973
WASHINGTON—Mrs. Betty Bagdikian, a Democratic Party staff-worker, glared over her spectacles at the rifled desks, gaping file drawers and the floor littered with memos, letters and correspondence of the Democratic National Committee.

"Who would dream of such a thing?" she exclaimed. "It's unconstitutional; it's an invasion of privacy. There's a conspiracy law, you know."

She was reacting to the brazen attempt by five men to install spy devices in the plush Watergate offices of the Democratic Party in one of the most bizarre episodes since President Nixon took office. The five spies were caught red-handed by D.C. metropolitan police as they crouched behind an office partition in the inner office of Democratic Party Chairman Lawrence F. O'Brien. They were carrying satchels of sophisticated eavesdropping equipment, cameras for microfilming and pens filled with tear gas when apprehended at 2:30 a.m., Saturday, June 17.

When police pointed their pistols at them, the spies held up their hands. They were wearing surgical rubber gloves, and one of them declared, "Don't shoot!"

Since then, in a series of spectacular disclosures, the agents have been linked directly to the Committee to Re-Elect the President. (CREEP) Top aides in the White

DAILY WORLD

STANS: I DIDN'T DO IT, ONLY RAISED THE CASH

House, the Republican National Committee, the Central Intelligence Agency, the FBI, and counter-revolutionary Cuban exiles. The leader of the spy plot is credited with masterminding the abortive Bay of Pigs invasion of 1961 in which the CIA attempted to overthrow the socialist revolution in Cuba.

Florette Lebow, a secretary, and Pat Johnson, editor of the Democratic Party publications, showed me the fire-door jimmied by the agents when they broke into the offices. Incredibly, the agents used tape to keep the door from latching; this was visible to the Watergate guard as he made his hourly rounds. The guard mistakenly thought the Democrats themselves had taped the door and simply removed it. An hour later, when he returned, the guard noticed that the door had been re-taped! He immediately telephoned the police.

The spies were especially interested in the Office of Youth affairs. They rifled through the files in this office before moving on to the Research Office. Finally, they jimmied the office door of Democratic Chairman Lawrence F. O'Brien, removed two acoustical tiles from the ceiling of his office but were caught before they had time to install listening devices.

The conspirators have been the subject of round-the-clock investigation by reporters seeking answers to endless questions about the operation. Some contend the bungling of the job indicates "amateurishness." But others say it was the result of overconfidence born of repeated success in similar plots.

'They must have been here before," declared Mrs. Johnson, "That is why they were so confident, so fearless, so brazen."

"It's scary," said Miss Lebow with a shudder.

White House Press Secretary Ron Zeigler pushed the "amateur" line when he characterized the break-in as a "third-rate burglary attempt" unworthy of comment either by himself or the President.

Senator Mike Mansfield (D-Mont) hastened to reject charges that the Republican high command was behind the break-in. He said it was inconceivable that the Republicans could have hired such miserable incompetents to undertake the mission.

Another argument is that the Democratic Party has no secrets worth discovering by such a risky enterprise as breaking into their headquarters. The political cost of being caught in the act, the argument goes, far outweighs anything that could be found in O'Brien's inner office, which can be read "like an open book," according to some.

All this speculation has one purpose: to throw the people off the trail, to dispel outrage, to pin the episode on the nearest patsy. The Democratic Party has made crystal clear who they believe inspired the plot. Its suit seeking $1,000,000 in damages for conspiracy to deny the civil rights of the Democratic voters names the CREEP as the guilty party.

This is tantamount to charging that the conspiracy was ordered by top circles of the Nixon Administration itself. It directly contradicts attempts by the Nixon Administration to pooh-pooh the episode as an activity of the "lunatic fringe."

Predictably, GOP Chairman Robert Dole lashed back, accusing the Democrats of using the break-in for electioneering purposes.

But the facts in the case are incontrovertible. They point in one direction: toward the White House.

According to Ken W. Clawson, Deputy Director of Communications for the Nixon Administration, E. Howard

Hunt was hired as a top consultant at the White House by Nixon's special counsel, Charles W. Colson. Hunt worked under Colson's command for sixty-three days in 1971 and another twenty-four days this year, as recently as March 29. Colson hired Hunt because of his "expertise" gained in years as a top Central Intelligence Agency spy.

About two weeks before the break-in, Hunt flew to Miami where he met Bernard F. Barker, identified as the "leader" of the break-in at the time of his arrest at Democratic headquarters. At this Miami meeting, Hunt handed Barker his business card with his suburban Maryland phone number penciled on the back and gave him "oral instructions to call him if he ever needed help," according to the *New York Times*.

Police tracked Hunt down because his name was written in Barker's address book, confiscated when he was arrested. Also in the address book were notations such as "W. House," and "W.H."

Hunt and Barker, a Cuban-born gusano, were top CIA operatives who carried out the infamous Bay of Pigs invasion of Cuba in 1961. This fact goes a long way towards exploding the argument that the Republican Party would never hire "bunglers" to do its dirty work. No operation was more stupidly conceived nor more criminally executed than the Bay of Pigs invasion, yet it enjoyed the full support of the White House.

Hunt, under the alias "Eduardo," was the CIA agent in top command of the Bay of Pigs invasion. Since the arrests, he has mysteriously disappeared.

Barker's role in the Bay of Pigs fiasco, according to Cuban exile sources, "was significant but more organizational than operational," a *Washington Post* article declared.

"He was said to be close to Manuel Artime, who commanded the landing force, and to have been a major conduit for Central Intelligence Agency funds.

"His association with the CIA is believed to have lasted at least through 1964 when commandos were being trained in Nicaragua for anti-Castro harassment raids."

Barker, who uses the code-name "Macho," which translates roughly as "Stud," is a virulent anti-communist. When President Nixon ordered the mining of Haiphong Harbor, Barker organized a motorcade through Miami of Cuban exiles supporting the aggression. He has urged gusanos "to oppose was protesters at this summer's two national political conventions here," the *Post* said.

Barker reportedly attempted to obtain the architect's plans of the Miami Convention Center, information useful to only an agent planning terrorism, assassination, or some other savage act at the Democratic convention.

James W. McCord, another of those arrested in the break-in, is also a direct link to the top command of the Republican Party. He began his career as an FBI agent, then spent nineteen years as a CIA agent before opening his own "rent-a-cop" agency in Rockville, Maryland.

John Mitchell, Nixon's Campaign manager, hired McCord at a salary of $1,209 per month to serve as the top security agent of the Committee to Re-Elect the President. McCord was assigned office space in the CREEP headquarters. McCord was also hired by the GOP as their top security agent.

McCord is a Lieutenant. Colonel in the U.S. Air Force. He is a member of a 15-man White House secret unit assigned to the Office of Emergency Preparedness whose duties reportedly include "compiling lists of radicals and developing plans for censorship of news and mail in the event of war."

The other arrested plotters are counter-revolutionary Cuban renegades including Frank Fiorini, alias Frank Sturgis, a gusano who claims to have fought with Cuban patriots in Oriente Province in 1958. He reportedly defected when socialism triumphed and showed up in Miami where he joined the John Birch Society. He founded a gangster outfit which calls itself "United Cubans."

Eugenio Martinez, alias Jean Valdes, a Miami real estate shark, and Virgilio R. Gonzales, alias Raoul Godoyn, a locksmith, also arrested at Watergate, were lieutenants of Fiorini, working with the aid of the CIA to overthrow socialism in Cuba.

Observers here note that New Orleans District Attorney Jim Garrison in his months-long trial of Clay Shaw directly linked these Cuban exiles to the assassination of President John Kennedy in 1963. The attempt to spy on the Democratic Party, therefore, fits into a consistent pattern of ultra-rightist terrorism by the exiles against democracy in the U.S. But what is new is the mounting evidence that links these plots to the White House itself, to the most reactionary pro-big business circles of the Nixon administration.

O'Brian criticized the White House for attempting to cover its tracks in this bizarre, chilling case of "political espionage."

The committee to Re-Elect the President, he said, is guilty of "police state tactics."

"We learned of this bugging attempt only because it was bungled. How many other attempts have there been? And just who was involved?" he asked. "I was appalled to hear that John Mitchell, the former attorney general who is now Mr. Nixon's campaign manager, tried immediately to make it appear that James McCord's employment by the Nixon Re-Election Committee ended some months ago.

"We know that as of the moment of his arrest at gunpoint just ten-feet from where I now stand, Mr. McCord was in the pay of the Committee for the Re-Election of the President, where he has an office, and of the Republican National Committee."

O'Brien has filed for a court order to subpoena records of McCord's security agency as well as the records of the Re-Election Committee in an effort to track down others involved in the plot. Evidence is mounting that at least three other men were actually at the scene of the crime as co-conspirators.

However, The Democratic Party has hailed the FBI investigation of the case and the Justice Department decision to convene a Grand Jury hearing on the episode.

This proposal has an "Alice in Wonderland" quality equal to the absurdity of the break-in itself. The fox is to guard the chicken coop. But pressure is mounting for a full investigation as reporters continue to expose the links in this Watergate caper.

Probe Stresses Peril to U.S. Constitution

Daily World

May 18, 1973
WASHINGTON. MAY 17— Senator Sam Ervin (D-NC) opened the Senate Watergate probe today with a grim warning that the spy and sabotage operations in last year's elections attributed to the Nixon Administra-

tion "affects the continued existence of this nation as a representative democracy."

A hush fell over the huge marbled Senate Caucus Room, jammed with a standing-room-only crowd as Ervin told the nation via television and radio that democracy itself is at stake in the Watergate hearings he is now chairing. Ervin, regarded as an outstanding Senate authority on the Constitution, cited the sweeping and ever-expanding charges that top Nixon Administration officials—including a former attorney general, the former acting FBI director, CIA officials and top White House aides—have been allegedly engaged in a massive assault on democracy.

"If the many allegations made to this date are true," said Ervin, 'then the burglars who broke into the headquarters of the Democratic National Committee at Watergate were, in effect, breaking into the home of every citizen of the United States . . . .What were they seeking to steal was not the jewels, money or other property of American citizens but something much more valuable—their most precious heritage, the right to vote in a free election."

In a grave warning to Nixon himself, Ervin added: "My colleagues on the committee and I are determined to uncover all the relevant facts surrounding these matters and to spare no one, whatever his station in life may be."

Ervin charged that the Watergate burglars were driven by "the same mentality as the Gestapo."

In this historic room, the Teapot Dome scandal was aired fifty years ago and since then the most spectacular hearings have been held here by the Senate but to all present, including 200 reporters from the world press, it was obvious that this hearing was the most significant of them all.

Already it is clear that a behind-the-scenes struggle was developing over the purposes of the hearings. Not every senator shares Ervin's stated purpose—to use these hearings to thwart what he regards as the greatest threat to democracy since the Constitution was framed in 1787.

A whitewash approach

Senator Howard Baker (R-Tenn), committee vice-chairman and one of Nixon's most reliable mouthpieces, sought immediately to channel the hearings to serve the purpose of what he called "national catharsis."

In an opening statement, Baker exonerated the national committees of both major parties from "any role in whatever may have gone wrong in 1972."

Thus, reactionary elements are already maneuvering to confine the investigation to criminal acts which they are apparently trying to pin on a handful of right wing "'zealots" acting without the knowledge of the White House.

Indeed, the first witness, Robert C. Odle, the twenty-eight-year-old former office manager of the Committee to Re-Elect the President (CREEP), was questioned by Baker and some others on his minute-by-minute actions on June 17, 1972, the day of the Watergate break-in.

Nixon men on the committee are not unaware that the endless talk of details will bury the essence of the matter—a plot to rig the elections and subvert democratic rights.

White House role

But despite the concentration on Odle's whereabouts and actions, one overriding fact emerged—the tight White House control over CREEP.

Odle conceded that key campaign personnel were recruited from the White House staff in 1971 by John Mitchell, the then Attorney General, and by H. R. "Bob" Haldeman, the White House chief of staff who resigned two weeks ago.

Odle is reported to have spent $4,000 in campaign funds to organize public "demonstrations" in support of Nixon's decision to mine Haiphong Harbor in the spring of 1972. Today he denied any knowledge of political spying and sabotage by CREEP people.

Wider plot charged

But if the senators were approaching Watergate gingerly as a threat to democracy, two youthful prize-winning reporters of the *Washington Post* were far more blunt.

Carl Bernstein and Bob Woodward, in a copyrighted story in today's *Washington Post*, branded the Watergate bugging and the burglary of the office of Daniel Ellsberg's psychiatrist as part of "an elaborate, continuous campaign of illegal and quasi-legal undercover operations conducted by the Nixon Administration since 1969."

Targets of the Administrations "continuing program of covert activity," the reporters wrote, were "radical leaders, student demonstrators, news reporters, Democratic candidates for President and Vice President and the Congress, and Nixon Administration aides suspected of leaking information to the press."

Among the clandestine operations carried on by the Administration, according to the *Washington Post* account, were "the use of paid provocateurs to encourage violence at anti-war demonstrations," the use of "undercover political activities against persons regarded as opponents of the Nixon Administration," as well as "political sabotage" and the use of "vigilante squads" of "professional wire-tappers and ex-CIA and ex-FBI agents."

To old-timers in the capital, the Post account had ominous overtones of the grim progression of fascist activities in Nazi Germany—from attacking "radicals" to wiping out bourgeois democratic opponents. Quoting an unnamed "high-level participant in many of the undercover activities," Bernstein and Woodward wrote:

" . . . the activities were aimed at whatever individual or group the White House perceived as a threat at any given moment.

"First it was the radicals," he (the source) said. "Then it was reporters and leaking White House aides, then the Democrats. They all got the same treatment: bugging, infiltration, burglary, spying, et cetera."

The Nixon activities included an FBI investigation of Daniel Schorr, a CBS-TV reporter who was critical of the Administration.

Other undercover activities included inspired campaigns to attack network news correspondents and telephone complaints to TV and radio stations carrying material critical of Nixon.

Honoring the Media, PA. FBI "Burglars"

2015

Broadcast on the PBS documentary program *Independent Lens* last May 18 was a film by Johanna Hamilton titled *1971*. It told the story of a brave band of peace activists in Pennsylvania who broke into the FBI office in Media, Pennsylvania, the night of March 8, 1971.

The burglars "liberated" thousands of top secret FBI documents exposing the surveillance of tens of thousands of law abiding people who were exercising their constitutionally protected right to protest the war in Vietnam, and many other injustices. Among the most dangerous projects exposed were documents that laid bare FBI Director, J. Edgar Hoover's COINTELPRO spy program, aimed initially at the Communist Party USA but expanded to target Senators, Representatives, the Reverend Martin Luther King, Jr. and millions of other advocates of peaceful, non-violent change.

I was the Washington correspondent of the *Daily World* and received a packet in the mail of those stolen dossiers. I opened the manila envelope that day. It had no return address. I perused the documents with growing amazement. Naively, I telephoned the FBI to ask for a comment.

"Those documents are classified. You must return them immediately," the FBI spokesman said in an officious voice. "We're sending an agent over to your office to pick them up now."

In a panic, I called Carl Winter, Editor in Chief of the *Daily World*. "Carl," I said. "I have about 200 top secret FBI files here. I called the FBI for a comment and the agent told me they are sending someone over right now to pick them up. What should I do?"

"Get the hell out of there," Carl shouted over the phone line. "And don't forget to take the files with you."

I grabbed up the documents and hastened out of my office and up the stairwell of the National Press Club where I hid for an hour or so. As far as I know, the FBI never sent anybody.

Finally I crept back to my office and wrote my story.

I never knew the names of the heroes who sent me that envelope until the release of *The Burglary: The Discovery of J. Edgar Hoover's Secret FBI* by Betty Medsgar in 2014.

Like me, Medsgar, a reporter for the *Washington Post*, received a packet of the stolen documents in the mail back on that cold spring day in 1971. The FBI never caught the burglars despite Hoover's assigning 200 agents to search for them.

In recent years, Medsgar convinced several to break their silence. They include Keith Forsyth, John and Judy Raines, and Bob Williamson.

Like Edward Snowden who "liberated" all those digitized National Security Agency files, exposing NSA spying on law abiding people, the Media, Pennsylvania burglars should be honored for their courage in defending the right of dissent protected by our Bill of Rights.

Here is the article I wrote about the Media, Pennsylvania break-in with the *Daily World* front page images.

Frenzied FBI Seeks to Choke Off Critics
The Daily World

April 17, 1971
WASHINGTON, APRIL 16—The FBI has unleashed a desperate fear campaign in the wake of the "liberation" of FBI documents by a citizens' group in Media, Pennsylvania, March 8.

The documents expose the massive apparatus headed by J. Edgar Hoover, engaged in spying on U.S. citizens, particularly citizens working for peace and Black liberation.

The FBI drive was unleashed as the attack on FBI czar Hoover reached storm proportions here with demands from senators and representatives that Hoover be fired.

Senator Edmund Muskie (D-Me) today repeated his charge that the FBI had conducted surveillance of "Earth Day" meetings at which Muskie had been a speaker.

The FBI's campaign of intimidation is widespread.

Columnist Nat Hentoff of the *Village Voice* reported (April 15) that two FBI agents knocked on his door and asked, "if I would show them material about which I had written a column, "Investigating the FBI.'"

Hentoff reported that he told them to see his legal adviser, a director of the American Civil Liberties Union. He refused to discuss the matter.

"You have a constitutional right to remain silent," Hentoff wrote.

FBI hunts copies

The FBI is trying to track down the thirteen documents, photocopies of the material from the Media FBI files sent out by Resist, a Cambridge, Mass. Anti-war group.

A total of about 1,000 dossiers and wiretap tapes had reputedly been lifted from the FBI Media office by a group known as the Citizens Commission to Investigate the FBI.

The Media action has been termed in some Washington circles "a modern Boston Tea Party."

FBI agent L. J. Heim, of Hoover's public relations staff, attempted to browbeat the *Daily World* reporter Wednesday into surrendering to the FBI a file of photocopies of the documents "liberated" from the FBI Media office.

Congressmen threatened

While threatening over the telephone to send FBI agents to "pick them up" and "have a talk" with this reporter, agent Heim revealed that other "individuals," including U.S. Congressmen, are targets of similar scare tactics.

The *Daily World* had received a set of thirteen of the photocopied documents here in the mail from Resist. The documents are marked "United States Government Memorandum" and "Pennsylvania State Police Intelligence Report" and are signed by several Special agents of the FBI.

One is a confidential report on Jacqueline Reuss, daughter of Representative Henry Reuss (D-Wis). The dossier is addressed to none other than J. Edgar Hoover himself, "Director, FBI."

The nation-wide fear campaign by the FBI to frighten those who are receiving the documents was confirmed when this reporter telephoned Resist in Cambridge. A spokesman for the organization who asked that his name be withheld said two agents came last week to the Resist office to question them in an attempt to round up copies of the documents. He said the agents left when they refused to cooperate.

Yesterday, FBI agents served a subpoena on Claudette Piper, assistant national director of Resist.

It was reported today that the FBI is scrutinizing serial numbers on Xerox machines in a drive to track down the members of the Citizens Commission to Investigate the FBI.

Informers tagged

The documents received by the *Daily World* name seven FBI informers on campuses, in banks, switch-board operators and in Black liberation organizations. Letters were sent by the commission to these people over a week ago as well as to two of the groups and individuals against whom they had been working.

Letters were also sent by the commission March 30, 1971, to each informer. The letter declares, "We realize that the FBI sometimes uses coercion of one kind or another in obtaining information from people like yourself. However, the people you have been spying on are on the whole attempting to work for a more just and open society. Your cooperation with the government is seriously hindering this work.

"Therefore, approximately one week after you receive this letter, the people you have been informing against will be notified of your activities. Later on your name will be made public.

"Don't expect the FBI to help you. They have a habit of using people like yourself and then forgetting about them once their usefulness is over.

"We regret that this action was necessary, but these are troubled times and the struggle for freedom and justice in this society can never succeed if people continue to betray their brothers and sisters."

Bank and college officials

The eleven informers named by the Citizens Commission include a cashier of the Southeast National Bank, Chester, Pennsylvania; an officer of the Computer Center, Southeast National Bank, Chester, Pennsylvania; an assistant manager of the Chester Credit Bureau, Inc., Chester, Pennsylvania; Margaret Turner, 3114 West Euclid, Philadelphia; William Gordon, detective, Police Department, Upper Darby, Pa.; Robert Bunker, assistant chief, Rutgers University Campus Patrol, Rutgers,

N.J.; described as an "established and reliable source"; Donald K. Cheek, Dean of Student Affairs, Lincoln University; a secretary to the Registrar, Swarthmore College, Swarthmore, Pennsylvania; Henry Peirsel, Security Officer, Swarthmore, College, Swarthmore, Pennsylvania; the chief switchboard operator, Swarthmore College, Swarthmore, Pennsylvania; and Charles Grier, Postmaster, U.S. Post Office, Swarthmore, Pennsylvania.

A hopeless search

The call to Resist in Cambridge indicated the hopelessness of the FBI's assignment to track down the documents. A spokesman for the anti-war group told the *Daily World* that forty news organizations had bombarded them with requests for the three batches of documents they released.

He said they receive the documents anonymously in ordinary manila envelopes in the morning mail. They Xerox them by the hundreds and mail them out to selected newspapers. He said they attempted to keep a balance between "straight" and "movement" newspapers to maximize both the analysis and the exposure of the files.

The thirteen documents in the *Daily World* Washington office reveal that no American who opposes war, racism, repression, pollution or any policy of the U.S. Government is safe from J. Edgar Hoover's anti-communist spy network.

Included is a photo-static copy of a report filed by the Media FBI office on the daughter of Representative Reuss filed by FBI spy Marjorie Webb.

Legalizing Watergate: Senate Bill Menaces Civil Rights

WASHINGTON, January 30 (1975)—Leaders of both parties are in a joint push for early Senate passage of the fascist-like dragnet law, S.1, to crush rising protests

Above, Frank Wilkinson, founder of the National Committee Against Repressive Legislation (NCARL). He played the key role in defeat of S.1. Wilkinson also organized the National Committee to Abolish HUAC which succeeded. Wilkinson and his close friend, Carl Braden, refused to testify before a HUAC (House UnAmerican Activities Committee) witchhunt hearing and were convicted of contempt of Congress and spent nine months in the Federal penitentiary. Photo courtesy of The Frank Wilkinson Centennial 1914-2014

against the Pentagon, big business and the economic crisis.

Senate Majority Leader, Mike Mansfield (D-Mont.) and Minority Leader Hugh Scott (R-Penn.) joined January 15 with rightwing Senator John McClellan (D-Ark.) and Senator Roman Hruska (R-Neb.) in making the bill the first one in the Senate hopper.

Esther Herst, Washington Coordinator of the National Committee Against Repressive Legislation, warned today that the Mansfield-Scott backing is a dangerous boost for the 753-page bill, the longest ever introduced in the Senate.

The bill is an agglomeration she said of the most repressive features of S.1400 and S.1 bills introduced in the last Congress by McClellan and Hruska which virtually rewrite the U.S. Criminal Code to unleash an assault on the Bill of Rights.

Media silent

She pointed out that aside from articles in the *Daily World* and other progressive outlets virtually nothing has been reported in the mass media about this ominous "law and order" bill originally authored by John Mitchell, the convicted Watergate conspirator (who served as Nixon's Attorney General and later as chair of Nixon's reelection committee, CREEP).

The bill has been variously described as an attempt to "legalize the Watergate", "a blueprint for fascism" and a "nightmare of repression."

S.1 resurrects and makes mandatory the death penalty, broadens the definition of "treason" "sabotage" and "espionage."

The focus of the anti-democratic measure is in two chapters, chapter two entitled "Offenses Involving National Defense" and Chapter 18, which contains a subchapter with a punitive definition of "riot offenses."

Crackdown on information

The bill provides for a crackdown on government workers, newsmen, editors, etcetera, who uncover and make public government conspiracies such as the Watergate plot and the Pentagon Papers expose of the Vietnam War.

In the name of "national defense," S.1 would legalize electronic surveillance without court orders such as that used by the FBI and CIA to compile dossiers on millions of citizens.

Jail terms are dictated for anyone who advocates refusal to serve in the Armed Forces. This could be used against those who, as in the Vietnam War, oppose wars of aggression.

The bill also prescribes jail for those who advocate "conduct that then or at some future time would facilitate the forcible overthrow or destruction "of the government and for anyone who "organizes, leads, recruits members for or participates as an active member" of an organization that advocates basic social change.

Ms. Herst charged that this section of S.1 would rewrite into law the anti-communist Smith Act overturned as unconstitutional. Communist Party members spent as much as eight years in jail under the Smith Act for expressing their belief that a basic change in the U.S. government is needed to end racism, war, and big business profiteering.

Ms. Herst urged a battle to pressure Mansfield, Senator Birch Bayh (D-Ind.) and other so-called liberals into reversing themselves and to keep S.1 from reaching the Senate floor.

Committee action in March

The full Judiciary Committee is expected to begin a markup session of S.1 in March.

Hearings have not yet been convened on similar legislation in the House.

"It is critical that letters get to the Senate," Ms. Herst said. "The Senators have to realize that people are opposed to this, that they are angry at attempts to push S.1 through."

She said S.1 preserves all the horrors of the version introduced in the last Congress.

"The section on 'treason' with a mandatory death penalty under some circumstances is still there," she said. "Expanded wiretaps are still there. The Smith Act is still there in all its repressive glory. It's really scary."

The bill codifies entrapment as a tactic of police repression. A person tricked by police into committing a crime and supplied by police with equipment to carry the crime out could not defend himself by claiming he was "entrapped."

Entrapment has become a standard practice of FBI and CIA provocateurs to disrupt democratic movements.

The bill also vastly expands government use of "conspiracy" as a criminal classification. More than seventy-five anti-racist and anti-war resisters have been tried in the past decade. In every one of these cases, the jury acquitted the defendants.

S.1 defines a "riot" as an "assemblage of five or more persons or damage to property."

Mary Ellen Gale, staff counsel of the Washington office of the American Civil Liberties Union, pointed out in recent Congressional testimony that in this definition of riot "discretion is left to the law enforcement officials by the vagueness of the term.

"Such broad provisions," she added, "can only encourage dragnet arrests where police make the arbitrary determination that everyone within sight or reach is engaging in a disturbance."

Postscript: Thanks to the work of NCARL led by Frank Wilkinson and Esther Herst, S.1 and "son of S.1" were defeated. Wilkinson deserved a White House "Medal of Freedom" for leading this struggle to victory.

Fred Haley defended my aunt, Margaret Jean Schudakopf (above), when witch hunters got her fired from the Tacoma schools

Candymaker, Fred Haley, Fought Red-Baiters

Posted on Facebook,

February 12, 2018
SEATTLE—Joyce & I stopped at a gift shop at SeaTac airport yesterday to pick up a couple of gifts for family and friends in Baltimore. As always, I chose a bag of "Almond Roca" by Brown & Haley in Tacoma. We always buy Brown & Haley chocolates, not only because the delicious candy is manufactured in Tacoma.

B&H is a UNION shop, the 350 or so workers represented by Local 9 of the Bakery & Confectionary Workers Union.

In 1954, Fred Haley, CEO of Brown & Haley came to my aunt, Margaret Jean Schudakopf's defense. She was a high school counselor at a Tacoma high school when red-baiters accused her of being a "communist." It went viral. She was hauled before witch hunt hearings. The anti-communist headlines shrieked! My aunt was a tall, handsome woman, dignified, very learned; a graduate of Reed College who obtained a PhD with a dissertation on the French Philosophes focused as I recall on Denis Diderot. Haley was an active, outspoken anti-racist who later attended the 1963 March on Washington for Jobs and Freedom. A member of the Tacoma School Board, he spoke out strongly against firing my aunt. There was never any question about her performance as a school counselor, he said. She is competent, conscientious and it is wrong to blacklist her for her political views. He and three other members of the Tacoma School Board voted against firing her. She spent years after that struggling to find jobs. She taught at small colleges in Oregon and Texas. (That job was at a historically Black college). I have no idea whether Aunt Margaret Jean was a member of the CP. I do remember that she was a staunch, unwavering member of the Methodist Federation for Social Action, close enough to communist to deserve the blacklist, according to the professional witch hunters.

I visited my aunt in Gig Harbor one summer day. I was playing my autoharp and singing folk songs on her patio. "Sing 'Die Gedanken Sind Frei,'" she said. I had never heard it so she sang it. I learned that wonderful German folk song and have sung it ever since. "Die gedanken sind frei/ My thoughts freely flower/Die Gedanken sind frei/My thoughts give me power/ No scholar can map them/No hunter can trap them/ No one can deny die gedanken sind frei...." As for Fred Haley, he was a man as sweet as the candy his workers made.

'We Charge Genocide': The cry rings true 52 years later

People's Weekly World,

November 4, 2005

NEW YORK—Just over half a century ago, Paul Robeson and William L. Patterson, two giants of the struggle for African-American equality, delivered to the United Nations a petition titled *We Charge Genocide: The Crime of Government Against the Negro People.*

Robeson was accompanied by signers of the petition December 17, 1951, when he presented the document to a UN official in New York. The same day, Patterson, executive director of the Civil Rights Congress (CRC), which had drafted the petition, delivered copies to the UN delegates meeting in Paris. The preamble of the petition reads:

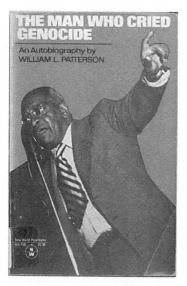

"Out of the inhuman Black ghettos of American cities," the introduction began, "out of the cotton plantations of the South, comes this record of mass slayings on the basis of race, of lives deliberately warped and distorted by the willful creation of conditions making for premature death, poverty and disease . . . "

Jarvis Tyner, executive vice chair of the Communist Party USA, says the power of the petition was its expose of culpability in genocide by the ruling circles in the U.S. Said Tyner, "The federal government claimed it had nothing to do with the lynchings. But this petition said: 'You knew about it and you did nothing. You knew about the super-exploitation and inhuman hardships inflicted upon the Black people and you did nothing.

Your inaction, your indifference in the face of oppression means that it was policy.'"

Among the signers were the eminent African-American historian and freedom fighter Dr. W.E.B. DuBois, George Crockett Junior, later a distinguished judge in Detroit who went on to serve many terms in the U.S. Congress, New York City Communist councilman Benjamin J. Davis, Junior, Ferdinand Smith, Black leader of the National Maritime Union, Dr. Oakley C. Johnson of Louisiana, Aubrey Grossman, the labor and civil rights lawyer, and Claudia Jones, a Communist leader in Harlem later deported under the witch-hunt Walter-McCarran Act. Also signing were family members of the victims of "legal lynching": Rosalee McGee, mother of Willie McGee, framed up on rape charges, and Josephine Grayson, whose husband, Francis Grayson, was one of the Martinsville Seven, framed and executed on false rape charges in Virginia.

In the section titled "Evidence," hundreds of cases of lynching were documented. The petition charged that since the abolition of slavery at least 10,000 Black people had been lynched. The full number, it stated, will never be known because the murders were often unreported.

The petition exposed a conspiracy to deny Black people the right to vote through poll taxes, literacy tests and outright terrorism. It brings to mind the "vote scrubbing" of 87,000 Black voters in Florida that enabled George W. Bush to steal the 2000 election.

Strom Thurmond, then South Carolina governor, was listed in the rogues' gallery. He had run for president on the segregationist Dixiecrat Party ticket in 1948. The petition quoted Thurmond denouncing the Fair Employment Practices Act requiring equal pay for equal work as "patterned after a Russian law written by Joseph Stalin." Thurmond scorned a proposed law against lynching as "tyranny," adding, "What could be more un-American?"

George W. Bush and Senator Trent Lott (R-Miss.) toasted Thurmond at his 100th birthday bash in

Washington a few weeks ago. Lott told the crowd the country would have been "better off" if Thurmond had been elected president. This racist remark touched off a furor that forced Lott to step down as Senate Majority Leader, but it also laid bare the poisonous racism of the Republican Party.

Patterson, a leader of the Communist Party USA, was an eminent civil rights attorney who had defended Sacco and Vanzetti. He spearheaded defense of the Scottsboro Nine, a group of African-American youth in Alabama framed up on phony rape charges in 1932. Patterson wrote in his autobiography, *The Man Who Cried Genocide*, that he had just returned from Richmond, Virginia, where he had struggled without success to save the Martinsville Seven, also falsely accused of raping a white woman.

"To me, it seemed clear that the Charter and Conventions of the UN had to be made the property of the American people as far as possible and especially of Black America," Patterson wrote. "It could be made the instrumentality through which the 'Negro Question' could be lifted to its highest dimension."

The UN Convention on the Prevention and Punishment of the Crime of Genocide, adopted December 9, 1948, flowed from the determination of the world community that never again would fascism be allowed to plunge humanity into holocaust and world war. Patterson pointed out that the U.S. stubbornly refused to ratify the convention even as American officials boasted of U.S. "democracy" and lectured other nations on human rights abuses, a "do as I say, not as I do" posture. (The U.S. did not ratify the Genocide Convention until Senator William Proxmire (D-Wisc.) finally pushed it through the U.S. Senate in 1987.)

The "prime mover" in the genocide against the African-American people "is monopoly capital," the petition charged. "Monopoly's immediate interest is nearly four billions of dollars in super-profits that it extracted from the oppression of the Negro people . . . " The racist wage differentials inflicted on Black workers drives down the wages for workers of all races, the petition charged. Despite gains for the African-American people, that wage differential continues today to pour tens of billions in extra profits into corporate bank accounts each year.

The petition answered the argument that "genocide" refers only to physical extermination, citing the UN's definition: "Any intent to destroy, in whole or in part, a national, racial, or religious group is genocide." The petition continued,

"We maintain, therefore, that the oppressed Negro citizens of the United States, segregated, discriminated against, and long the target of violence, suffer from genocide as the result of the consistent, conscious, unified policies of every branch of government . . . If the General Assembly acts as the conscience of mankind and therefore acts favorably on our petition, it will have served the cause of peace."

The courageous act of Robeson and Patterson ignited a firestorm with Cold Warriors slurring them as "traitors" in the service of the Soviet Union.

The attempts to silence Patterson began while he was in Paris. Packages with copies of the petition sent to London and Paris never arrived. He had brought twenty copies in his luggage and had sent sixty more to Budapest. He called Budapest and friends there expressed them back to him.

All the UN delegates received a copy. During a recess at the Palais de Chaillot where the UN was meeting, Dr. Channing Tobias, a U.S. delegate, chided Patterson for "this attack upon your government." Patterson snapped, "It's your government. It's my country. I am fighting to save my country's democratic principles."

Later, Eleanor Roosevelt, head of the U.S. delegation, delivered a speech, attempting to answer the charges without mentioning the petition. When Patterson arrived back in the U.S., federal agents hustled him into a room and strip-searched him, the first of many acts of retaliation.

The charge of disloyalty was aimed at diverting attention from the irrefutable evidence in the petition. Yet the Cold Warriors could not hold back the rising tide of outrage against racist segregation enforced by lynch terror. The "We Charge Genocide" petition was only the opening shot. The Supreme Court's Brown v. Board of Education decision in 1954 inflicted a huge blow on the system of legal segregation by reversing the Plessy v. Ferguson doctrine of "separate but equal." The high court ruled that "separate is inherently unequal." Then came Rosa Parks' refusal to move to the back of the bus in Montgomery, Alabama, and the boycott that followed. The floodgates of the civil rights revolution were opened.

Jean Damu, chair of the California Coalition for H.R.-40, the reparations bill introduced by Representative John Conyers (D-Mich.), wrote recently that the "We Charge Genocide" petition "may be seen as much the ideological stimulus for the civil rights movement as Brown v. Board of Education," and "must be seen as the seminal act." Damu points out that while the petition did not call for reparations, "here for the first time in regards to African-Americans, a crime is charged and documented, a victim is specified and a perpetrator is pinpointed."

Robert Taylor, a spokesperson for "Millions for Reparations," based in Brooklyn, New York, likewise hailed the "We Charge Genocide" petition as an antecedent of the struggles to win reparations for the African-American people for centuries of slavery, genocide and continued oppression today.

"Think of all the police killings of Black people in which the white officers were exonerated," Taylor said, citing the case of Amadou Diallo who died in a hail of forty-one bullets fired by eight white New York City cops. "All the white police officers were exonerated. Consider the Central Park jogger case where those innocent young Black men spent thirteen years in prison for a crime they didn't commit. Yes, things have changed, but the essence remains the same."

The struggle against racist oppression has won many victories and made long strides toward equality. But contrary to the assertions of Bush and the ultra-right, the U.S. is far from the "color blind" oasis of "equal opportunity" they proclaim. There are more African Americans in prison than in college. A Human Rights Watch report revealed that Black men are imprisoned for drug offenses at an astounding rate of 1,146 per 100,000, thirteen times higher than the rate of 139 per 100,000 for white men. "This is nothing short of a national scandal," the report charged.

During the past decade, an estimated 2,000 African Americans died at the hands of police, almost always white officers, the slaying invariably ruled "justifiable homicide." The most recent is Michael Ellerbe of Uniontown, Pennsylvania, a twelve-year-old Black youngster shot in the back by Pennsylvania state troopers just before Christmas. The troopers were exonerated by the State's Attorney.

January 1 was the 140th anniversary of the Emancipation Proclamation. Yet African-American life expectancy is 71.8 years, compared to 77.4 years for whites. Infant mortality for African Americans is 14.6 per 1,000 live

Paul Robeson and fellow Civil Rights Congress workers present "We Charge Genocide" petition to a UN official Dec. 17, 1951

births compared to 5.8 per 1,000 live births for whites. In these two vital statistics, the gap between white and Black is once again widening. Last year, 1.3 million people fell below the poverty line. There are now 33 million poor people in the U.S., 7.8 percent white, 22.7 percent Black, and 21.4 Hispanic. Unemployment is at six percent and again the Black jobless rate is twice that of whites.

With his demagogic attack on affirmative action at the University of Michigan, falsely branding it "racial preferences" and "reverse discrimination," Bush makes plain that he seeks to roll back the gains of the African-American people.

In his foreword to the 1970 edition of "We Charge Genocide," Patterson wrote:

> Racism U.S.A. is an export commodity breeding aggressive wars and threatening the peace of the world . . . I assert that the wantonly murderous and predatory racist attacks on Korea, Vietnam and Cambodia . . . are inseparably related to the equally criminal murders of rebellious Black youth in Chicago . . . New Haven . . . Augusta, Georgia, and Jackson, Mississippi. "We Charge Genocide" will ring with the truth until racism is banished and the African-American people have won full equality.

Pentagon Drug Test Victims Seek Justice
Daily World

September 26, 1979
WASHINGTON, September 25—Victims of Pentagon drug testing yesterday demanded that the government prosecute high officials who have made their lives a nightmare of suicidal depression, memory loss and ruined marriages and careers.

The ten victims appeared at a Capitol Hill news conference sponsored by Representative Ronald V. Dellums (D-CA) to denounce the decades long Pentagon program at Edgewood Arsenal in Maryland in which hundreds of victims were unwittingly administered mind altering drugs such as LSD and an agent ten times more powerful, called BZ.

The CIA had a similar program called "MK Ultra" and "Artichoke" in which several victims are known to have died. Under a blanket of cold-war anti-communism, the Pentagon and the CIA were searching for a mind-altering drug to be used against socialist countries, newly independent nations of the third world, and against domestic dissidents.

The U.S. government claims the programs have ended, but the army has stockpiled fifty tons of BZ at its Pine Bluff Arsenal in Arkansas, enough to destroy the minds of ten times the world's population.

Given promises

Gary S. Wagner, of Royal Oak, Michigan told the news conference he was lured to Edgewood with promises of "a vacation-type atmosphere," "extra pay" and "no duty." He said he was assured that all the drugs were "already on the open market" with no danger that he would suffer after effects.

One day, in the base hospital, his arm was tied down, a pencil-thick needle was inserted and an unknown drug was injected. Said Wagner, "I was terrified and asked the nurse and doctor . . . what drug they were going to use on me. I was told it was 'top secret' and they were unable to tell me."

Another victim at the Longworth Building news conference who asked that he be called "Roger" said the drugs made him "violently sick . . . my mental state at the time was one of utter desperation and helplessness, to the point of wishing for death in order to end the torment."

Can't concentrate

He said he has been "plagued" ever since by an inability to concentrate. He said he has not "received a reply" to his numerous requests to the Pentagon for information and assistance on these after effects.

Representative Dellums said he has written to the Attorney General Benjamin Civiletti demanding to know "how the Department of Justice operates regarding prosecution of alleged illegalities in human experimentation programs conducted by the military or civilian agencies."

In a separate letter to Secretary of Defense Harold Brown, Dellums demanded to know "why there has been no medical follow-up for the thousands of servicemen who underwent the Edgewood Testing with drugs other than LSD in spite of repeated reports of long range ill-effects currently being suffered by these men and their families."

"In recent years . . . we have learned that our own government has been training, encouraging and subsidizing the same kind of experimentation that has made the name of Joseph Mengele and others of his ilk the symbol for wanton murder by the state," he asserted.

The press conference was arranged by American Citizens for Honesty in Government.

The CIA Helped Jail Mandela. Will Bush Apologize?
People's Daily World

June 23, 1990
WASHINGTON—When Nelson Mandela arrives at the White House June 25, will President Bush apologize to him for the CIA's role in his arrest twenty-eight years ago? Will Bush promise to put an end to the CIA's collusion with South Africa's spy agency in acts of terror against the freedom movement?

Those are pertinent questions in the wake of news that the CIA provided information that enabled South Africa's Bureau of State Security (BOSS) to arrest Mandela August 5, 1962. "Congress should investigate the CIA's role in Mandela's arrest with the same urgency that Senator Frank Church investigated CIA assassinations in 1975," declared Tony Monteiro, a Rutgers University professor and expert on Africa. Monteiro listed the African leaders assassinated or overthrown in CIA-instigated coups—Patrice Lumumba, president of the Congo in 1961; Kwame Nkumah, president of Ghana, overthrown in 1966, Amilear Cabral of Guinea Bissau, assassinated in 1973; Eduardo Mondelane, and Samora Machel of Mozambique, assassinated in the 1980s.

No movement has suffered losses heavier than the African National Congress (ANC) of South Africa—Ruth First and Dulcie September murdered and Albe Sachs wounded, in addition to thousands of other rank-and-file freedom fighters. "This is the CIA's strategy of beheading the African liberation movement," Monteiro said.

A retired CIA agent told *Cox News Service* that hours after Mandela's arrest, a fellow CIA officer named Paul Eckel walked into his office in Pretoria and declared, "We have turned Mandela over to the South African security branch. We gave them every detail, what he would be wearing, the time of day, just where he would be. They have picked him up. It is one of our greatest coups." Eckel died in 1986.

Retired CIA and BOSS agents told Cox that in 1962, the CIA "devoted more money and expertise to penetrating the ANC than did the tiny, fledgling intelligence service of the South African government."

Asked about the reports, Bush's press secretary, Marlin Fitzwater, snapped, "Don't beat me up for what the Kennedy administration did." The CIA declined comment.

But the record is clear: CIA collusion with South Africa continued throughout the 1960s, 1970s, and 1980s. It extended across the African continent and cost millions of lives in "low-intensity" wars instigated by the United States and South Africa. Angola, for example, was a target of Lieutenant Colonel Oliver North's Iran-contra enterprise. Representative Howard E. Wolpe (D-Mich.), chair of the House Africa Subcommittee, wrote letters to the chairmen of the Iran-contra committees explaining the ties between southern Africa and the Iran-contra affair. Wolpe even offered a witness who was willing to testify that Saudi Arabia had agreed to arm and train Jonas Savimbi's UNITA mercenaries in Angola if the U.S. delivered AWAC planes in exchange. The committees refused to hear him.

The *Cox News* article does not identify the CIA spy who betrayed Mandela in 1962. But he is named in an article by John Kelly in the Fall-Winter 1986 *National Reporter*, headlined, "The arrest of Nelson Mandela: Uncovering the American Connection." Kelly quotes *CBS Evening News* for August 5, 1986: "There can be no doubt at all that Mandela was betrayed by, at that time, the American counsel in Durban, who told us he was working for the CIA." CBS identified this officer as Donald C. Rickard.

Rickard, who reportedly had infiltrated the Durban branch of the ANC, passed on all the details of Mandela's movements to Colonel Daniel Bester of the Duban branch of BOSS. In exchange, Bester gave Rickard sensitive information about South Africa's plans to force the Black majority to resettle in bantustans. With Rickard's help, Bester "traced the identities of ANC members," which set the stage for the infamous Rivonia treason trial, Kelly reports. It led to Mandela's imprisonment for twenty-seven years.

Serving in Pretoria at the same time as Rickard was Frank C. Carlucci, a man destined to become Washington's favorite covert troubleshooter. President Reagan appointed Carlucci as his national security adviser after the cover was blown on the Iran-contra affair. Considering his background, preserving the deep cover on CIA covert actions in southern Africa may have been one of Carlucci's most important assignments. U.S. multinational corporate profits are at stake—Angola's oil, southern Africa's fabulous reserves of gold, platinum, diamonds, copper, vanadium, chrome, manganese, uranium. Carlucci himself owns substantial stock in the South African diamond conglomerate, DeBeers.

In March 1960, Carlucci was transferred to Leopold-ville, Congo—now Kinshasa, Zaire. Less than two months later, the CIA began plotting the murder of Lumumba, a brilliant poet and independence leader who favored a socialist path of development for his country. According to a report by a Senate Church Committee, that assassination was probably approved by President Eisenhower. Carlucci played a major role in the CIA coup that installed Mobutu Sese Seko as dictator of Zaire. Mobutu has been a key CIA asset ever since.

The U.S.—South African collaboration escalated with the collapse of Belgium's and Portugal's colonial empires in the 1960s and 1970s. Washington saw an opportunity to grab a piece of the action. One of the first steps was the formation in 1960 of CIA stations throughout Africa, especially in the Belgian Congo. By 1984, according to William J. Pomeroy, the CIA had forty stations and 3,500 agents on the African continent. During a series of South African invasions of Angola in the mid-1970s, "CIA chiefs met with BOSS . . . representatives regularly in Kinshasa . . . and the BOSS director visited Washington secretly twice to confer with the CIA's African Division Chief, James Potts," writes Pomeroy. Another element of the strategy was sending Carlucci as Ambassador to Lisbon in December 1974 to orchestrate a counterrevolution against Portugal's left-progressive, anti-colonial government.

Meanwhile, in Zaire, the CIA set up "Operation Feature," directed by a young agent named John Stockwell, to intervene across the border in Angola in collusion with the South Africa Defense Force (SADF) and BOSS. Because of the 1974 Hughes-Ryan Amendment, the Ford administration was compelled to reveal Operation Feature. In January 1976, Congress passed and President Ford reluctantly signed the Clark Amendment barring aid to the Angolan rebels. Ford's Director of Central Intelligence at the time was George Bush.

But the contra war against Angola did not stop—and it escalated sharply after Reagan's election in 1980. In September 1982, CIA Director William Casey visited South Africa. Ruth First had just been murdered and Pomeroy writes that the aim of Casey's visit "was to map out a campaign for the expulsion of the ANC from the countries bordering South Africa which gave the ANC refuge." Tactics included murderous cross-border raids by SADF, terrorism and assassinations—all with the assistance of the CIA. Another likely aim of Casey's trip was circumvention of the Clark Amendment. Kenneth Mokoena, a researcher at the National Security Archives (NSA), said his group submitted a list of questions to the Iran-contra committees, including whether Savimbi received some of the profits from the arms sale. Did Oliver North secretly deliver arms to Savimbi through the port of Lagos, Nigeria, in violation of the Clark Amendment? The Iran-contra committees "brushed our questions aside," Mokoena charged. Congress later repealed the Clark Amendment and a flood of arms for the UNITA terrorists followed.

Among the documents released by the Iran-contra committees are ship logs for Oliver North's freighter, the Erria, showing that it made stops in several West African ports, including Lagos. The owner of the Erria was Dolmy Business Inc. of Panama, one of several dummy "offshore" companies set up by North to conceal arms shipments. A flow chart of these companies prepared by Casey's Swiss bank, Credit Suisse, lists several of these firms. Under Dolmy Inc. appears one word: "Africa."

A tilt towards Africa also surfaced in a memo by General Jack Singlaub, head of the World Anti-Communist League, one of North's closet accomplices. Singlaub laid out a scheme, authored by Casey, for "three-way trade" to ensure continuous flow of weapons to "freedom fighters in Nicaragua, Afghanistan, Angola, Cambodia, Ethiopia, etc." The arms would be funneled through an offshore trading company operating with "neither the consent or awareness of the Department of State or

Congress." Again, senators questioned Singlaub extensively about this memo but never about its application to Africa. Yet Singlaub and his cohorts were so enthusiastic about Savimbi and his South African allies that the World Anti-Communist League convened a meeting of contras from around the world at UNITA headquarters in Jamba, Angola, in the spring of 1987. It was bankrolled by Rite Aid drug store billionaire Lewis Lehrman.

Mokoena said he has in his possession a U.S. Embassy memo stamped "top secret" that was leaked in Pretoria in 1962. "It describes Nelson Mandela's whereabouts. It is clear that the CIA was tracking his every movement."

Name CIA Men In Afghanistan

WASHINGTON, February 21, 1980—The CIA began a program of armed intervention in Afghanistan at least one year before Soviet troops ever entered that nation it was charged today by a prominent Washington magazine that specializes in information on the spy organization.

To back up its charges, the magazine "Counter Spy" published names of prominent CIA operatives involved in the armed activities. "Counter Spy" has made national news over the past years for its articles which have reliably named prominent CIA operatives in various nations around the world.

Konrad Ege, an editor of the magazine and author of an article in its December issue titled "U.S. Intervention in Afghanistan" told the *Daily World* today that his research shows that for well over a year a special CIA task force under the command of CIA agent Robert Lessard has conducted counter-revolutionary activities against Afghanistan using the U.S. Embassy in Islamabad, Pakistan as its headquarters.

Ege's charges cast a light on President Carter's drive to establish a new anti-Soviet, anti-national liberation war alliance in the Persian Gulf with the U.S., China, Israel, Saudi Arabia and Pakistan supplying arms to the so-called Afghan rebels.

Carter lied

Ege said the Carter Administration is lying when it says CIA covert operations are a response to the movement of Soviet troops in Afghanistan last December. "The point of the story is that the U.S. involvement in Afghanistan is at least a year old—far longer than the Soviet troop presence in Afghanistan," he said.

In a press release, issued yesterday, Ege had charged that "it is important to note that these CIA operations were in support of Afghans violently opposing progressive improvement for their fellow citizens such as needed land reform and equality for women."

He charged that Lessard was a CIA undercover agent in Iran for ten years, an exceptionally long period, during which the CIA tutored SAVAK, the Shah's secret police in torture techniques and other methods of mass terror.

Lessard, Ege, continued, also was assigned to the U.S. Embassy before the April 1978 democratic revolution. Lessard has been assigned to Pakistan since July 1977.

Names CIA officers

Other CIA officers in Pakistan include John J. Reagan, David E. Thurman (both in Islamabad) and Richard D. Jackman (in Karachi). Ege pointed out that the State Department and the Pentagon have met with Ziya Nezri, a U.S. citizen of Afghan nationality "who is one of the leading figures of the reactionary forces which began fighting the Afghan government in 1978."

Another "rebel leader," Zia Nessery, is a U.S. Citizen who has received support from the Rockefeller funded Asia Society, Ege said. Bashir Zikria, a principal organizer of the counter-revolutionary commandos is a professor at the Columbia University College of Physicians and Surgeons and "commutes" to Pakistan, Ege charged.

"These facts prove that the U.S. is deeply involved in the internal war of the Afghans," Ege continued. "U.S. governmental support for them not only violates national sovereignty and international law but also U.S. law," he said.

Against the law

He cited Section 960, Title XVIII of the U.S. code which prohibits "any military or naval expedition or enterprise to be carried out from thence against the territory or dominion of any foreign prince or state . . . "

Ege continued, "Obviously the people of the United States have a right and a need to know of the U.S. governmental support for the so-called 'Afghan rebels'

I stumbled on this story I forgot I wrote while Googling. It was posted on the CIA website after they "sanitized" it in 2010, thirty-one years after I wrote it.

particularly since in their name and with their taxes a 'secret war' is being carried out.....Such CIA operations ultimately undermine the interests and national security of the U.S. people by bringing us all closer to war."

Ege's article also charges that the U.S. Drug Enforcement Agency has a team working in Pakistan. Ege pointed out that the DEA "has rarely limited itself to 'pure' prosecution of drug traffickers."

Ege referred to a recent article in the Canadian magazine *McCleans* that Afghan rebels have been purchasing arms from the U.S. with massive deliveries of heroin . . . now reportedly reaching the streets of U.S. cities in massive quantities.

Dark Alliance: CIA Gun Runners Linked To Cocaine Trafficking.

This article was reprinted from the September 7, 1996 issue of the *People's Weekly World*.

The Los Angeles City Council and Senator Barbara Boxer (D-Calif.) last week called for a full-scale probe of evidence that the CIA smuggled tons of cocaine into California during the 1980s and used the profits to buy arms for the Contra terrorists in their deadly war against the Nicaraguan people.

The new evidence of the CIA "drugs-for-guns" conspiracy came in a series of articles Dark Alliance in the San Jose *Mercury News* starting August 18 by staff writers Gary Webb and Pamela Kramer. Based on a year-long investigation, the articles filled eight full pages of the Mercury News. The series does not answer whether the CIA drug trafficking continues to this day.

The L.A. chapter of the Black American Political Association of California convened a news conference on the L.A. City Hall steps, August 23 to demand a "complete investigation . . . to determine not only the identities and roles of those who participated in the activity but also those who covered it up, protected it and knowingly tolerated it."

L.A. City Councilman Nate Holden pushed through a council resolution which asks Attorney General Janet Reno to investigate "serious and credible allegations" of CIA involvement in the drug trafficking in Los Angeles.

Senator Boxer wrote to CIA Director John M. Deutch August 28 demanding an investigation of charges that the CIA "raised over $50 million each year" for the Contras "by selling cocaine to drug dealers in California at the same time that the crack epidemic was beginning." Federal, state, and local law enforcement agencies, Boxer continued, "have complained that their operations were mysteriously thwarted . . . that the CIA had compromised their investigations in an effort to sustain the Contras."

The articles turn the spotlight back on the Iran-Contra scandal, a subject the Republican extremists want voters to forget in this election year. GOP Presidential candidate Bob Dole is attacking President Clinton for the increase in use of drugs by young people. But Dole was a loyal defender of President Reagan throughout the Iran-Contra affair. The *Mercury News* series helps expose that plot as a racist enterprise that continues to decimate the nation's African American communities with crack cocaine and gun violence.

The first article, headlined "80s' Effort to Assist Guerrillas Left Legacy of Drugs, Gangs in Black L.A.," points out that cocaine was an expensive narcotic used mostly by the affluent until CIA-connected traffickers started shipping it in to L.A. where it was converted to crack for street sale in African American communities across the country.

At the center of the cocaine operation uncovered by the Mercury News were Norwin Meneses and Oscar Danilo Blandon, with close family links to Nicaragua's deposed dictator, Anastasio Somoza. After the Sandinista army overthrew Somoza in 1979, Meneses and Blandon moved to the San Francisco Bay Area where Blandon became active in efforts to raise money to support the CIA's Contra army in Nicaragua, an effort orchestrated by Lt. Col. Oliver North from the White House basement.

On December 1, 1981, President Reagan signed a secret executive order that gave "the CIA the green light to begin covert paramilitary operations against the Sandinista government," the *Mercury News* reported. Within days Blandon received a telephone call from Donald Barrios, a wealthy friend in Miami ordering him to travel to Honduras with Meneses where they met with Enrique Bermudez, commander of the FDN, the largest Contra army. Bermudez had served as Somoza's liaison with the Pentagon and had been on the CIA payroll since 1981. The Reagan administration had assigned him to pull together the remnants of Somoza's defeated National Guard for the terror war against Nicaragua.

Last March, Blandon, now a highly paid informer for the Drug Enforcement Administration (DEA), told about the operation during a drug trafficking trial in San Diego. The Justice Department obtained a court order barring any defense questions on Blandon's links to the CIA.

Yet Blandon told the court of his trip to Honduras with Meneses. After getting their marching orders from Bermudez, Blandon testified that he and Meneses returned to the Bay Area and "started raising money for the Contra revolution . . . There is a saying that the 'ends justify the means' and that's what Mr. Bermudez told us in Honduras . . . "

The volume of cocaine skyrocketed after they made connections with Ricky Donnell Ross, alias "Freeway Rick," a ringleader in L.A. drug trafficking. There is no evidence that Ross knew about the CIA's role. Blandon later helped the DEA set up a sting that resulted in Ross' arrest and conviction. Ross' attorney recently won a delay in sentencing so that he can present new evidence drawn from the *Mercury News* series.

In the first year of the operation, the Meneses-Blandon ring sold a ton of cocaine to L.A. street gangs reaping $54 million in profits. "It arrived in all kinds of containers: false bottomed shoes, Colombian freighters, cars with hidden compartments, luggage from Miami," the *Mercury News* reported. "Once here, it disappeared into a series of houses and nondescript storefront businesses scattered from Hayward to San Jose, Pacifica to Burlingame, Daley City to Oakland."

Blandon told the San Diego trial that they not only supplied L.A. gangs with drugs, he also provided Uzi submachine guns and Colt AR-15 assault rifles. One source for this weaponry, he said was ex-Laguna Beach detective Ronald J. Lister who claimed he worked for the CIA and the DEA.

Meneses was known in Nicaragua as the "Rey de la Droga," (King of Drugs). Despite a "stack of law enforcement reports describing him as a major drug trafficker" in forty-five federal drug investigations, he was "welcomed into the United State in July 1979 as a political refugee and given a visa and a work permit," the *Mercury News* reports. "He settled in the San Francisco Bay Area and for the next six years supervised the importation of thousands of kilos of cocaine into California."

Meneses became a multi-millionaire and bought restaurants, car rental agencies and real estate throughout northern California. The *Mercury News* features a photo of Meneses posing with Adolfo Calero, a North crony and the FDN's representative in Washington.

The enterprise suffered a setback five years later when Congress approved $100 million in "legal" aid to the Contras. Soon after, on October 27, 1986, agents of the FBI, DEA local and L.A. police raided more than a dozen locations in Blandon's network. But someone on the inside had tipped off Blandon and when the law enforcement officers arrived, the incriminating evidence had been removed.

Nevertheless, Blandon and his wife were arrested. The search warrant for this dragnet sweep, signed by L.A. County Sheriff's Sergeant, Tom Gordon, stated, "Danilo Blandon is in charge of a sophisticated cocaine smuggling and distribution organization operating in Southern California. The monies gained from the sales of cocaine are transported to Florida and laundered through Orlando Murillo who is a high-ranking officer of a chain of banks in Florida named Government Securities Corporation. From this bank the monies are filtered to the Contra rebels to buy arms in the war in Nicaragua." This investment bank, with the aroma of one of North's notorious dummy corporations, has since gone bankrupt.

Blandon, himself, was tried and convicted on drug trafficking charges in 1992 but the DEA won his release on unsupervised parole after only twenty-eight months in prison. The *Mercury News* points out that young African American men are serving life sentences for selling a few vials of crack. Blandon has sold tons but is now living in luxury mansions in Managua and San Diego and is on the DEA payroll which has paid him $166,000 as an informer.

After the Sandinista government lost the elections, Norwin Meneses returned to Managua. He was arrested while attempting to smuggle 750 kilos of cocaine into the United States. His chief accuser during his sensational 1992 trial was a close personal friend, Enrique Miranda, who had been serving a drug trafficking prison term in Managua. In a long handwritten statement, obtained by the *Mercury News*, Miranda testified that Meneses "had financed the Contra revolution with the benefits of the cocaine they sold." This operation, he testified "was executed with the collaboration of . . . officials of the Salvadoran Air Force who flew planes to Colombia and then left for the U.S., bound for an Air Force base in Texas as he told me."

Meneses has stated that one of his closest friends is a former Contra pilot named Marcos Aguado, a Nicaraguan who works for the Salvadoran Air Force high command.

"Aguado was identified in 1987 congressional testimony as a CIA agent who helped the Contras get weapons, airplanes and money from a major Colombian drug trafficker," the *Mercury News* reported. Aguado's name "also turned up in a deposition taken by the Iran-Contra committees. Robert W. Owen, a courier for

Lt. Col. Oliver North, testified he knew Aguado as a Contra pilot and said there was 'concern' about his being involved in drug trafficking." Miranda mysteriously disappeared a year ago during a routine weekend furlough from prison, hours before he was scheduled to meet with a *Mercury News* staff writer.

The CIA has had a longstanding alliance with the criminal underworld in heroin and cocaine trafficking, much of it exposed in *The Politics of Heroin in Southeast Asia*, by Alfred W. McCoy (*Harper & Row*, 1972).

The CIA, McCoy writes, formed an alliance with the drug-dealing mafia in Sicily after World War II to prevent the Italian Communist Party from winning Italy's national elections. The spy agency worked with Corsican gangsters in Marseille, France, to smash dockworker strikes in 1947 and 1950. Once the left-wing dockworkers union was smashed, Marseille became the "French connection" for smuggling tons of heroin into the United States.

Mafia godfathers, Meyer Lansky and Santo Trafficante Jr., ran gambling casinos, and drug peddling rackets in Havana until they were driven out by Cuba's 1959 revolution. Then they moved to Florida, McCoy writes, where, they formed an alliance with the CIA. Trafficante flew to Hong Kong and Saigon in 1968 to set up the infrastructure for a flood of heroin from the "Golden Triangle."

During the Vietnam War the CIA's Air America flew tons of heroin out of Laos, destined for the growing heroin market in the U.S., McCoy writes. Lt. Col. Oliver North, a U.S. Marine officer was already connected to the CIA in Vietnam.

In the late 1980s, Senator John Kerry (D-Mass.) convened hearings before his Subcommittee on Narcotics in which Ramon Milian-Rodriguez, now serving a prison sentence as the "accountant" of the Medellin cocaine cartel, testified that billions of dollars in drug profits were being laundered through the Panama City branches of the wealthiest U.S. banks. It was confirmed by a report from the State Department that narcotics production "unfortunately remain big business. And drug abuse levels all over the world continue to rise . . . banks and bankers alike, have fallen victim (willing or unwilling) to the huge profits which result from laundering activities."

Newsweek ran a story headlined "Guns for Drugs?" about a CIA "Arms Supermarket based in Honduras and funded by cocaine profits" that was traced to the office of Vice President George Bush. North's notebooks contained a cryptic entry, July 12, 1985, that the White House "plans to seize all . . . when Supermarket comes to bad end. $14 M(illion) to finance comes from drugs."

Nothing was done to root out Reagan's high crimes and misdemeanors exposed in the Iran-Contra conspiracy. North did not spend a day in jail and in 1994 ran for the U.S. Senate. His campaign donors included the same wealthy right-wing extremists, like Peter and William Coors, who funded the Contra war. Now they are pouring dollars into Bob Dole's coffers. These latest revelations should spark calls for long overdue action, the abolition of the CIA.

Chapter 6

Scoundrel Time

ART SHIELDS, who taught me how to be a good reporter, once told me that good news reports have heroes and villains like any other good story. His own stories offered plenty of examples. He covered many coal miner strikes. The miners were heroes. The mine owners were villains.

I took that to heart and in my career as a reporter I have found plenty of heroes and far too many scoundrels. It is in the nature of scoundrels, especially political demagogues, to hide their knavery behind a lot of rectitude, patriotism, piety, and devotion to family. It takes digging to lay bare the sorry reality. Ronald Reagan is a perfect example, a demagogue who knew how to hide the rotten truth behind an "aw shucks" grin.

The role of *Fox News* is to serve as an ad agency for the corporate ultra-right. To cite just one example of this exercise in massive, nonstop prevarication, they are presenting air-brushed images all seventeen Republican candidates for President in the 2016 election. If we manage to survive this onslaught of GOP knavery, it will be thanks to the "off" button on our TVs.

My job as Washington correspondent was to expose, expose, expose, and expose again. I inherited a love of research and spent hours at many libraries, including the Library of Congress, digging up the truth and putting it on the front page of the *Daily World/People's Weekly World*.

Washington is really an excellent place to dig up dirt on Presidents, Representatives, Senators, and lobbyists. I learned from people who knew how to do it. I.F. Stone, for example, who put out a little newsletter, *I.F. Stone's Weekly*, that I subscribed to for many years. He was diminutive and wore spectacles. He was hard of hearing so he relied heavily on reading exhaustively from Federal documents. He put excerpts from these documents in *I.F. Stone's Weekly*. He was peerless in his skill at skewering the crooks with words from their own mouths.

Izzy, as he was fondly known, had met me when I was an undergraduate at Amherst College, already a subscriber to his weekly. He had come to meet with subscribers in Springfield, Massachusetts and I went down to meet him. We struck it off right then and there.

So when I showed up as the *Daily World* correspondent in Washington a few years later, I ran into him at a news conference. He greeted me like a long lost brother.

He read my articles and I read his. He praised me warmly and encouraged me to dig deeper to expose the scoundrels who exploit and oppress millions of ordinary working people.

I selected for this part of my book some of the exposes I wrote over many years, laying bare some of the meanest, most vindictive demagogues who defile our nation. Most—although not all—are Republicans. But all of them fit Art Shield's definition of villains.

Marine Corps General, Smedley Butler. Photo courtesy U.S. Marine Corps

Plot to Overthrow FDR
People's Weekly World

February 1999
NEW YORK—Was it coincidental that A&E Television's *History Channel* aired a documentary February 14 titled *The Plot to Overthrow FDR* hours after the Senate voted to acquit President Clinton? The Senate's vote was a fatal blow to the Republican extremist drive to force Clinton from office.

But this film focused on a similar plot sixty-six years ago to force President Franklin D. Roosevelt from office. The *History Channel* will air it again Monday, May 26 at 8 p.m. eastern time and 9 p.m. Pacific Time. The little known episode centered on General Smedley D. Butler, a maverick retired Marine, a two time Medal of Honor winner, who had been selected by the richest Wall Street banks to serve as the "man on a white horse" in a coup d'état modeled on Benito Mussolini's "March on Rome."

After winning election in November 1932, Roosevelt took the U.S. off the gold standard and pushed through the WPA public works jobs program. The way had been opened for enactment in the years that followed of the forty hour workweek, the minimum wage, unemployment compensation, workmen's compensation, and Social Security, and the first laws against racist discrimination. The Wagner Act was passed upholding union organizing rights.

A press release from The *History Channel* explains how corporate America reacted: "During the summer of 1933, a group of wealthy and powerful financiers and industrialists, alarmed by FDR's economic policies and inspired by the political trends taking place in Italy and Germany, began to discuss the idea of creating a fascist state in the United States. It was to be secretly financed and organized by leading officers of the Morgan and Du Pont empires . . . such as Irene Du Pont, . . . Grayson Murphy, director of Goodyear, Bethlehem Steel and a group of J.P. Morgan banks."

Interviewed in the film is Jules Archer, author of the 1973 *The Plot to Seize the White House*. He writes that the "savage hatred of 'that cripple in the White House' represented the most bitter animosity big business has ever manifested toward any President in American history." Greater, even, than that of the Clinton-haters.

The financier's first choice for leading the coup was General Douglas MacArthur since he was the son-in-law of a Morgan Bank director. But MacArthur had driven the "Bonus Army" from the Mall in Washington and burned their shantytown in the Anacostia flats using tanks, tear gas and rifle fire. Several World War I veterans were killed. They had come to Washington to demand that President Herbert Hoover and Congress redeem the bonus coupons given to them for their service in World War I.

MacArthur was so hated he could never muster the 500,000 disgruntled war veterans that Wall Street needed to overthrow FDR. By contrast, retired Marine General Smedley Butler was a perfect candidate. He had gone to the veteran's shantytown on a sweltering day in July 1932 and denounced Congress for killing the Patman Bonus Bill that would have met the Bonus Army's demands.

"Old Gimlet Eye," a veteran of U.S. interventions in Cuba, the Philippines, China, Haiti, Mexico, and Nicaragua, drew a thunderous ovation from the vets. That November, Butler, a lifelong Republican, campaigned to turn Hoover out of the White House and put Roosevelt in.

A year later, July 1, 1933, two men visited Butler at his home in Newtown Square, Pennsylvania, Bill Doyle, commander of the Massachusetts American Legion, and Gerald C. MacGuire, chairman of the "distinguished guests committee" of the American Legion. They told Butler they represented an influential group that wanted to remove the current leadership of the American Legion.

It was the first of many meetings between Butler and MacGuire who turned out to be an employee of the House of Morgan on Wall Street. MacGuire revealed a plan for Butler to attend the American Legion convention in Chicago. Handpicked veterans planted in the crowd would lead the cheering for a speech Butler would deliver calling for a return to the gold standard.

Butler played along, and MacGuire let slip that he was speaking for the most powerful financiers in the country. The gold standard speech had been written by John W. Davis, chief attorney for J.P. Morgan and Co. These financial titans, MacGuire disclosed, were prepared to ante up $3,000,000 immediately to pay for the recruitment of a paramilitary army from the Legion's ranks. Ultimately, they were ready to pay $300 million for a veterans march on Washington to remove or neutralize Roosevelt.

Weapons to arm the fascist army would be provided by Remington Arms Company owned by the Du Ponts. MacGuire told Butler he had been sent to Europe to learn how Mussolini and Hitler came to power. MacGuire reported that the American financiers had preferred the French stormtroopers, the Croix de Feu, (Burning Cross). While in Paris, MacGuire had used the offices of Morgan &Hodges another link to the House of Morgan.

MacGuire told Butler that within a year, a new movement aimed at promoting the takeover would be announced, the American Liberty League (ALL). Sure enough, in September 1934, ALL was announced with MacGuire's boss, Morgan banker, Grayson Murphy, as the treasurer.

Archer reports that among ALL'S heaviest contributors were Andrew W. Mellon, the Pitcairn family of Pittsburgh Plate Glass, Rockefeller Associates, E.F. Hutton Associates, Alfred P. Sloan, president, and William S. Knudsen, vice president of General Motors, and the Pew family, owners of Sun Oil. J. Howard Pew was a longtime friend and generous supporter of Robert Welch, founder of the John Birch Society.

Butler had decided to blow the lid on the conspiracy. He went to Tom O'Neil, city editor of the *Philadelphia Record*. O'Neil assigned an investigative reporter Paul Comly French, who confirmed the conspiracy in even greater detail. The *Record* broke the story November 20, 1934 under a headline, "$3,000,000 Bid For Fascist Army Bared."

On the same day, the McCormack-Dickstein Committee of the U.S. House of Representatives, better known as the House un-American Activities Committee (HUAC) convened a hearing in secret executive session in New York to hear the testimony of Butler and French.

Butler told the hearing that early on, he concluded that the first assignment for this army of paramilitary thugs would be "strike-breaking" and forcing workers to accept "wage cuts" to bail big business out of the crisis it had created. He had sworn an oath to uphold the Constitution and would never be part of a fascist plot to overthrow an elected president. McCormack and Dickstein vowed to subpoena the top financiers named in their testimony But the fix was in. Mysteriously, all the financiers were excused from testifying. *Time Magazine* featured a savage parody of General Butler making him out as a crazed Don Quixote. The media joined in the ridicule. The committee issued a sanitized transcript with all the names—the Morgans, Du Ponts, Rockefellers, and Mellons—deleted.

There were muckraking journalists like John Spivak and George Seldes and at least one newspaper, the *Daily Worker*, that joined Butler and French in the struggle to expose the fascist plot. Spivak even obtained an uncensored version of the Committee's report. Committee co-chair. Representative John McCormack (D-Mass.), later Speaker of the House, confirmed that the Committee "received evidence showing that certain persons had made an attempt to establish a fascist organization in this country . . . the formation of a fascist army under the leadership of General Butler . . . (the) Committee was able to verify all the pertinent statements made by General Butler . . . "

Soon after that, HUAC abandoned the search for Hitler lovers in the ranks of American financiers in favor of a witch hunt that targeted Communists, trade unionists, and other progressives as "Un-American." HUAC had joined forces with the fascists it was supposed to investigate. Yet the fascist coup was nipped in the bud and after many years of struggle HUAC eventually was abolished.

A little over a year ago, First Lady Hillary Rodham Clinton warned of a "vast right wing conspiracy" that targets her husband. Richard Mellon Scaife, who bankrolled the "get Clinton" plot, is a direct descendant of Andrew Mellon who helped bankroll the "get FDR" plot.

And what about the armed militias training in the woods for a racist, anti-Semitic war in the U.S. Aren't they the reincarnation of the armed rabble the House of Morgan tried to recruit in 1933?

And what do we make of Senate Majority Leader Trent Lott of Mississippi and Representative Bob Ban of Georgia, both Republican leaders of the "Get Clinton" vendetta. They have been linked to the white supremacist Council of Conservative Citizens. Aren't they the descendants of Ku Klux Klan nightriders, the U.S. version of the Croix de Feu? Wall Street underestimated the American people in 1998 just as they underestimated the people—and General Smedley Butler—in 1933.

I am a Guest on the Bill O'Reilly Show

(posted on Credo website petition calling for Bill O'Reilly to be removed from Fox)

I once appeared on the *O'Reilly Factor* show. I was the editor of the *People's Weekly World* and was invited to come and represent the "anti-American" position when the Chinese Air Force forced an American plane to land on an island. Bill O'Reilly was really salivating about the possibility of a U.S. war with China. Just before the program began, the Chinese resolved the issue and the plane flew home. I told O'Reilly I was happy to answer his questions but as an American, not an "anti-American." I kept returning over and over to a basic point: "It is not in the interests of the American people for us to have a war with China."

After I made that point half a dozen times, O'Reilly got pissed off and dismissed me during a commercial break. Then he put on a Chinese exchange student at NYU. His father was one of China's representatives at the UN. He too refused to be brow-beaten by this *Fox News* bully. He was cool, calm, and also made clear that war was not in the interests of either China or the USA. I had a chance to meet and talk with this brilliant young Chinese man after the interview. He spoke diplomatically but agreed with me: O'Reilly is a liar, a bully, and a warmonger. He should be removed from the airwaves. That was more than ten years ago. O'Reilly is still a warmonger and should be removed from the airwaves.

Postscript: Reilly is gone. He is no longer a factor having followed in the footsteps of Roger Ailes also fired by Fox News owner, Rupert Murdoch. O'Reilly raked in tens of millions in his twenty years as host of Fox News' flagship O'Reilly Factor, the most-watched news program on cable television. It has played a key role in making Fox News the dominant cable news program, a major factor in Murdoch's strategy of polarizing the American people along race, ethnic, and class lines.

The movement for women's equality was the sparkplug in the drive to force both Roger Ailes and O'Reilly off the air. A procession of women employees of *Fox News* stepped forward to accuse first Ailes and then O'Reilly of sexual harassment forcing Murdoch to pay at least $15 million in settlements to buy the silence of the victims. The National Organization for Women and other women's groups waged an increasingly effective campaign to convince businesses to pull their advertising from the *O'Reilly Factor*. Murdoch obviously didn't care about sexual assaults and harassment. But when advertisers started hitting *Foxes* bottom line, Murdoch wasted no time in pulling the plug on both Ailes and O'Reilly).

Hacking Scandal Rocks Murdoch Media Empire

July 12 2011
Billionaire Rupert Murdoch tried to squelch the hacking scandal engulfing his media empire by closing down his London-based tabloid, *News of the World*, but the firestorm continues to spread.

It was revealed July 11 that two more Murdoch newspapers engaged in hacking including electronic

spying on former Prime Minister Gordon Brown's bank
account. The hackers also
stole the medical records of
Brown's four-year-old son,
a victim of cystic fibrosis.
The Murdoch publications
also bribed bodyguards
assigned to Queen Eliza-
beth II for information about
the monarch, a potential

Photo: Rupert Murdoch, corpor-
ate guru, at the World Economic
Forum annual meeting in 2009.
World Economic Forum CC 2.0

danger to her safety and a clear breach of national
security.

Peter Hart, activism director of Fairness and Accu-
racy in Reporting (FAIR), the media watchdog group,
told the *People's World*, "Murdoch may have hoped that
he could close down *News of the World* and make it go
away, but the story is getting bigger by the day if not by
the hour."

He cited an article in *Newsweek* by journalist Carl
Bernstein, who exposed Richard Nixon's Watergate
scandal in the 1970s. In the article, titled *"Murdoch's
Watergate?"* Bernstein points out that this scandal now
threatens to engulf the Tory regime of David Cameron,
whose press secretary, Andy Coulson, previously served
as editor of the Murdoch tabloid.

It couldn't come at a worse time for Cameron, facing
a nationwide revolt as 750,000 public workers went on
strike last week to protest his austerity policies including savage cuts in pensions and other benefits.

Morning Star, the British left-wing daily, reported that
the scandal has rocked the prime minister on his heels.
Their story quoted veteran left Labour MP Dennis Skinner, who called Murdoch "a cancer on the body politic"
and denounced Cameron as a "smug, arrogant man"
with deep crony ties to Rebekah Brooks, current head of
Murdoch's *News International,* who was editor of *News
of the World* at the time it was involved in the cell phone
hacking that has now been exposed.

Cameron, Murdoch and Brooks are part of the so-called "Chipping Norton set" who wine and dine together in Oxfordshire or even at Number 10 Downing Street, official residence of the prime minister, *Morning Star* reports.

When the scandal broke, Murdoch fired 200 *News of the World* reporters instantly but is defending Brooks.

Among those hacked by Murdoch's *News of the World* minions was actor Hugh Grant and Prince William, an heir to the British throne. But even more outrage has greeted the revelation that Murdoch reporters hacked into the cell phone of a thirteen-year-old murder victim, making deletions and alterations that gave her parents false hope that she was still alive. Also hacked were the private phone calls of relatives of soldiers killed in Iraq and Afghanistan.

"The behavior was so widespread and shocking that reporters are now keeping this scandal alive," said Hart. "This isn't just some rogue correspondent. They are asking the question: Who was in a position of power to approve this hacking? Does it trace back to Murdoch himself?"

The hacking went on for years and involved many news-gatherers. Tens of thousands of dollars was paid to police and others in exchange for lurid and salacious gossip to be used against targeted people, including elected officials.

There is a long history of this brand of sensational, scurrilous media on both sides of the Atlantic, Hart continued, but Murdoch is the "purest expression of this brand of partisan journalism."

He added, "At least in England, people in the Labour Party are saying we have to be more vigilant in curbing the power of one media owner to control so much of the media."

Murdoch's central role in promoting right-wing extremism stretches back to British Prime Minister Margaret

Thatcher, who owed her hold on power to Murdoch's vicious incitements against embattled British coal miners as well as locked out union printers who produced his newspapers.

He played a role in the election of Ronald Reagan, cheerleading the "Great Communicator" for his attacks on workers and union rights including the mass firing of PATCO air traffic controllers.

Murdoch, an Australian by birth, began his invasion of the U.S. by buying the *New York Post*, turning the once respected liberal newspaper into a gossip-mongering rag. Then he bought the *Wall Street Journal* and moved its editorial page even further to the right, into the ideological center of far-right extremism. His empire generates an estimated $33 billion in profits annually.

Murdoch created *Fox News* in 1996. It has served as the round-the-clock mouthpiece of right-wing "attack journalism" featuring charlatans like Glenn Beck, who spout a fake brand of "populism" aimed at giving a grass-roots veneer to the corporate takeover of all branches of government. Beck spread so many patent falsehoods that he became an embarrassment even for Murdoch, who fired him recently.

Between the *Post, Fox News* and the *Wall Street Journal*, Bernstein writes, "it's hard to think of any other individual who has had a greater impact on American political and media culture" than Murdoch. "But now the empire is shaking and there's no telling when it will stop."

He continues, "It will remain for British authorities and presumably disgusted and/or legally squeezed News Corp. executives and editors to reveal exactly where the rot came from and whether Rupert Murdoch enabled, approved, or opposed the obvious corruption that infected his underlings."

Many of those same questions could be asked on this side of the Atlantic.

I Visit a "Killer School" in Georgia
Based on Tim Wheeler's story in the March 26, 1981 *Daily World*.

ATLANTA, GEORGIA—In the spring of 1981 I was sent with Pam Mincy, a young African American fellow staffwriter of the *Daily World*, to Atlanta to cover the grisly murder of twenty-six African American children. Pam and I took the train down to Atlanta.

We stayed with Pam's aunt and uncle in the Atlanta suburbs. We plunged into the assignment, working hard, attending the regular news briefings by the Atlanta police. We joined volunteers in a search through the woods and beside streams on the outskirts of Atlanta where bodies of the victims had been found. We were not finding any "smoking guns" that would expose the criminal or criminals who committed these heinous crimes. But we were helping lay bare the climate of racism and racist violence that pervaded Georgia.

Pam and I spoke by phone with *DW* Editor, Mike Zagarell at least once a day. One day Mike said to us, "I'm reading a book right now about a guy named Mitchell Livingstone Werbell III. He is a real nut case. I think he is located right outside Atlanta. Maybe you should check him out."

I said it would go on the top of my agenda.

I checked the Atlanta area white pages. Bingo! There he was, listed in the phone directory.

I called the number and a woman answered. I told her who I was and could I please speak to Mr. Mitchell Livingstone Werbell III.

"Just a moment, please. I'll see if the General is here." A minute later, a man with a gravelly voice said, "Werbell here. Can I help you?" I told him I was a *Daily World* reporter and could I come and visit him on his farm?

He invited me.

Pam and I did not have a car so I left the next morning early. I was traveling to Marietta, Georgia, seat of Cobb County, and then hitchhiking down some country road or other to get to the Werbell plantation, how I did not know.

Yet I had done some research of my own and discovered that the infamous Klan racist, J.B. Stoner lived in Marietta. He was implicated as the ringleader in the 1963 murder of the four Black school girls at the 16th Street Baptist Church in Birmingham, Alabama. In 1980, he had been convicted of bombing Bethel Baptist Church in 1958. No one was injured in that earlier church bombing, also in Birmingham. Stoner was in the midst of a three-year appeal against that conviction when I decided to seek an interview with him that same day.

The bus from downtown Atlanta to Marietta was one of those airport style mini-buses and it was so early in the morning that few passengers were on board. So I sat right behind the driver and engaged him in conversation. I told him I had been invited to visit Mitchell Livingstone Werbell's farm. He glanced at me, his eyebrows raised. "Werbell? I know that place well. I drive by it every day going to and from work. It's scary. You sure you want to go there by yourself? How are you planning to get there?"

I told him I was hitchhiking.

"Well, my shift ends at noon. If you want a ride I'll be driving right by the front gate." I told him I would be back at the bus depot when his shift ended.

When I got off the bus, I stepped into a phone booth and checked the phone directory. Bingo again! There was a listing for J.B. Stoner. I dialed the number. This time, it was a man's voice. I told him I was a *Daily World* reporter trying to contact J.B. Stoner. "This is Stoner."

I told him I was in town and needed the interview immediately. He was a lawyer and he invited me to visit his office and home. It turned out to be only a thirty-five or forty minute walk from downtown Marietta.

I trudged the whole way, working up a good sweat. When I arrived at his office and knocked on the door, he called out, "Come in." I opened the door and there was Stoner sitting behind his desk, natty in his bow tie.

Behind him on the wall was a giant Confederate "Stars & Bars" flag.

I plied him with questions about the bombings of two churches in Birmingham. He refused to comment on the Birmingham murders but he was very ready to level charges on the Atlanta killings. It was the Black community that was guilty, he ranted. They are "savages" who "murder their own children."

He predicted that white people would rise up and strike down African Americans. Clearly relishing the thought, he said the streets would run red with the blood of those who would die in this "race war."

I made my escape from Stoner's ghoulish office, walking back toward the bus stop as fast as I could. Sure enough, the bus driver arrived a few minutes after I did. He drove me down a country road about fifteen miles. He dropped me off at the entrance to Mitchell Livingstone Werbell III's estate.

Werbell was a veteran of the Office of Strategic Services (OSS) whose founding director was William "Wild Bill" Donovan. OSS, forerunner of the Central Intelligence Agency, was famous—or infamous—for its role in spying and commando operations behind enemy lines during World War II. One of its agents was Allen Dulles who spent World War II in Switzerland seeking to negotiate a separate peace with the Nazi Third Reich so that Germany, the U.S. and Britain could turn their combined forces against the Soviet Union.

Dulles went on to become the first director of the CIA. Werbell was an enthusiastic accomplice.

Werbell described himself as a millionaire "exiled Russian count," a covert OSS agent in China and Southeast Asia and in recent decades a "contractor" for the CIA.

Werbell's family made a fortune manufacturing safety pins after they fled the October Revolution in 1917.

Werbell was operating a paramilitary training academy, Cobray Inc. on his sixty-six acre estate charging $3,000 for a twenty-day course in the most up-to-date methods of killing. With officials saying the Atlanta slayings were the work of professionals, this school, or a place like it, may have housed the children's killer(s).

In 1967, Werbell joined with anti-Castro Cubans and other CIA-connected riff-raff to plan an invasion of Cuba from bases in Haiti. The U.S. Coast Guard halted a flotilla of boats as the Werbell group left Florida for this abortive counter-revolutionary attempt.

Peddled arms to CIA

Werbell invented a super silencer, to be attached to sniper rifles, which he has peddled to gangsters, CIA assassins and right-wing death squads around the world through his Military Armaments Corporation.

Werbell was a top member of the ultra-right American Security Council and a well-known international arms dealer.

I was given a tour of the shooting range, unconventional-weapons range and stress range, where students are subjected to live automatic weapons fire. I was shown a classroom and a martial arts gymnasium at the training center.

The school turned out to be not only a training facility for assassinations here in the U.S., but also a nest of international intrigue aimed at overthrowing the democratic revolution in Afghanistan and progressive regimes elsewhere.

My guide was "Colonel" Edward Wandel, a beefy soldier of fortune and veteran of the Vietnam War. Wandel said he had spent three and a half years as a mercenary "Grey Scout" in Rhodesia, named for the racist gold and diamond billionaire, Cecil Rhodes. (Rhodesia has since been re-named Zimbabwe).

Led anti-liberation forces

Wandel boasted that he had led incursions across Rhodesia's border to Mozambique and Zambia to attack the liberation forces in these "sanctuaries."

There was an air of lunacy about this operation. Werbell's "students" were nowhere to be seen, despite Wandel's claim that a class of eleven had just completed the course and a fresh batch of "students" was on the way.

Wandel told me he has twenty-six "instructors," all of them veterans of counter-insurgencies in Africa, Asia, and Latin America. I did not see any of them. But the M16 automatic rifles, high-powered sniper guns with telescopic sites, the live ammunition, silencers and daggers displayed were chillingly real.

"Colonization was the best thing that ever happened to the Black man. The worst thing that ever happened to the African continent was the overthrow of Ian Smith," said Wandel in an interview in his office at the training center. "Rhodesia was at the pinnacle of civilization; now it is degenerating into tribalism."

Killer symbolism

On the wall was a poster that proclaimed, "Fight terrorism—join the Rhodesian army." Opposite this was a flag with the insignia of Cobray Inc.—a hooded Cobra grafted on to a Moray eel entwined around the globe. "It symbolizes our ability to strike both above and below the surface anywhere in the world," Wandel boasted.

Wandel claimed that 600 students, including many Atlanta area police officers, bankers and businessmen, have "graduated" from the school. He said the students take courses in "instinct shooting," martial arts, and hand-to-hand combat with unconventional weapons—including hammers, chisels, ice picks, screw drivers, tomahawks, and piano wire.

Students learn to load, fire, strip down and reassemble automatic weapons. They are "familiarized with Communist weapons," he said. "Convoy ambushes" are staged on roads that cross the sixty-six acre training ground, to teach "evasion and escape" tactics.

Denies terrorist link

Wandel vehemently denied that the school instructs terrorists and mercenaries. "We have all kinds of kooks showing up here asking to be trained as mercenaries and we tell them to go somewhere else," he said.

He cited the example of Wade Lane, a would-be soldier of fortune employed as a paramilitary instructor at "Cobray, Inc."

Said Wandel, "We found out he was a kook, a megalomaniac, who wanted to take over the world, and we fired him."

Lane has since organized his own paramilitary camp "Force Ten" on a 200-acre site near Calhoun, Georgia.

A few minutes later, however, as Wandel led me on a tour of the camp, he became carried away with enthusiasm. "This is the sniper range," he said gesturing toward a 300-yard stretch of open ground with human profile targets erected at the far end. The targets had been mutilated recently by high-powered rifle fire.

"Of course, this was only for a select few," he said. "We don't teach just anybody to load and fire a poison dart gun to put somebody away."

One of the favored instructors at the school, he said, is Colonel Morgan Smith, U.S. army, "who set up the unconventional Warfare Camp in Panama. He designed part of our curriculum here."

CIA torture instructor

He was referring to the notorious CIA-operated training center in the Canal Zone where Latin American dictators send their "death squads" to be instructed in the most effective U.S. techniques of torture and assassination.

Wandel predicted insurrection in U.S. cities, which he said will eclipse upheavals anywhere else in the world.

"It's definitely coming," he said. "Reagan is cutting back on the social programs. And the Blacks say they are going to fight him. They are going to take to the streets. Look at those coal miners; they are fighting him.

They have been claiming all those Black Lung benefits and you know as well as I do they aren't qualified."

He said corporate executives, bankers, policemen and many other affluent suburbanites "want to prepare to defend themselves."

Afghanistan connection

I asked about the unfamiliar tri-colored flag flying from the flagstaff at the camp entrance, which I had noticed when I arrived. "That's the flag of Afghanistan," Wandel explained. "I'm a colonel in the Royal Free Afghan Army. I was appointed by his royal majesty, King Hassan of Afghanistan."

As he led me back across the sniper range, a limousine drove through the electronic gate and sped up the driveway to Werbell's mansion. "That's the General," Wandel said.

A few moments later he introduced me to the squat, paunchy little man with a close-cropped Prussian style haircut and a monocle in one eye, carrying a cane with a carved ivory head.

Werbell, ever eager for publicity, invited me into his sumptuously decorated house with magnificent oriental rugs, original paintings and statuary.

Secured against eavesdropping

"Come into my den," he said, leading me into a large, dimly lit walnut paneled room. The walls were covered to the ceiling with Mauser pistols and automatic weapons, most of them mounted with sniper stocks.

I asked him about an assault rifle mounted with a telescopic site. I could tell by looking closely that it was a Soviet weapon. "That is a superb weapon," he said, "Unfortunately; it is made by the Russians"

His office was an inner sanctum "absolutely secured against penetration by any electronic eavesdropping devices," according to Werbell.

He punched the intercom on his desk and ordered scotch and ice. During the interview he again called his "servant" and told her to "find Jack Singlaub, wherever he is." General Jack (John) Singlaub is the former commander of U.S. forces in Korea who was dismissed from duty for contradicting President Carter's policy of withdrawing troops from South Korea. Carter later promoted Singlaub and cancelled the troop withdrawal.

Darling of the fascists

Since then Singlaub has been the darling of fascist elements in the U.S. An autographed portrait of Singlaub and other top Pentagon brass decorate one wall of Werbell's office.

Werbell told me that Singlaub is peeved with him because he, Werbell, outranks him, being a three-star general while Singlaub only has two stars.

Asked to explain his military rank, Werbell boasted, "I'm a three-star general in the Royal Free Army of Afghanistan. I'm his majesty's chief of intelligence.

"He's around here somewhere."

Werbell punched the intercom again and ordered his servant to summon the "monarch."

A few moments later an elegant, dark-complexioned man entered the room and sat down.

"His royal majesty, King Hassan of Afghanistan," Werbell announced. (Hassan never actually held the throne, even when Afghanistan was a monarchy. The former king of Afghanistan, Mohammed Zahir Shah, was deposed in 1973.-Ed.)

Hassan explained that he had left Kabul, Afghanistan as a child and that his title was purely a dynastic one. "I'm just trying to give some help to the simple, tribal people of my country. I want to keep the claim to the throne alive."

Arming Afghan 'rebels'

Hassan said his main activity in his frequent trips to Washington to consult with Reagan Administration officials is raising funds and material for the Afghan rebel bands hiding out across the border in Pakistan.

The main recipients of the aid, he said, are Sayed Ahmed Gailani and his bandits, based near Peshawar, and a Colonel Ishnatullah, based near Chaman, Pakistan.

"We've raised money and sent tons of supplies but we have had trouble getting it to the rebels because of Zia," he said referring to the fascist dictator of Pakistan.

"Sire, the son-of-a-b—h, is nothing but a thief," snorted Werbell, giving his cigar a vicious chomp.

The "king" agreed, "Gailani tells us that less than ten percent of what we ship ever arrives at their camp. Zia takes all the rest."

Another problem, Hassan said confidentially, is that virtually all the "simple people" in the bands raiding across the Pakistan-Afghan border are "in the drug trade."

Underworld drug smuggling

A gleam appeared in General Werbell's eye at the mention of drugs. He has been deeply implicated in CIA and underworld drug smuggling operations from Latin America. "There's lots of drugs over there," Werbell said enthusiastically.

The general said it is essential for Reagan to immediately ship massive arms to the rebels. "It takes money. It costs $2.50 for a single round to kill one Soviet."

As he ushered me from his office, he pointed at an evil-looking M16 rifle lying carelessly on a couch next to several clips of ammunition.

"That's for killing Soviets," he said. "It's my favorite hobby."

I left the farm dizzy at the bizarre unreality of what I had seen that day. J.B. Stoner, natty in his bow tie, barely hiding his relish at the death of Black youngsters. And here was General Werbell and his crazed minions, training bank executives in the most advanced methods of killing whether with handguns or piano wire. Werbell lusted for an outright shooting war whether against the African people, the Soviet people, or poor people and people of color right here in the U.S. Stoner and Werbell were cut from the same cloth.

Neither Werbell nor his Chief of Staff, questioned me about the weird circumstance of a reporter showing up without transportation. I walked down the long, curving drive to the gate and trudged up the road, laughing out loud at the insanity. I heard a vehicle behind me and turned and stuck my thumb out. It was a pickup truck and the driver stopped, I trotted up and climbed into the front seat. It was a young guy who sized me up quizzically. "What are you doing out here?" he asked.

"Well, thank you for picking me up," I said, shaking my head, still in a state of shock and disbelief. "You won't believe it, I was just in there interviewing Mitchell Livingstone Werbell. You won't believe what I saw," I repeated.

"Oh, I believe it. I'd believe anything you say. Around here we call that the 'Killer School.'"

Reagan and the Iran Connection
People's Daily World

November 20, 1986
The "Iran Connection" has thrown a spotlight on the Reagan administration's increasing use of covert action in carrying out U.S. foreign policy. The National Security Council (NSC) in the White House has been exposed as the nerve center and command post for clandestine global warfare, which the administration delicately calls 'secret diplomacy."

Police mug shot, Lt. Col. Oliver North

The revelations that President Reagan authorized the NSC to

make secret arms deliveries to Iran comes on the heels of disclosures that Reagan's national security advisor, Vice Admiral John Poindexter, orchestrated an NSC "disinformation" campaign against Libya.

It follows statements by Eugene Hasenfus, the cargo handler captured after his plane was shot down over Nicaragua, that the contra gun-running operation was supplied and directed by CIA agents under the command of Vice-President George Bush and officials of the NSC.

Such covert activities "Undermine our Constitutional system," warned Henry Steele Commager, professor of U.S. history at Amherst College. Taken together, he said, they could be grounds for preparing articles of impeachment against Reagan for "high crimes and misdemeanors."

The White House hoped that it could tough out disclosures of the Iran Connection. White House spokesman Larry Speaks and communications director Patrick Buchanan attempted to squash the story.

But when the issue would not go away, the administration abruptly changed course. On the evening of November 13, Reagan delivered a twelve-minute television speech in which he admitted that he had authorized the transfer of arms to Iran, but denied it was an attempt to exchange weapons for U.S. hostages.

He claimed the intention was to "send a signal" to factions in Iran that the U.S. favors improved relations. But NATO allies are citing the hypocrisy of the White House delivering arms to Iran for use in its war against Iraq at the very time Reagan was demanding a trade embargo on grounds that Iran is a "terrorist" state.

The Iran Connection began over eighteen months ago (Israel says it began as far back as 1982), when Michael Ledeen, a long time CIA agent and a consultant to the NSC, was sent to Europe to meet with an expatriate Iranian businessman, Manucher Ghorbanifar, to discuss an overture to "moderate" factions in Iran.

Ledeen met with Israeli agents to expand the connection. It came to a head last January, when President

Reagan signed an executive order authorizing the secret contacts and lifting the ban on arms deliveries to Iran. Later, former National Security Advisor Robert C. McFarlane traveled to Teheran to meet with Iranian officials.

Reagan claims that the arms delivered to Iran would "fit into a single cargo plane" and could not influence the outcome of the Iran-Iraq war. But the Danish Seamen's Union insists that the administration has used Israel over a long period of time as a conduit to deliver "many thousands of tons" of U.S. arms to Iran aboard a Danish freighter.

Further, delivering just enough arms to keep the blood flowing but not enough for Iran to win would be consistent with a strategy of "bleeding both sides white," according to Eqbal Ahmed, a professor of international relations at Hampshire College in Amherst, Massachusetts. Ahmed is one of many who charge that the administration's real aim was to use the fratricidal war to reassert U.S. military, political and economic hegemony in the oil-rich Persian Gulf.

Leaders of the Senate and House have promised a full-scale investigation of the Iran Connection. But many are wondering how thorough that probe will be. Will Congress pursue the constitutional issues raised in Reagan's increasing use of covert action as an instrument of U.S. foreign policy? Did he comply with requirements of notification of the House and Senate Intelligence Committees? And where did the money come from to pay for these wide-ranging covert operations? Who will be subpoenaed? Vice Admiral Poindexter? His predecessor McFarlane? Oliver North, head of the NSC's military arm? President Reagan himself? Will they call Vice-President Bush and ask him about the charge by Hasenfus that Bush has met several times with the Cuban exile CIA agents involved in the contra supply operation from El Salvador?

At the heart of Reagan's increasing reliance on clandestine warfare is his transformation of the National Security Council—an unelected body—from a presidential advisory body to an operational command staff for covert action.

The National Security Council was established as an advisory body in 1947, at the beginning of the Cold War, by the National Security Act. The Act also established the CIA, ostensibly to be supervised by the NSC. The members of the NSC include the president, vice-president, the secretaries of state and defense, the director of the CIA, and, of course, the NSC director. The director is appointed by the president but is not confirmed by the Senate. He is thus not subject to oversight by Congress, as are the secretaries of state and defense, and the director of the CIA.

Historically, the NSC has been used to promote the "imperial presidency" and has undercut the State Department's authority in carrying out foreign policy.

Reagan is trying to shield the NSC's clandestine activities from congressional investigation by claiming "executive privilege." But many assert that it should be subject to the same congressional oversight as the CIA.

Evidence is growing that over the past six years the NSC has assembled a network of "assets"—mercenaries and agents who are carrying out counter-revolutionary activities around the world under the direction and coordination of the NSC.

What has surprised lawmakers is how closely the White House NSC staff supervises these activities on a day-to-day basis. Lieutenant Colonel North exercised a command role over the nominally "private" network that supplied the anti-Nicaraguan contras. He led a commando team to Turkey's border with Iran in a scheme to free U.S. hostages and was a planner of the U.S. invasion of Grenada and the bombing of Libya. He also accompanied McFarlane to Teheran.

There are supposed to be curbs on the gangsterism coming to light in the Iran arms deal. The final report of the Watergate Committee charged that over the years successive Republican and Democratic administrations had "institutionalized" assassinations, chillingly called "executive actions," as the ultimate weapon of foreign policy intrigue. Congress soon thereafter enacted a law forbidding the plotting or execution of assassinations of foreign leaders. Other curbs, including the requirement that the House and Senate be informed in advance of covert actions, were also enacted.

Rolling back and destroying democratic people's revolutions while they are still weak and unconsolidated has emerged as a top foreign policy goal of the Reagan administration.

The "Reagan Doctrine," as this state terrorism is widely called, has been practiced in Nicaragua, Angola, Afghanistan, Ethiopia, North Yemen, Grenada and Kampuchea. Its implementation in Iran required the re-establishment of a full-blown covert warfare capability.

A revolutionary upsurge with an anti-U.S.-imperialist thrust in 1979 overthrew the shah of Iran, who had been installed in 1953 in a CIA-orchestrated coup directed by Kermit Roosevelt. But that revolution has been short-circuited by reactionary Islamic fundamentalist clerics.

In 1985 the Heritage Foundation, a right-wing think-tank whose analyses and politics have been closely adhered to by the Reagan administration, published "Mandate II," an update of an earlier blueprint. It included advice on the Iran-Iraq war.

The Reagan administration, the document stated, should maintain a public posture of "strict political neutrality" in the war but "quietly give military help to whichever side is losing . . . The U.S. interest continues to be that neither side wins . . . . In the long term, good relations with Iran remain far more important. With a population of 45 million and borders on the Soviet Union and the Persian Gulf, Iran undeniably is a strategic prize."

This is what is behind the Reagan administration-National Security Council strategy for Iran and the president's violation of laws outlining democratic procedures for establishing and carrying out foreign policy.

Irangate Reveals 'fascist international'
People's Daily World

June 25, 1987

WASHINGTON, D.C.—There was a time when rightwing extremists were dismissed as the "lunatic fringe" and their crazed anti-Communism was so discredited, it received little more than ridicule.

But after 110 hours of testimony by eighteen witnesses in the Irangate hearings, the U.S. people are confronted by a sobering reality: The "lunatic fringe" has migrated from the fringe to the seat of political power in Washington. The hearings have shown that the lunatics were, and perhaps still are, operating from the White House with the full blessing of the president.

Testimony proves that they were provided with tens of millions, perhaps billions, of dollars in covert funds hidden in Swiss bank accounts, with sophisticated CIA encrypting devices, with a private air force and access to Pentagon weapons stockpiles. There is massive documentation of the fact that, with the full backing of the president, they recruited mercenary armies that are now waging terrorist wars of counterrevolution on at least three continents.

Their migration to the center of power has not moderated their lunacy. It was lunacy to fly to Tehran with a chocolate cake, a bible autographed by President Reagan and a cargo bay full of TOW missiles. It was lunacy to divert the profits through a maze of Swiss bank accounts to buy arms for the contras, and to shred documents and smuggle other incriminating evidence out of the White House in underwear.

But even more crazed than these Keystone Cops antics is the policy itself—pathological anti-Communism.

A key figure in implementing that policy has been retired General John Singlaub, head of the World Anti-Communist League. Acting at the behest of Senator Jesse Helms (R-NC) and CIA Director William Casey, Singlaub mobilized fascist-like mercenaries and criminal elements such as Tom Posey of Civilian Material Assistance.

His role was revealed in a memo Singlaub wrote to Oliver North at the White House, calling for a permanent apparatus for funneling arms secretly to anti-Communist forces all over the world. This apparatus would use Taiwan, South Korea and other rightwing dictatorships as conduits. It would be "unaccountable to Congress or even the State Department," he wrote.

Singlaub worked to mobilize extreme rightwing anti-Communists all over the world—Reverend Sun Myung Moon and his Unification Church, Reverend Pat Robertson, the Knights of Malta, and many others—in a supranational apparatus molded in the image of the transnational banks and corporations that it was to serve.

It is now clear that Singlaub's plan—to create the secret infrastructure of what could be called a "fascist international" dedicated to anti-communism, anti-socialism, and counter-revolution by any means necessary, including mass murder—was being implemented.

Assistant Secretary of State Elliott Abrams arranged for extreme rightwing activists to be hired at government expense. Carl "Spitz" Channell's National Endowment for the Preservation of Liberty (NEPL) worked under contract to the State Department's Office of Public Diplomacy. In an August 25, 1986 draft memo to White House Chief of Staff Donald Regan, Abrams boasted that NEPLS $4.1 million "lobbying campaign" reached twenty-five states. It broadcast television messages in thirty-two congressional districts, produced two thirty-minute television documentaries supporting the contras, actively lobbied Congress with a staff of five and ran newspaper ads in major media markets. Abrams own draft memo reported that Channell had engaged in "continuous work with Assistant Secretary Abrams," a fact Abrams has consistently denied.

Noting that Congress buckled under White House pressure and repealed the Boland Amendment, Abrams wrote that this high pressure campaign "carried the support program for the President" in "Thirty-two of the fifty-one Democratic districts that ultimately stood with Ronald Reagan on this issue." He did not mention that the TV ads were scurrilous redbaiting messages questioning whether contra foes were "standing with President Reagan or Daniel Ortega."

Channell, we now know, worked as North's fund-raising partner, actively soliciting money from wealthy donors and escorting them to the White House to meet with President Reagan. It is still not clear how much NEPL's anti-Communist brainwashing slush fund was misappropriated State Department funds. But misappropriation is the least of the crimes uncovered in these hearings.

Channell's activities were the domestic counterpart of Singlaub's overseas activities. They, too, were part of a secret drive to build the infrastructure for a "fascist international"—in this case, inside the U.S. It had to be kept secret because the U.S. people, by a large majority, had rejected Reagan Doctrine wars around the world.

Reagan, Vice President George Bush and Attorney General Edwin Meese all claim they knew nothing about the secret activities of their subordinates. But polls show the people do not believe them. Suspicion is growing that Reagan, Bush, Meese and others were keeping the lid on the conspiracy until their secret agents completed the infrastructure of that "fascist international"—when it would have been too late to stop them.

David Duke is Down, Still Deadly
By Tim Wheeler
People's Weekly World

November 23, 1991
NEW ORLEANS—Outside the Monteleone Hotel last Saturday night a Dixieland band played "The Saints Come Marching In." Louisiana's raucous gubernatorial

election was over and the results had poured in: Democrat Edwin Edwards had won by a landslide.

But two days after his defeat, David Duke, Grand Wizard of the KKK, the Republican candidate for governor of Louisiana announced he is considering a run for the presidency in 1992 elections to "make George Bush adhere to the principles of the party and stop drifting to the left." He denounced Bush for signing the Civil Rights Act of 1991 which he branded a "civil wrongs act" and called for a repeal of all affirmative action programs.

Duke has been given a forum to spout his racial views on every talk show—ABC's *Nightline, Phil Donahue* and *David Brinkley.* Polls show that his name recognition is higher than any of the announced Democratic presidential candidates.

The people outside Monteleone hotel in the French Quarter were celebrating the stunning defeat they had inflicted on Duke. And a stunner it was. Final returns showed Edwards, a three-term former governor twice indicted for corruption, swamping Duke, sixty-one percent to thirty-nine percent. Edwards' total was 1,056,263 to Duke's 665, 409. As recently as three days before the election, pollsters had said it was too close to call. The nation was facing the menace of a Hitler-lover capturing the governorship of this state.

In a victory speech in the packed hotel ballroom, Edwards said, "Tonight, Louisiana became the first to turn back the merchant of hate, the master of deceit."

Edwards warned that Duke clones are being groomed as office-seekers across the country. "I do not know where [they] will rise again, but America needs to be on guard," he said.

At the news conference the next day, Edwards accused President Reagan and Bush of "setting the stage" for Duke with their divisive policies and campaign tactic. "I think the days of Willie Horton ads are over," he said. "We have many problems. Race-baiting, name-calling, suggesting it is the fault of someone else is not going to solve the problems."

Duke was defeated by a powerful interracial, interfaith coalition. It was spearheaded by African-American voters, twenty-seven percent of the states total. Over eighty percent of Black voters cast ballots, two percentage points higher than the white vote, a first. And ninety-six percent of them voted for Edwards.

A sampling of the precincts by pollster Ed Renwick underscored the discipline of the Black vote in every region of the state. In New Orleans's Seventh Ward, precinct 7-9A, the vote was 438 for Edwards, zero for Duke. In Pontchartrain Park, precinct 9-31D, the Edwards vote was 457, Duke zero. It is the home precinct of City Councilwoman-at-large Dorothy Mae Taylor, who coordinated the awesome get-out-the-vote effort in her city. Edwards swept eighty-seven percent of the votes in New Orleans, 173, 279 to Duke's 25,923.

"This is the first time I have seen a coalition this broad and this deep come together," she told me in an interview at Edward's campaign headquarters hours before the polls opened. "We have the religious community, the labor community, the business community, the Jewish, Hispanic and Black communities, lower income, middle income, upper income. They have all come together to stop the racism that David Duke represents."

Anticipating Duke's' defeat, she warned that his style of racist demagogy will remain a danger. "He has succeeded in convincing many voters to cast their ballot for racism," she said. "It hurts to realize that people will vote for a man who projects racism and Nazism and all the other things that Duke uses to divide us."

Ben Jeffords, Edwards' statewide coordinator, led me on a tour of the Edwards' campaign headquarters. Scores of young women volunteers were phone-banking. Vanloads of canvassers were departing for one last sweep of crucial neighborhoods. At the rear of the storefront was what Jeffords called the "War Room," with big precinct maps of New Orleans on the walls and the votes Edwards had tallied in the October 19 primary.

Jeffords said the aim was to sharply exceed those totals in the runoff. Poll watchers at each polling place would report by walkie-talkie any precinct with a low turnout. Teams of twenty canvassers would then be rushed to the neighborhood to go door-to-door to get people out and if necessary transport voters.

It may have been redundant. Every utility pole in the impoverished neighborhoods of this graceful city was plastered with red stop signs and the slogan, "Stop David Duke. Vote November 16." Men, women and children spoke of little else in the days before the election other than the menace of the Ku Klux Klansman occupying the Governor's Mansion in Baton Rouge.

Peter Babin, vice president of the New Orleans AFL-CIO, coordinated the work of nearly 1,000 trade unionists in the "Stop Duke" campaign. They canvassed door-to-door, phonebanked, stuffed envelopes and drove people to the polls. An eight-page *Labor-Links* newsletter exposing Duke's racism and his anti-labor voting record was mailed to 51,000 trade unionists in the New Orleans area.

I interviewed Babin the day after the election. "This is a great victory for organized labor and the people of Louisiana," he said. Yet he, too, warned that Duke-style racist politics remain a danger to the nation. "I don't think the struggle is ever over against someone like David Duke," he said. "I think Ronald Reagan began sending these coded messages very subtly when he talked about too much government and started cutting back on poverty programs, job training programs, anything that helps low-income people. He didn't cut defense.

"Bush picked up on that. The Willie Horton ad was sending messages to white people, appealing to their fears and prejudices. I think the Republicans are totally responsible for how they conducted their campaigns. Duke just says straight out what Bush says in coded language."

Babin said it was "solidarity" that produced the victory over Duke. "We had a coalition that embraced such a wide spectrum of the people of this state, there was no way Duke could have won," he said. "If the Democrats could put together a coalition like this at the national level, at next year's convention, if we can unite around a candidate who is willing to fight on the issues, like jobs for the unemployed, they could capture the White House."

Duke has hoped to offset Edwards' enormous lead in New Orleans with big majorities in the affluent and working-class white suburbs, in conservative north and west Louisiana. Based on exit polls in thirty precincts by Voter Research and Surveys, Duke did get fifty-five percent of the white vote—a grim reminder of the deep and entrenched racist influence among white voters. But Edwards' forty-five percent white vote proved that he cut deeply into the voting block Duke was counting on. Babin said their analysis of the election returns showed that the coalition made deep inroads into Duke's presumed base. "We succeeded in turning many voters around, convincing them not to vote for Duke," he said.

Edwards ran well in virtually all parishes across the state, even defeating Duke in his own bailiwick, Jefferson Parish, a white middle and upper income suburb of New Orleans that he had represented as a first term state representative. He had to give up that seat in running for governor. Edwards confidently predicted that this erosion of Duke's base means he will never hold statewide office in Louisiana.

This may be true, but interviewing voters in Arabi and Chalmette, mostly white working-class suburbs in the Duke stronghold of St. Bernard Parish, is a chilling experience. With Mobil, Shell and other oil refineries looming on the horizon, a mood of anger and discontent hung over the lines that stretched out of the polling places on the sunny election-day afternoon. "We can run our own state. We don't need any outsiders," snapped one man in denying me an interview as he emerged from his polling place. This "outsider" line is one of Duke's standard applause getters.

Eunice Price, an Edwards supporter, a native of Arabi, escorted me and a *Los Angeles Times* reporter from polling place to polling place. A legal secretary for a major oil company, she said the angry mood is traceable to ten years of double-digit unemployment in the Bayou State. "Kaiser Aluminum just shut down a plant, a loss of about 1,500 jobs," she said. "Amstar is trying to bust the union at their sugar refinery. People are hurting and they are angry."

She attended the Duke rally the night before. "He sounded like he's running for president," she said. "There was violence and hatred right under the surface. Duke keeps feeding it and feeding it. He's reminiscent of Hitler, simply put."

She said she had attempted to organize a pro-Edwards committee in Arabi. "When we put up Edwards signs, they were torn down. People with Edwards bumper stickers had their car windows smashed. It was intimidation. It's' typical Klan tactics."

Torture in Iraq: Buck stops with Bush

People's World

May 14 2004

WASHINGTON—George W. Bush and his minions are toiling to contain worldwide outrage over the torture of hundreds of Iraqi detainees by U.S. occupation soldiers at the infamous Abu Ghraib prison. Slip-sliding to shift blame to a few low ranking soldiers, Bush and Defense Secretary Donald Rumsfeld swear they learned of the repellent photos of U.S. military police torturing naked Iraqi prisoners only when they saw them on television.

But this is like one of those raging California wildfires, out of control and spreading. Rumsfeld himself told the Senate Armed Service Committee the "worst is yet to come" with even more photographs and videos of depraved and criminal abuse of Iraqi detainees.

In his fifty-three-page classified report on the war crimes, U.S. Army Major General Antonio Taguba charged that U.S. soldiers and commanders at Abu Ghraib committed "egregious acts and grave breaches of international law . . . sadistic, blatant and criminal abuses."

He reports, "The various detention facilities operated by the 800th Military Police Brigade have routinely held persons brought to them by Other Government Agencies (OGAs) without accounting for them, knowing their identities, or even the reason for their detention."

The MPs called them "ghost detainees," who were moved around within the facility to hide them from a visiting International Committee of the Red Cross survey team.

This maneuver was "deceptive, contrary to Army Doctrine, and in violation of international law," Taguba charged.

Staff Sergeant Ivan L. Frederick, one of the MPs facing court martial, told Taguba one inmate died during interrogation. "They stressed him out so bad that the man passed away," Frederick said. "They put his body in a body bag and packed him in ice for approximately twenty-four hours in the shower . . . the next day the medics came in and put his body on a stretcher, placed a fake IV in his arm and took him away."

Frederick said the prisoner had not been recorded in the prison system "and therefore never had a number." But the ghoulish prison guards snapped photos of a smiling soldier kneeling beside the bruised and beaten corpse.

Was this one of the "ghost detainees" of the CIA, FBI, Defense Intelligence Agency, private contractors and profit-seeking mercenaries like CACI and Titan? Taguba told the Senate Armed Services Committee, May 11, that the MPs deferred to these private contractors as the "competent authority" during interrogations.

Investigators are looking into the death of at least twenty-five Iraqi and Afghani prisoners who died in U.S. custody.

Former Representative Mary Rose Oakar (D-Ohio,) president of the American Arab Anti-Discrimination Committee, charged at a May 7 National Press Club news conference that the racist abuse flows from the "demonizing and dehumanizing of Arabs and Muslims in general." She cited scurrilous anti-Muslim statements by General William Boykin, chief of U.S. Military Intelligence, and Attorney General John Ashcroft that fanned the flames of bigotry. "Nothing short of the dignity and honor of our country is at stake here," she said.

Representative Dennis Kucinich (D-Ohio,) a candidate for president, said, "It's not enough that Rumsfeld be fired. It's the war that's wrong. . . . As long as Bush is in the White House, it doesn't matter who is in the Pentagon. Nothing will change except that it will get worse."

Kucinich urged people to sign his on-line petition to the Democratic Party (at www.kucinich.us) urging them to adopt a policy of "UN in and U.S. out of Iraq."

The media is now reminding readers that prison inmates here at home are victims of racist abuse. The torture of Abner Louima by New York police officers comes to mind when one reads that an Iraqi inmate was "sodomized with a chemical light and perhaps a broom stick" in an effort to "soften him up" for interrogation.

The Geneva-based International Committee of the Red Cross revealed May 10 that they had visited Abu Ghraib prison last October and discovered that methods forbidden under the Geneva Conventions were being used. The U.S. officer in command of the prison told the Red Cross team the abuse is "part of the process." The Red Cross report was delivered to the Bush administration in February documenting the humiliation and abuse of prisoners, also charging that several inmates were murdered.

"The nine men were made to kneel, face and hands against the ground as if in prayer position," the report states. "The soldiers stamped on the back of the neck of those raising their head." One corpse had a broken nose, broken ribs and facial wounds indicating a beating. "He was heard screaming for help before he died."

At the coalition's Camp Bucca jail, Red Cross monitors "observed burns on the buttocks of a sixty-one-year-old detainee who told them he had been tied, hooded and forced to sit on a hot surface that he believed to be the engine of a vehicle, causing him to lose consciousness."

In another case, the Red Cross charged, a prisoner "required several skin grafts and had a finger amputated after receiving burns to the face, abdomen, foot and hand when he was forced to lie on a hot surface." Between seventy and ninety percent of the detainees were arrested "by mistake," military intelligence officers told the Red Cross.

The Bush-Cheney administration brushed this report aside.

Critics charge these crimes flow from the Bush administration doctrine of preemptive, unilateral war policies and reflect the arrogance of a conquering imperialist power. The tactics of humiliation recall the strategy of "shock and awe" aimed at instilling fear and forcing the masses to surrender to U.S. occupation.

General Taguba charges that the Pentagon sent Major General Geoffrey Miller, then in charge of interrogations at the U.S. detention center at the Guantanamo Navy Base in Cuba, to Iraq in August 2003 to shake up the prison system because so little "actionable intelligence" was being squeezed from the 8,000 inmates.

Taguba reports, "General Miller's assessment was that Coalition Joint Task Force 7 did not have . . . procedures in place to affect a unified strategy to detain, interrogate and report information from detainees/internees in Iraq." Gen. Miller argued that, "Detention operations must act as an enabler for interrogation." The occupation army must "dedicate and train a detention guard force to facilitate successful interrogation."

Taguba charged that General Miller's call for "consolidation and coordination" of Military Police and Military Intelligence was contrary to U.S. Army Regulations, that the duty of the MPs is to insure order and the safety of the detainees.

The *New York Times*, in an editorial calling for removal of Rumsfeld, points out that it was after General Miller's trip to Iraq that the worst abuse of Iraqi detainees began. Miller bragged to the media, "We used the models we had made at Guantanamo . . . to assist in the success of interrogations [in Iraq]." Guantanamo detainees have been denied the protections of the Geneva Convention by Bush, Rumsfeld and Ashcroft. Now the evidence proves the coercive methods used in Guantanamo were used on Iraqi detainees in flagrant violations of the Geneva Convention.

The photo of a naked Iraqi detainee on a leash held by a female soldier or one of a hooded man standing on a box with electric wires hooked to his fingers, toes, and penis, was taken after General Miller's visit.

Incredibly, Bush and Rumsfeld have sent Miller back to "clean up" the mess despite evidence that he was a ringleader in the atrocities.

Amnesty International sent an open letter to Bush May 7 charging that the U.S. has rejected their calls that detainees held in U.S. prisons around the world be brought before a "competent tribunal" to determine their status as required by Article 5 of the Third Geneva Convention.

"When the USA unilaterally decides whether or not to affirm the rights of individuals protected by international treaties and agreements, this may send a message to troops and others that the government is set on a course in which international agreements can be ignored or set aside at the discretion of the executive for the sake of expediency," the letter states.

As Rumsfeld sweated in the witness chair May 7, Senator Robert Byrd (D-W.Va.) said, "I see arrogance and a disdain for Congress. Given the catastrophic impact that this scandal has had on the world community, how can the United States ever repair its credibility? How are we supposed to convince not only the Iraqi people but also the rest of the world that America is, indeed, a liberator and not a conqueror, not an arrogant power?"

Blood Money
People's Weekly World

April 5, 1997

WASHINGTON—The story of Nazi Holocaust survivors struggling to regain family assets hidden in Swiss bank accounts has stirred such indignation that at least half a dozen investigations of the scandal are underway. Swiss bankers claim they have found only 774 "dormant" accounts with deposits totaling $32 million.

Attention has shifted to the far larger question: What was the total value of the loot stolen by the Nazis during the twelve-year Third Reich, and what happened to it? Not all of the loot ended up in Zurich.

There is the 377 metric tons of Nazi bullion confiscated under the 1946 Washington Agreement and stored

Nazi General, Karl Wolf (left) U.S. Spy Chief, Allen Dulles (right)

in the Federal Reserve bank vaults in Manhattan and the Bank of England in London.

The lion's share, worth $4 billion in current dollars, "was long ago returned to the central banks" of Europe, the *New York Times* reported February 4. President Clinton announced the $68 million in gold bars that remains may be used to compensate Holocaust victims.

Clinton has ordered an investigation of the U.S. role in the seizure of the Nazi assets. A report by the State Department is due in April. The investigators have at their disposal more than a ton of recently declassified documents stored at the National Archives here.

In 1943, the U.S. set up "Project Safehaven" to track down Nazi loot. According to the cover story in the February 24 issue of *Time*, Allen Dulles, then an agent of the U.S. Office of Strategic Services (OSS) assigned to Zurich, "warned the Swiss government that much of the 100 tons of gold bullion the Reichsbank was selling for Swiss francs was stolen . . . Eventually, Safehaven agents concluded that some $6 billion in Nazi assets had been transferred into Switzerland from 1938 to 1945 under cover of bank-secrecy laws."

Dulles buys Italian election with Nazi loot

But investigative journalist Christopher Simpson presents a far different picture of Dulles' role. It is contained in his book *Blowback*, which exposes the recruitment after the war of hundreds of Nazi war criminals by the CIA of which Dulles was a founder and director.

In 1947, the Communist Party of Italy, admired for leading the fight against Mussolini, was expected to win major gains in Italy's first post-war election. The Truman administration unleashed a covert operation to block the anti-fascist victory. Simpson quotes New York's Francis Cardinal Spellman, who served as a liaison between the CIA and the Vatican:

The U.S. government, the Cardinal declared, had secretly "released large sums in 'black currency' in Italy to the Catholic church . . . a substantial part of this funding for clandestine activities in Italy came from captured Nazi assets including money and gold that the Nazis had looted from the Jews."

The trail of this tainted money, Simpson continues, dates back to 1941 when the War Powers Act authorized the U.S. Treasury's Exchange Stabilization Fund to serve as a holding pool for captured Nazi valuables—currency, gold, jewels, and even stocks and bonds.

The Exchange Stabilization Fund, Simpson adds, "was authorized to safeguard the portion of the Nazi hoard that had been uncovered and confiscated by the United States in the Safehaven program . . . In reality, this pool of money became a secret source of financing for U.S. clandestine operations in the early days of the CIA."

The CIA "was a young organization in those days," the book continues. "Therefore much of this (Italian) campaign was handled on an ad hoc basis out of the offices of Allen and John Foster Dulles at the Sullivan & Cromwell law firm in New York."

Italy's Christian Democrats, with thousands of fascists hiding in its ranks, won the election. The undertaking became the model for CIA covert operations worldwide, sometimes using "velvet glove" tactics but more often assassinations, paramilitary warfare and military coups—tactics that bear a striking resemblance to Hitler's Brown Shirt terrorism.

A bank's dalliance with the Nazis

Before World War II, the Dulles brothers had been appointed to the board of the J. Henry Schroder Bank with offices in Wall Street, London, Zurich, and Hamburg. The Dulles brothers were senior partners in Sullivan & Cromwell, the Wall Street law firm that represented the legal interests of the Rockefeller empire. Allen Dulles was general counsel of the Schroder Bank, which served as a link between the Rockefellers, London banks, and German high finance. His clients included the I.G. Farben chemical trust and the Fritz Thyssen steel trust.

The Soviet magazine *New Times* carried a two-part series on the J. Henry Schroder Bank in February 1947 by *Trud* correspondent A. Leonidov. Leonidov charges that this Anglo-German-U.S. bank's influence "spread literally to every artery of modern capitalist society: banks and heavy industry, diplomacy and military staffs, influential political parties, military and political intelligence."

A scion of the Schroder family was Baron Kurt von Schroder, grandson of the founder of the Schroder Bank. Kurt von Schroder was head of the I.H. Stein Bank of Cologne, the personal bank of both Adolf Hitler and Heinrich Himmler. The J. Henry Schroder Bank served as the official agent of the I.H. Stein Bank in London.

Writes Leonidov, "This was the Baron Schroder who . . . arranged the notorious meeting of Hitler with the Ruhr kings when the latter decided to turn over power to the Nazis and to furnish Hitler with funds, thereby paving the way to World War II."

Financiers back Hitler

The German financiers decided to back Hitler after the Nazi's suffered a disastrous defeat in the November 6, 1932 elections, losing two million votes and thirty-five seats in the Reichstag. The vote for the German Communist Party increased by 750,000, gaining eleven more deputies. The German masses, facing mass unemployment and starvation in the Great Depression, were turning toward socialism.

The German financiers counted on Hitler to save German capitalism by annihilating the Communists, socialists, the Jews, smashing Germany's Communist-led unions, preparing Germany for a war to conquer the world.

During the prewar period of the appeasement of fascism, the Schroder Bank sought to strengthen Germany's ties with Britain and the U.S. "to open the road to the East and to create a great Western bloc pointed against the Soviet Union."

Leonidov reports that during World War II, Kurt von Schroder served together with the Third Reich's Finance Minister, Walther Funk, as a director of the Bank for International Settlements (BIS) in Basel Switzerland. By 1944, the BIS was dominated by Axis bankers but the president was an American, Thomas McKittrick. After the war, he was appointed vice president of the Rockefeller-controlled Chase National Bank.

Nazis launder their loot in Switzerland

Simpson corroborates Leonidov's findings in his recent book *The Splendid Blond Beast: Money, Law, and Genocide in the 20th Century.* Writes Simpson, "BIS cooperated with the German Reichsbank's efforts to launder gold stolen from the mouths of death-camp victims." The BIS, he continued, participated in "a complex Nazi scheme to use currency manipulations and bank clearing procedures to loot the economies of entire countries."

Thus, while Allied soldiers were fighting and dying to defeat fascism, these U.S. and British financiers were helping launder Nazi loot in Switzerland.

Dulles' deal with the SS

The Nuremburg War Crimes Tribunal shed some light on Allen Dulles' wartime activities as OSS chief in Zurich. Leonidov writes: "His chief adjutant in intelligence work was another director of the New York Schroder bank, a certain Lada-Moscarski, who held the official post of American vice consul in Zurich . . . building up contacts with the 'anti-Hitler' opposition in Germany." He was referring to top Nazis like financier Hjalmar Schacht, who, late in the war, realized that Hitler was doomed and should be eliminated to clear the way for Germany's "separate surrender" to the U.S. and Britain, excluding the Soviet Union.

Allen Dulles' obituary in the January 31, 1969 *New York Times* reports that in his communiques to Washington from Zurich, Dulles argued vehemently that "the insistence on unconditional surrender . . . made it impossible to promise the German dissidents less rigid terms for peace if Hitler were overthrown."

In an OSS project code-named "Operation Sunrise," Dulles, Major General Lyman L. Lemnitzer and a British officer, Major General Terence S. Airey met with SS General Karl Wolff and with SS General Walter Rauff at a villa near Ascano Switzerland to arrange the surrender of all German forces in Italy, May 2, 1945, one week earlier than the Nazi surrender to the Soviets in Berlin.

Dulles' intrigues in Switzerland failed. The worldwide-united front, spearheaded by the Soviet Union, smashed the Third Reich. But even in defeat, the Nazis had their CIA collaborators who schemed to rescue them. Their numbered bank accounts were swollen with SS loot.

The other loot: profits from slave labor

After the war, General Wolff lived openly at his villa on Starnberg Lake south of Munich. He operated a profitable arms export business. It took seventeen years to bring Wolff to trial. He was sentenced to fifteen years but served seven years and was released. There is widespread suspicion that Dulles and the CIA aided in Rauff's escape to Chile. Rauff was the inventor of the hideous "gas wagon" in which thousands of innocent men women and children were murdered.

The German Democratic Republic (GDR) released a *Brown Book* in 1965, which states that SS General Karl Wolff "bore the main responsibility for the murder of 300,000 Polish Jews in the Treblinka extermination camp." In Italy, he had ordered the extermination of

15,000 Jews, Communists, partisans, and other anti-fascists.

Wolff, an "expert witness," not a defendant, at the Nuremburg War Crimes Tribunal, bragged that he participated in the monthly meetings of Heinrich Himmler's "Circle of Friends of the Reichsfuhrer SS." He testified that he observed chieftains of German high finance making cash contributions to the SS at the sessions. Himmler frequently took them on tours of Auschwitz and Dachau to see the system of slave labor first hand, Wolff testified.

"Over 20 million people from almost all countries of Europe were dragged by the fascists into Hitler Germany as slave labor," the Brown Book charges. "Hundreds of thousands of them were tortured, beaten to death, shot and gassed."

The Krupp "Family Enterprise" alone exploited 97,952 prisoners of war and concentration camp inmates in their Ruhr steel mills. "Already in the first five years of the fascist rearmament drive, Krupp could book a net profit of 500 million Reichsmark," the GDR expose charged. "In the fifth year of the war, his war criminal family had an accountable profit of over 110 million Reichsmark—gathered from the exploitation of 250,000 people . . . of which tens of thousands perished as prisoners in the trusts own concentration camps."

Doctor Alfried Krupp was found guilty at Nuremburg, stripped of his huge empire and sentenced to twelve years in prison. Five years later, at the request of West German Chancellor Konrad Adenauer, Krupp was released and all his property was restored to him.

The Schroder Bank client, I.G. Farben, producer of Zyklon- B, the cyanide gas used in the death camps, reported profits of 32 million Reichsmark in 1932. By 1943, with thousands of slave laborers, I.G. Farben reaped 822 million Reichsmark in profits. They kept it all.

It was a flagrant violation of the Potsdam Agreement signed by Josef Stalin, Winston Churchill and Harry

Truman, a treaty that bound the wartime Allies to break up the giant trusts that bankrolled Hitler. In contrast, I.G. Farben's vast petrochemical complex at Buna, in the Soviet sector of occupied Germany, was confiscated, later made the socialist property of the citizens of the GDR.

A warning across five decades

Senate Banking Committee Chair Alfonse D'Amato (R-N.Y.) is shouting about the skullduggery of the Swiss banks. But don't expect him to investigate this other Nazi loot, a thousand-fold greater than that hidden in the Swiss banks. Now these same German, British and U.S. banks are gobbling up socialist property in East Germany, Poland, the Czech Republic, and Russia that 20 million Soviet soldiers and citizens defended with their lives in World War II.

Leonidov's revelations convey a warning across five decades. The Bechtel Corporation, a Schroder subsidiary, placed two of its directors in the Reagan Administration in 1980—George Shultz as Secretary of State and Caspar Weinberger as Secretary of Defense. Allen Dulles' old OSS crony, William J. Casey, was named as director of the CIA. They and their underling, Lieutenant Colonel Oliver North, utilized a numbered bank account at Credit Suisse in Geneva to launder stolen money for the Reagan Administration's illegal Iran-contra wars in Nicaragua, Angola, Afghanistan, in which millions of innocent people died.

In 1995, President Clinton named James D. Wolfensohn as president of the World Bank. His bio identifies him as the former president and chief executive officer of the J. Henry Schroder Bank of New York.

Chapter 7

Rip-Off Nation

A friend and I were strolling along Kalinin Ave, in downtown Moscow one afternoon in November 1980. We were delegates attending a series of seminars at the Lenin Institute. Ronald Reagan had just won the presidential election and one of the assignments of our twenty member delegation was to reassure the Soviets that the American people had not all gone insane in electing this Grade-B movie cowboy as our chief of state. It was a lovely afternoon and our seminar ended early. My friend, who knew more about Moscow than I did, suggested we take a walk on Moscow's main shopping thoroughfare. Out of the crowd bounded a slim young man wearing spectacles. He was smiling widely and exclaimed in British-accented English, "Hello! You are Americans, right? I could tell a mile off! My name is Dmitri. May I walk with you? I am a student at the English Language Institute at Moscow University. I need to practice my English. I am so tired of this British English! I really, really welcome you! It will be such a treat to hear REAL American English."

We invited Dmitri to join us in our walk. "We learn English out of the textbook. It is soooo boring!" His voice dropped to a near whisper and he looked back over his shoulder to see if we were being followed "Tell me, please: What is the latest slang. If I get some really hot American slang from you, my fellows at the Institute will be GREEN with envy!"

I thought hard. "Rip-off. That's a pretty recent addition to our vocabulary and we hear it every day," I replied.

Dmitri's eyes grew wide.

"Rap-off."

"No, not rap-off. Rip-off. Rap is a good word too, but in this case the word is 'rip' not 'rap.'"

"What is this 'rip-off'? What does it mean?"

"Rip-off is one of the main activities of banks and corporations in the United States. The term refers to their cheating, stealing, and other nefarious ways of robbing us of our money. Of course, we could call it 'thievery' but the word is too tame to describe the swindling by the banks and corporations in the United States during the era of Ronald Reagan. Rip-off is a great word to describe the way they fatten their accounts at our expense."

"I see," said Dmitri, nodding earnestly as we strolled along. "Rip-off. Rip-off," he muttered the word under his breath to commit it to memory.

"Are you communists?" he asked.

"Yes, we are."

"Members of the Communist Party of the United States of America?"

"Yes we are."

"Do you know Gus Hall?"

"Yes we do. We know him well," I replied. "My wife and I were guests in the home of Gus and Elizabeth Hall for over a month."

"You've got to be kidding," Dmitri exclaimed. "Wait until I tell my classmates about this! Gus Hall! He's a very foxy guy!"

Dmitri was a student at an excellent university that charged no tuition. In fact he was paid a stipend to attend. A job was guaranteed once he graduated. He was provided free cradle-to-grave health care. Rents were about 5% of income. Now all that is gone. Once the Russian billionaire oligarchs took over, Dmitri, like us, was living in a "rip-off nation."

He was learning firsthand the meaning of the word.

It is remembering this little episode on a Moscow street that made me decide I needed to add a section to my book: "Rip-off Nation."

Youngstown Workers Hit Shutdowns
Daily World

January 17, 1980

YOUNGSTOWN, Ohio, January 16—The furnaces of Briar Hill Works of Youngstown Sheet and Tube are cold as the dead and the skeleton crew that left the doomed mill this January afternoon looked like mourners filing out of a graveyard. On November 28, the day after U.S. Steel announced it would close its Ohio and McDonald works here destroying 5,000 jobs, Youngstown Sheet and Tube, a subsidiary of the LTV Corporation, announced it would close the Briar Hill Works by December 27, liquidating an additional 1,500 jobs.

The plague of plant closings has raged through the Mahoning River Valley, third largest steel-making center in the nation, since 1977 when Youngstown Sheet and Tube closed its Campbell Works, destroying nearly 5,000 jobs. Altogether, the steel trusts have slated 12,000 steelworker's jobs in this area for the scrap heap, destroying the economy of the valley.

Every steelworker job supports two or three jobs in other sectors of the economy, meaning that 36,000 or more jobs will be destroyed if U.S. Steel is permitted to go through with its plan.

Already, the effects of the plant shutdown can be seen in downtown Youngstown, which stretches in a narrow valley by the banks of the Mahoning River. The A&P grocery chain has closed all its outlets in the area. Fazio's, a Cleveland-based grocery chain, closed all but one of its outlets and Western Auto shut down eight of its stores here.

William Monroe has toiled for thirty-three years at the Briar Hill Works, which produced some of the highest quality steel pipe in the world. With his lunchbox under his arm, he paused in front of the Briar Hill mill as he left the day shift today to speak with a Daily World reporter. "It's' just unbelievable," he said. "I started here when I was a kid. I didn't think there was any end to steelmaking in Youngstown. But I was wrong."

Monroe, a maintenance worker, father of six children, two of the teenagers living at home, said he would receive $800 per month on early retirement if he is unable to find a new job when he is finally laid off in June. "I could probably just about make it on that but just barely, the way the economy is going today," he said. "Two years from now, $800 a month won't be nearly enough. I don't want to just sit in a rocking chair. I'll try to find something to do."

James Mitchell, grievance committeeman in the conditioning plant at Briar Hill, said the Works will close completely by next June. "There are 350 working in the plant right now, but that won't last long. We are just going to clean up." Mitchell, a Black man, father of nine children, has worked at Briar Hill for twenty-nine years.

Ohio Works

Just down the river from the Briar Hill Mill is U.S. Steel's Ohio Works. Smoke still rises from the towering blast furnaces. When the steelworkers tap into the base of the furnaces, molten steel pours out in a white-hot stream into stools lined up on the railroad siding.

But U.S. Steel has scheduled this plant too for extinction. The corporation has not yet announced a date for the termination of the 1,700 jobs at the Ohio Works.

Just up the road from the Ohio Works, at United Steelworker Local 1330, scores of Afro-American and white workers were organizing a fightback against U.S. Steel to keep the Ohio and McDonald Steel Mills open.

In an interview in his office, Bob Vazquez, president of USWA Local 1330, told the Daily World, "We don't take what U.S. Steel says as the absolute truth. We think there is a lot of life in these facilities. If they don't want to operate them, we, the workers, should be given the chance to keep them running."

Suit filed

Vazquez said the steel union locals affected by the scheduled shutdown have joined in a suit against U.S. Steel. The suit was filed by Representative Lyle Williams (R-Ohio) and asks the courts to issue an injunction to force U.S. Steel to postpone the closing.

"What we are alleging in the suit is that David Roderick, chairman of U.S. Steel, give us assurances that these facilities would remain open as long as they are profitable. We are saying they are profitable and that U.S. Steel broke an agreement. They are guilty of a breach of contract," Vazquez said.

He cited statements by Roderick on national TV as well as direct quotes to the *Wall Street Journal* in which the steel corporation president gave these assurances.

On the basis of this promise, Vazquez charged, steelworkers made important concessions to the company, allowing job combinations and other moves to enhance the mill's profitability.

Cynically, a few weeks after making these promises, Roderick turned around and announced the mills will be closed.

Services eliminated

Vazquez said that the Youngstown City Council met a few days ago to plan next year's budget and projected a loss of $1.2 million in income tax revenues because of the closings. 'They are talking about eliminating garbage pickup in Youngstown," he said. "That means the end of hundreds of sanitation workers jobs."

The young steel local president denounced the Carter Administration and Congress for refusing to take action to declare Youngstown a disaster area and come up with massive federal assistance.

Angrily, he referred to the supersonic speed with which Washington approved a $1.5 billion taxpayer bailout for the Chrysler Corporation.

He said, "If they can come up with a billion and one half dollars for Chrysler then they can come up with enough to save this community. You'd think we'd be entitled to the same kind of consideration that a company would get. They said they were bailing out Chrysler because of the loss of jobs: the impact on the country. Why shouldn't that apply here too?"

More for Chrysler, Less for Workers
Daily World

December 20, 1979

WASHINGTON, December 19—While Congress was debating how much it should pick from the pockets of Chrysler workers, Rep. Ronald Dellums (D-Calif.), proposed an investigation of corporate mismanagement, plant closings and runaway shops.

Dellums' proposal, made on the floor of the House yesterday, was supported today by Marc Stepp, vice president of the United Auto Workers, who said that "corporate behavior" should be investigated and that massive companies like Chrysler should be "brought to task for their policy of throwing tens of thousands of workers out of their jobs."

Meanwhile, the Senate leadership met behind closed doors and boosted to $525 million the amount Chrysler workers would be ordered to "sacrifice" as a price for a loan guarantee to the company.

An even greater wage cut of $800 million, equivalent to a three year wage freeze, was contained in a bill introduced by Senator Richard Lugar, (R-Ind.). It was rejected, however.

The House version, passed yesterday 271 to 136, would cut $400 million from the workers contract. It imposes on each Chrysler worker a wage cut of about $4,000 or the equivalent of a nineteen month wage freeze.

Labor lobby

Scores of UAW and AFL-CIO legislative representatives, including 18 Chrysler local presidents crowded the Senate reception room, a gilded crystal, chandeliered chamber just off the Senate, for today's debate. UAW president Douglas Fraser told the *Daily World* the main goal of the UAW at this point is to save the 700,000 jobs that would be destroyed if Chrysler goes bankrupt.

"I live in Detroit and if Chrysler goes under, it's going to be total devastation," he said. At the same time he said Chrysler workers have rejected a three year wage freeze and he said the UAW leadership is fighting to persuade the Senate to approve legislation introduced by Sen. Donald Riegel (D-Mich), which is similar to the House-passed version.

Filibuster **possible**

Fraser told reporters that the House version was adopted and the Eagleton amendment approved a clear mandate against the Lugar version. He warned however, that a Senate filibuster is still possible to kill the legislation. "After all, the will of the majority was similarly thwarted on Labor Law Reform," he said, referring to the killing of labor's top priority legislation in the last Senate.

Don Stillman public affairs director of the UAW, told the *Daily World*, "this is going to have to be ratified by our members, and if the Senate goes above $400 million, we're going to have problems."

Marc Stepp, was also present in the ornate Senate reception room. He blasted Lugar for betraying the 18,000 Chrysler workers in his native state of Indiana.

Stepp told the *Daily World*, "For every one of those 18,000 Chrysler workers in Indiana, there are five other jobs at stake. So Senator Lugar is risking the jobs of 90,000 workers in Indiana by his demand for a three year wage freeze."

Stepp pointed out that even if the bailout loan for Chrysler is approved, the legislation will not assist the

2,700 workers at Chrysler's Dodge main plant in Hamtramck nor the tens of thousands of other Chrysler workers on indefinite layoff across the nation.

"On January 4th, the Dodge Main plant will close down flat," he said.

The UAW, he added, is demanding that Chrysler transfer all the Dodge Main workers to its yet to be opened Jefferson Avenue plant in Detroit. He said these workers must suffer no loss of seniority or benefits.

Dellums' proposal

During House debate yesterday, Dellums told his colleges he supported the loan guarantee for Chrysler because of the 700,000 jobs at stake. However, the legislation would "perpetuate a demonstrated record of managerial incompetence and sustained corporate failure," Dellums said.

He added, "and the workers and consumers are supposed to bear the economic burden of their incompetence. Why?"

He called for a special congressional committee "to investigate the entire spectrum of corporate bankruptcies, plant closings, and dissolution of private investment savings.

"The time is now to search for new directions in using industrial potential for maximum benefits for all the people, not the corporate few," he said.

Meanwhile, yesterday, a group of Black ministers came to Washington with petitions signed by more than 40,000 citizens of Detroit demanding that Congress act to save the Chrysler workers.

Frank Lumpkin: "Always bring a crowd"
By Tim Wheeler

CHICAGO—"Epic" is the best word to describe Beatrice Lumpkin's recent book *Always Bring a Crowd: The Story of Frank Lumpkin, Steelworker.* It is lucky that we have this book in the waning days of the 20th century when so many people are paying homage to the achievements of heroic men and women over the past 100 years.

I recommend Bea Lumpkin's book as a holiday gift. It you are looking for a book that will lift your spirits and convince you that capitalist war, racism and exploitation can be ended in the new century, then this is a "must" read. Frank Lumpkin looms out of the pages of her book as a larger than life working-class hero.

You don't need to take my word for it. Frank Stanley reviewed *Always Bring a Crowd* for The Bell Ringer, a publication of the United Methodist Church. "I was fortunate to have met and appreciate this man," Stanley writes. "He was a giant, a legendary figure, an icon of the struggle to gain what was the workers' just due after the huge Wisconsin Steel Works unceremoniously closed its gates . . . "

International Harvester sold its giant Wisconsin Steel Works mill on Chicago's South Side to a shell corporation, Envirodyne. In turn, Envirodyne spun off the mill to two other shell companies. On March 28, 1980, without warning, the shadow owners of the mill padlocked the gates. The 3,500 Wisconsin Steel employees were locked out, stripped of their jobs forever - many after twenty-five or thirty years of service. Their final paychecks bounced. The company defaulted on the wages, health benefits and pensions they owed the workers.

The company had engaged in a legal subterfuge to evade the estimated $65 million in financial obligations to the workers. In her book, Beatrice Lumpkin called it the "perfect corporate crime." Tom Geoghegan, a lawyer for the workers later wrote, "It was like a game of Chinese boxes, and when you got to the last box, nothing was in it. Nobody would be paying the pensions."

This swindle took place only a few months before Ronald Reagan's election, ushering in a decade of ruthless union busting with his smashing of the striking air traffic controllers' union, PATCO. It was to be a decade of plant closings and relocations to regions of cheap labor. Padlocking factory gates without notice became corporate America's normal operating procedure. The steel industry was a special target of this policy of de-industrialization that would destroy more than three million union jobs and transform the midwest into another "rust belt."

This was capitalism run amok and it is little wonder that the owners of Wisconsin Steel thought they could get away with their sleazy scam. There was only a company union misnamed the Progressive Steel Workers Union (PSWU). It didn't even convene a membership meeting to discuss the disaster.

Envirodyne might have made a clean get-away if not for Frank Lumpkin. He had toiled for 30 years at the Wisconsin Steel mill and when the disaster struck, he stepped forward.

He convened a meeting of the workers to set up the Wisconsin Steel Save Our Jobs Committee (SOJ). Beatrice, his wife, who was helped organize the Women's Committee, writes that part of the legal subterfuge was a deal between the company and the PSWU that nullified the right of the workers to file a class-action lawsuit on behalf of the workers. Consequently, SOJ had to contact every worker and get them to sign individual complaints that Wisconsin Steel owed them back wages, health care and pension benefits. Thousands signed these complaints.

Bea Lumpkin's style lets the people in her book speak for themselves. She conveys the immense tragedy of the mill closing, like a death in the family, by inserting the testimony of the workers: Florencio (Floyd) Ortega, billet dock; Rafael Huerta, pickler in the scarfing dock; Herman Caldwell, 6-mill. Caldwell said, "Its a poor system that allows this to happen. And we had a poor union. When the mill closed down we found out it wasn't like they said. Then Frank Lumpkin formed this Save Our Jobs Committee and that's the only thing keeping people informed about their jobs . . . ."

Frank Lumpkin could not know that this struggle would rage on for 17 years. A man of less determination would have surrendered. But Frank Lumpkin was a former prize fighter, "heavy-weight champion of the South," He earned a reputation as a hard counter-puncher in and out of the ring. As a convinced Marxist, a leader of the Communist Party, Lumpkin knew that the cause of the Wisconsin Steel workers was winnable if they could be convinced to stick together and keep slugging. It is a tribute not only to Frank but to those hundreds of rank-and-file workers - African American, Latino and white - that they refused to be divided or bought off.

Bea writes that many in the Wisconsin Steel Save Our Jobs Committee thought of their organization as a "union." Frank disagreed. He called it a "movement." He knew that it could be held together only if it became a grassroots organization that engaged constantly in direct action to buttress the lawsuits they filed seeking restitution of the money stolen from them. In the years since 1980, the members of the SOJ staged hundreds of their own rallies, picket lines, and mass meetings. They joined other groups' picket lines and rallies, and conducted petition drives. They organized a march on Springfield and traveled by bus twice to Washington to make their case before Congress.

I remember vividly as a *World* Washington correspondent covering their two trips to D.C. where they were greeted by Reps. Harold Washington, Gus Savage, Rep. Charlie Hayes, and other lawmakers. They made common cause with steelworkers at Pullman Standard when that historic shop that made the Pullman sleeping car was closed down. They joined with the steelworkers in fighting the closing of U.S. Steel's Southworks.

They threw their backing to "Jobs Or Income Now" (JOIN), a movement fighting to reopen the steel mills under federal ownership to produce steel needed to rebuild the infrastructure of our crumbling cities. Their program is as timely today as if was a decade ago.

Lumpkin also led SOJ into independent political action. They played an important role in the election of Harold Washington as mayor of Chicago, a historic victory over the most entrenched, reactionary political machine in the U.S. Bea writes that "At that time, Washington and Lumpkin had a special relationship . . . Washington seemed to draw strength from Lumpkin's participation.

At meetings rallies, street encounters, whatever, Washington would call Frank over and say, 'When I see you, I know things are in good hands.'" SOJ was also an important factor in the election of Charles Hayes, African-American leader of the Meatcutters union, to take the Congressional seat vacated by Washington, and the election of Carol Moseley Braun, the first Black woman to serve in the U.S. Senate.

SOJ won a series of partial victories including a ruling by the Pension Benefit Guaranty Corporation that 500 of them were entitled to 40 percent of their pensions. After they were awarded a $14.8 million settlement, Frank, himself, ran twice for the Illinois legislature as an independent, on the slogan, "Send a Steel Worker to Springfield."

Bea's book brings to life the tremendous enthusiasm generated by the campaign. R.C. Longworth, a *Chicago Tribune* correspondent called Frank, "An amazing man . . . Lumpkin who is probably as close to a saint as Chicago has these days, rallied the workers, kept them together, labored to keep their spirits up." He got eighteen percent of the vote in one race and fifteen percent in another.

This biography illuminates the sources of Frank Lumpkin's strength as a mass leader. A strong working-class family is part of the answer. The several Lumpkin families lived so close together "they could smell what was on the stove for dinner and drop in for a taste," she writes. The parents, Elmo and Hattie Lumpkin, were sharecroppers. Frank, one of ten children, was born October 13, 1916 just outside Hilliard Station, Georgia. The family moved to an orange grove near Orlando, Florida where Frank grew up.

Before World War II, the family moved to Buffalo where Frank became a steelworker at Bethlehem Steel.

His sister, Jonnie, now Pat Ellis, was the first to join the Communist Party USA in Buffalo and this was to become another wellspring of the family's strength. It brought them into the nationwide and worldwide movement against fascism, for national liberation and socialism. She led the fight against racist hiring practices at the Bell Aircraft plant during the war. Her mother Hattie soon joined the Party and became a leader in the Ellicott community of Buffalo.

Frank served five years in the Merchant Marine, running arms and ammunition to the allies through the U-boat infested North Atlantic during the war. He became an active member of the National Maritime Union and he, too, joined the Communist Party.

They became part of a movement with strong leaders like Paul Robeson, Henry Winston, Benjamin Davis, Claudia Jones, and Elizabeth Gurley Flynn. Over the years, Frank became a close friend of Gus Hall, a fellow steelworker and General Secretary and later, National Chair of the CPUSA.

"Through Jonnie, the whole family was introduced to the ideas of Marx, Engels, and Lenin," Bea writes. "The family always had confidence in their 'own people.' They began to broaden their idea of their 'own people' to include people of other races. They began to think in terms of class and see racism as an attempt to weaken and divide the working class. A united working class could end capitalist oppression just as earlier generations overthrew slavery."

That struggle for the unity of African-American, Latino and white workers forms the bedrock of Frank Lumpkin's leadership of the Wisconsin Steel workers.

Bea chose for the title of her book, *Always Bring a Crowd*, one of Frank Lumpkin's favorite mottoes. It expresses his optimism that victory is possible in the face of heavy odds if workers unite and mobilize by the millions. Edward A. Sadlowski, who served for six years as executive director of the SOJ Committee recalls in the book the incessant picket lines the SOJ organized outside the corporate offices of Envirodyne, leafletting the expensively dressed executives as they stepped from their limousines along Chicago's "Magnificent Mile."

Sadlowski remarks that workers were transported to these picket lines on school buses. "Frank always travels with a loaded school bus," Sadlowski quips. Finally Envirodyne closed its offices and fled to a suburb forty-five miles away. The workers tracked them down and marched with placards that read, "Envirodyne, you can run but you can't hide."

Bea reports that Frank often used the motto *"Always bring a crowd."* He had another motto that he used to rally his fellow workers: "Fight or die." It took special courage, determination, as well as strategic and tactical brilliance to lead the struggle of the Wisconsin Steel workers in a struggle that continues to this day. He is a broad-shouldered man in the city of broad shoulders.

This was a turning point struggle in the last decades of the twentieth century. Only a worker could lead this fight. Frank Lumpkin, an African-American steelworker, Chair of the Communist Party of Illinois, led it. His continuing leadership proves that we are on course as we head into a new century."

Ken Lay, George W. Bush Dance Their Last Tango

Tim Wheeler,
Editor of PWW

March 20, 2002
HOUSTON, TEXAS—A friend who has lived in Houston for thirty-five years took me on a tour of the Bayou City recently. Our first stop was Enron's gleaming twin towers.

In front of the building is the famous upended "E" glowing in the East Texas sunset like a cattle rustler's branding iron. "We call it the 'Crooked E,'" my friend said with a rueful laugh.

Attorney General John Ashcroft was busy with the war on terrorism, so he looked the other way as, behind the tinted glass at Enron headquarters, paper shredders ran at full throttle for two months. They were destroying evidence of Enron's grand larceny.

The crimes are legion: massive corporate fraud, insider trading, price fixing, influence peddling, tax evasion, obstruction of justice. Already the signs of a coordinated cover-up are becoming clear. The first priority is to protect George W. Bush, whose "good ole boy" ties to Enron's former CEO Ken Lay are as fresh and malodorous as a steaming cow pie.

Like Ashcroft, Bush is so preoccupied as "commander-in-chief" that he has no time to answer the overriding questions in this debacle: "What did you know and when did you know it?"

Yet the real story of Enron is the corporation's incestuous relations with the Bush family and the ultra-right. Track the rise of Enron and you are tracking the career of George W. Bush from a callow college frat rat to a cunning corporate-government insider who always knew what was best for the oil and gas billionaires.

Like his one-term dad, George W., Richard Cheney, House Majority Leader Tom DeLay and hundreds of other Republican and Democratic officials fed at Enron's trough. Enron contributions added up to at least $6.6 million in the years of Bush's rise to power. So many were on Ken Lay's dole, it is hard to find anyone with hands clean enough to investigate the company's collapse.

Enron's ties to the ultra-right are so well-known in Texas that a website was set up with the address, "EnronOwnsThe GOP." It reports that Texas Governor Rick Perry, a Republican, accepted $227,075 from Enron while Attorney General John Cornyn—who is "investigating" Enron—received $193,000 from the defunct energy trading giant.

By far the biggest recipient of Enron largesse was George W. Bush, who received an estimated $2 million in Enron cash, starting with his race for Texas governor in 1994.

Bush, who calls Lay "Kenny Boy," flew to campaign stops during the 2000 presidential election aboard

Enron corporate jets. Enron, of course, was not the only oil and gas company that rallied for Bush. The nation's oil and gas monopolies poured $41 million into his election campaign.

When Bush lost the popular vote nationwide and in Florida, Enron-connected lawyer James A. Baker, Secretary of State in the elder Bush's cabinet, was rushed to Florida to orchestrate the termination of the vote count.

DeLay, another lawmaker on the Enron dole, recruited a fascist-like goon squad that rushed down to Florida to bully election officials to halt the count.

The U.S. Supreme Court installed Bush in the White House. It was a very American coup brought to us by Enron and other banks and corporations.

Craig McDonald, executive director of Austin-based Texans for Public Justice, cited letters Ken Lay wrote to Bush during his tenure as governor. The Texas Archives released them pursuant to a Freedom of Information lawsuit.

"They show a very close personal relationship between Lay and Bush," McDonald said.

"The visibility of the corruption is astounding, the degree to which the rich and the powerful were controlling policy. Ken Lay knew he had to be a political broker if he was going to broker electricity. He needed deregulation of the energy market to gain control of it."

Richard Cheney's notorious Energy Policy Task Force produced a report that embraced Enron's quest for total gas and electric deregulation. Lay met with Cheney and other Task Force members six times to dictate the language of the report.

"Cheney may have been talking, but the words were Lay's," McDonald said. Bush and Cheney tried to keep the proceedings of the task force hidden under a blanket of "executive privilege." But a federal court has ordered them to surrender the records of this secretive outfit.

The sewer of corruption promises to pour out more filth for the rest of Bush's term in office. McDonald scoffed at the Bush administration's clumsy damage control efforts, reducing the scandal to a "corporate scandal" while covering up its political essence.

"They want people to see Enron as one rogue corporation. In fact, people are beginning to understand that Enron is one of many," McDonald said. "The problem is the system. This is good government if you are Enron. But the policies promoted by the moneyed class benefit them, not us."

Senator Barbara Boxer (D-Calif.) cites a memo from the task force obtained by *The San Francisco Chronicle*, which she calls the "smoking gun" of Enron's role, with help from the Bush administration, in the California energy crisis of 2001.

"As we connect the dots," she wrote, "it is becoming increasingly clear that California's sky high electricity prices were brought about by Enron's methodical plan to free itself from all government oversight to hike up energy prices in secret."

Enron played the leading role in pushing through deregulation of California's electricity market with the help of Dynegy, Duke Power, and other natural gas suppliers.

"Deregulation allowed Enron to buy and sell electricity behind closed doors in an effort to trade up the price of energy through futures contracts before it reached the consumer," Boxer said.

Their control became so extensive, they could manipulate supplies minute by minute, she wrote. Sure enough, spot shortages began to cause rolling "brownouts," while rates paid by consumers skyrocketed in the space of weeks.

Governor Gray Davis pleaded with the Bush administration to impose price caps. But Bush, at Ken Lays' request, stiff-armed these pleas for months as the people of California suffered.

Then the Federal Energy Regulatory Commission, headed by Pat Wood, Enron's hand-picked nominee, approved caps that locked in high utility rates in California. Davis has accused Enron and other energy providers of overcharging consumers at least $8.9 billion.

Part of the scam was to shift blame for the crisis from Enron and the Bush administration to Davis and other Democratic officials. The hope was that outraged voters would oust them from office and elect a Republican governor and legislature in 2002.

But Boxer's answer was to demand the confiscation of Enron's loot, hidden in offshore dummy corporations in the Cayman Islands, and use it to reimburse California ratepayers.

A California Senate committee called for the arrest of Lay and other Enron executives and their return to California to stand trial for contempt in refusing to honor a state legislature subpoena.

Carl Wood, a member of the California Power Commission, says that the Enron debacle has brought to a standstill, at least for now, the drive for deregulation of electric utilities. There is, he said, a renewed interest in public ownership of energy as an answer to fleecing the public by pirates like Enron.

Debra Johnson, who served as a senior administrative assistant in Enron's Human Resources Division in Houston explained to me that the sorrow among Enron workers over Lay's betrayal is now turning to anger.

"We had high respect for Kenneth Lay," she said. "He would walk down the halls saying 'good morning' to everybody, just like a regular person." Then after seven years of devoted service she was fired on one day's notice.

"The executives paid themselves, but they left us with nothing," she said. "I have two young grandchildren I am raising. I never thought I would be forced to wait in a welfare line for food stamps, but I am."

Johnson is a member of the Enron Employees Committee that has filed a lawsuit with the bankruptcy court in New York demanding that the 4,000 furloughed employees receive severance pay.

She debunked the sob story from Lay's wife and children that they are broke, pointing out that Lay owns a dozen homes scattered across the U.S., each of them worth millions. Lay is now hiding out in his condo at the lavish Huntington condominiums in wealthy west Houston.

"I don't care how many mansions he has as long as he gives the workers the severance pay they deserve," Johnson said. "I think Kenneth Lay owes us an apology."

Harris County AFL-CIO President Richard Shaw said Enron workers gave their all for the company. "They believed the company line that Enron was going to take care of them," said Shaw.

"Many viewed Ken Lay almost like a father. But when the company unraveled Lay and the rest of them took care of their own interests and left the workers to fend for themselves."

The Texas and national AFL-CIO, Shaw said, came to their assistance, shouldering the cost of the lawsuit and helping the dazed workers get jobless benefits and other forms of public assistance. "During meetings people would ask us, 'Why are you here?' They didn't even know what the initials of the AFL-CIO stand for. We told them: 'We are here because an injury to one is an injury to all.'"

"Corporations like Enron will never subordinate their profit interests to the rights and needs of their workers," Shaw said.

"That's what unions are for. Workers must learn to join together and defend each other."

Reagan-Style Taxes: "Steal From Poor, Give To The Rich"

WASHINGTON—Thirty-two years ago, I wrote the story below about an outrageous tax swindle that President Reagan and the Republicans were preparing to ram through Congress. The story speaks for itself.

A few weeks after my story appeared, they did it! My story exposes the Reaganite drive to redistribute the nation's income from the pockets of hard-pressed wage earners to the coffers of the millionaires. Yet at the end of 2017, the Republicans bowed to billionaire President Donald Trump and rammed through an enormous tax swindle that lavishes billions in tax cuts on the super-rich while adding a trillion dollars to the federal deficit. Already the Republicans are citing the deficit they created as the reason they must slash Social Security, Medicare, Obamacare, federal aid to public education, etc.

Trump's tax swindle makes Reagan's tax scam seem like child's play. Yet my story proves that the corporate ultra-right has been working non-stop for many, many decades to use the tax code to redistribute our wealth from the 99% to one-tenth of one percent billionaires.

Economy Falters as Tax Bills Are Ironed Out
People's Daily World

July 19, (1986)

WASHINGTON—Fear of economic recession is taking hold in Congress just as House-Senate conferees meet to iron out differences in the tax bill approved by both bodies.

James Miller, President Reagan's budget director, admitted last week that economic stagnation will add $10 billion to the $200 billion deficit announced earlier this year. Industrial production fell 0.5 percent last month, the fourth decline in five months.

Economist Albert Sindlinger reports that 31 states dependent on farm, energy, steel, textile, mining, and timber production are now suffering what he calls 'local recession" that could prove a major factor in the 1986 Congressional elections. Other states are "borderline" and could plunge into recession with mass layoffs in the weeks before November 4.

Underlying the statistics is a report last week in the *New York Times* entitled "The Average Guy Takes it on the Chin," which reveals that average hourly earnings adjusted for inflation have declined a staggering 14.3 percent since 1973.

Already some are calling for a regressive tax increase to offset the ballooning deficits—even though this would further slash the purchasing power of working people adding to recessionary pressures.

Rep. David Obey (D-Wis.), chairman of the Joint Economic Committee, opened a hearing on "Progressivity and the Federal Tax Code" this week. He announced that a study to be released soon by his committee proves "the rich are getting richer and the poor are getting poorer" with the nation's wealth "increasingly concentrated in the hands of the super-rich few. With the deficit threatening to zoom past last year's huge $212 billion, it makes no sense to consider another bonus for the rich while potentially adding to the tax burden of the middle class."

He challenged the idea promoted by the Reaganites on the tax committee that everyone will enjoy a tax cut. A study by the Joint Committee on Taxation shows that "more than thirty percent of all households with incomes between $20,000 and $75,000 would pay higher taxes" if the Senate version prevails.

Obey said the Senate version cuts the tax rate for the rich by another forty-six percent—on top of the twenty-nine percent cut they enjoyed in 1981.

Released at the hearing was a Roper Organization survey, "The American Public and the Federal Income Tax System." Pollster Burns W. Roper said his firm's interviews with 1,500 randomly selected taxpayers "shows quite clearly that the public wants a more progressive tax system, not a simplified, flatter tax system. Tax reform to the American public means fairness; and their perception of fairness is more progressive, not less progressive."

Both the Senate and House versions undercut a progressive, ability-to-pay tax system and move towards a flat tax.

Meanwhile, Citizens for Tax Justice (CTJ) released another report, "Corporate Freeloaders," which identified 130 corporations that "managed to pay absolutely nothing—or less—in federal income taxes" in at least one year since 1978.

The biggest tax cheat is AT&T. It reported $25 billion in profits yet paid no federal taxes between 1982 and 1985. In fact, AT&T received tax refunds totaling $636 million.

Other top avoiders were DuPont, Boeing, General Dynamics, Pepsico, General Mills, Transamerica, Texaco, International Paper Co., Greyhound, and IC Industries. These corporations paid no taxes on 1982-85 profits totaling $39.7 billion and received $1.5 billion in tax rebates. The top six military contractors reported total profits of $21.7 billion in those years and paid taxes at a 3.5 percent rate.

CTJ Director, Robert McIntyre said, "For the vast majority of American families who pay their federal income taxes year in and year out, the idea of a 'no tax year' is almost inconceivable. . . . But for most of America's largest corporations, no-tax years are now commonplace . . . . Voters are fed up with a tax system that produces such inequities and forces middle-income families to pay the freight for hugely profitable freeloaders."

The House-approved tax bill is marginally more progressive than the Senate bill. Both close some of the worst corporate tax loopholes and impose a twenty percent minimum tax on corporations urgently needed to end embarrassing disclosures like McIntyre's. Big Business is flocking to support the tax revision scheme because it slashes the maximum corporate tax rate to as low as thirty-three percent.

Senator Carl Levin (D-Mich.), voted against the tax bill charging that thirty percent of middle income taxpayers will end up paying $340 to $525 more in taxes. "This shock may turn to anger when taxpayers learn that more than half of the taxpayers making over $200,000 may get a tax cut averaging over $50,000 a year," Levin said.

Reagan decries the progressive income tax as a Marxist scheme to "redistribute wealth." But the tax revision schemes he supports in Congress are redistributing wealth from the pockets of working people to the pockets of the rich."

Home Owners Fight Foreclosures
By Tim Wheeler
People's Weekly World

BALTIMORE—Louis Beverly, an ACORN leader here, used a bolt cutter to break the lock on Donna Hanks foreclosed home so she could move back into the house in east Baltimore she lost in foreclosure. Baltimore Police issued a warrant for their arrest on "burglary" charges February 24 and both have surrendered and are now awaiting trial. ACORN calls the project "Homesteading," an emergency measure in the absence of the moratorium on foreclosures the grassroots community organization is demanding.

Hanks owed $260,000 on the modest home with a monthly payment of $1,600, ruinous given her income of about $1,200 a month as a hotel employee. She had fallen more than $7,000 behind in her mortgage payments.

Joe Cox, a leader of the Baltimore Chapter of the Association of Community Organizations for Reform Now (ACORN) told reporters, "People say we're breaking the law but we don't see how putting a person back in an abandoned property is hurting anyone."

ACORN is expanding the homesteading project to twenty-two cities. It has enlisted 500 volunteers to serve as "home defenders," blocking evictions and disrupting auctions of foreclosed properties. An estimated 2.3 million homeowners have lost their homes in foreclosures in 2008. Another 9 to 11 million foreclosures are forecast in 2009.

Rep. Marcy Kaptur (D-OH), distressed at how many of her Toledo constituents were being foreclosed, urged them to stay put. "You be squatters in your own homes," Kaptur thundered in a speech on the House floor. "Don't you leave!" Kaptur pointed out that the mortgage market is so tangled that no one knows for sure who legally owns tens of thousands of foreclosed properties in Ohio. A judge in Cleveland refused to proceed with several foreclosures because the banks could not certify which financial institution owned the mortgages.

While lobbying for foreclosure relief on Capitol Hill, recently, Phoenix ACORN President Alicia Russell greeted Kaptur's "squatter" proposal. "I think it is a good idea," she told the *World*. "The banks have sold and resold these mortgages so many times that no one knows who actually owns them. The banking industry is out of control. These are families that do not want to be homeless." Phoenix, she said, is the sixth hardest hit city in the foreclosure crisis.

President Obama traveled to Phoenix to unveil his $275 billion package aimed at stabilizing the housing market and helping 11 million homeowners keep their homes. ACORN hailed Obama's initiative.

Art Perlo, chair of the Economics Commission of the Communist Party USA also greeted Obama's plan but stressed it is only a first step. "Too much is voluntary, not compulsory, starting with an indefinite moratorium on evictions," Perlo said. Homeowners shouldn't have to declare bankruptcy and depend on a bankruptcy judge's whim for relief. The principal of loans (not just interest rates) "should be written down to a level that reflects realistic home values and families' ability to pay," he continued.

This should be done universally, not on a case-by-case basis by courts which are in no position to deal with 10 million individual cases. Perlo assailed bailouts of the banks. "The plan should have less carrot and more stick," he said. "Instead of spending billions to bribe them to make changes in mortgages, the executives and managers of these banks should be told to modify ALL loans favorably if they want to escape doing serious jail time for fraud, conspiracy, and economic terrorism."

The plan ameliorates the crisis "but does not alter that 10 million to 20 million families are so burdened by mortgage debt that it dominates their lives" and leaves them at risk of losing their homes. As for squatting and homesteading, "These actions will have to be multiplied a hundred-fold in order to overcome this crisis," he told the *World*. Indeed, the financial meltdown is so catastrophic that nationalization is openly proposed by mainstream economists as the only remedy.

ACORN warned that a moratorium on foreclosures is urgently needed. Many major lenders have already agreed to abide by a voluntary moratorium. Yet these voluntary moratoriums "only cover a small portion of the troubled loans that may slip into foreclosure in the immediate future," said ACORN CEO Bertha Lewis.

Lewis pointed out that the banks voluntary moratorium covers only the loans they "own." That leaves the vast majority of at-risk homeowners without protection. Take for example Wells Fargo. They "own" only 6 percent of the mortgages they deal with. Fully 94 percent of the mortgages they "service," i.e. collect homeowner payments on, are owned by some other financial entity.

"Especially worrying is the vast majority of the subprime loans at the heart of the foreclosure crisis," Lewis continued. "At least seventy-five percent of these subprime loans were securitized and sold to investors rather than held onto by the banks....so none of the announced moratoriums will protect those borrowers stuck with subprime loans from losing their homes in the coming weeks and months."

Banks bilk homebuyers, cities say
People's Weekly World

January 18 2008
BALTIMORE—Mayor Sheila Dixon has filed a lawsuit charging Wells Fargo bank with targeting African American homebuyers for subprime loans. The groundbreaking

initiative has thrown a spotlight on discriminatory lending across the nation in violation of federal law.

Dixon's suit, filed January 9, was followed a few days later by a lawsuit filed by the city of Cleveland against twenty-one banks, including Wells Fargo, charging "reverse redlining," in which Black and Latino home buyers are pressured to accept unpayable loans.

Cleveland is described as the "epicenter" of subprime foreclosures, with 17,000 vacant, foreclosed homes. The city expects 8,000 foreclosures in 2008.

Cleveland Mayor Frank Jackson accused the banks of knowingly luring people into mortgages with impossible payments. "The money was too good," he said. The banks "were living large off the misery and suffering of people."

The Rev. Jesse Jackson, president of RainbowPUSH, called for a massive march on the Department of Housing and Urban Development January 22 to force President Bush to address the foreclosure crisis in his State of the Union message that night.

"We need to take mass action for mass results," Jackson told a Washington news conference Jan. 15.

Predatory lending has unleashed a flood of foreclosures in a housing collapse that is pushing the economy toward recession. The U.S. Conference of Mayors released a report last November predicting that 1.4 million homes will be foreclosed in 2008, with a combined market value of $316 billion.

Homeowners will lose $1.2 trillion in equity, and the ten hardest hit states will lose an aggregate $6.6 billion in tax revenues, the report warned.

Since 2000, more than 33,000 Baltimore homes have been foreclosed. Wells Fargo, the city's second largest mortgage lender, made 1,285 loans a year since 2004, totaling more than $600 million. Two-thirds of Wells Fargo foreclosures were in Baltimore census tracts with sixty percent African American population.

Rose Taylor, a Baltimore housing activist who years ago lost her home in foreclosure, told the *World*, "This crisis is devastating for working class people. We pull together the money to purchase a home. Predatory lenders then take our property in outrageous foreclosures. We need a moratorium on foreclosures. Shelter is a basic human right."

President Bush assigned the banking industry to write his plan for dealing with the crisis. Only those whose mortgage payments are current will be assisted. Those behind in their payments are on their own.

Public interest lawyer Matthew Lee, author of "Predatory Bender: A Story of Subprime Finance," published by Inner City Press in 2003, told the *World*, "The fact that cities like Baltimore and Cleveland are taking legal action against predatory lending shows that the federal government has been asleep at the switch."

The Federal Reserve and other federal regulators, Lee said, "have known about these practices for years and did nothing. Whole blocks of our cities are vacant and abandoned because of these practices."

The publisher's web site includes a "Wells Fargo Watch," featuring hundreds of complaints by Wells Fargo customers of being bilked by the San Francisco-based bank, fifth largest in the nation.

Wells Fargo bought out Island Finance, a mortgage bank based in San Juan, Puerto Rico, and has spread its predatory loan business to Aruba, the U.S. Virgin Islands and Panama, the web site reveals. CEO Richard Kovacevich bragged that Wells Fargo is the "number one NAFTA bank, with more banking stores and assets than any competitor within sixty miles of Mexico and Canada."

Wells Fargo violated the Service Members Civil Relief Act, which requires banks to reduce mortgage interest rates for military personnel. One soldier filed a complaint with the Office of the Comptroller of the Currency (OCC), saying that he informed Wells Fargo just before he was deployed to Iraq in January 2003 that the interest on his two home equity loans should be reduced to six percent. "In mid-July when I returned to my residence from the Persian Gulf, I learned from my wife that Wells Fargo never reduced our interest rate to six percent as required by law," he wrote.

The United Steelworkers put up picket lines at Wells Fargo banks to protest their bankrolling of Oregon Steel/CF&I in its five-year drive to bust the union at its Pueblo, Colo. steel mill a few years ago. The workers ultimately won that fight.

Wells Fargo is donating $250,000 to fund the Republican convention in Minneapolis later this year.

Wal-Mart—Nation's Worst Workplace Bully

January 23, 2003
WITH $9.1 BILLION in profits squeezed from the labor of one million workers at 3,250 stores across the country last year, Wal-Mart deserves its reputation as the nation's worst "workplace bully."

But the grievances against the huge discount chain, the largest private employer in the U.S., are not limited to its workers. A vast coalition of grassroots organizations is rising up in rage against Wal-Mart on issues ranging from its importation of sweatshop garments, its predatory underselling of independent retailers in towns and cities across the nation, as well as the starvation wages it pays its workers.

It's also being challenged for its Scrooge-like practices. Just before Christmas, managers of a Wal-Mart store in Sterling, Colorado agreed to permit a local charity group to place a big box outside the store for customers to donate toys for needy tots.

Susan Kraich, who had organized the project, said she had been elated one day to find the box nearly full. She returned a few hours later to find it empty.

When she confronted the manager, he admitted that he had ordered the toys put back on the shelves on grounds that customers may have stolen them. He told her he would replace the toys only if she produced receipts proving they had been bought in the first place.

"I don't know how I'm supposed to prove what was in there," Kraich told the press. "I thought since Wal-Mart agreed to place the box, they were agreeing to keep an eye on it."

Then there's Wal-Mart's "dead peasants insurance."

Wal-Mart takes out life insurance policies on their employees, coyly referred to as "associates." Wal-Mart names itself as the beneficiary. Wal-Mart took out about 350,000 "dead peasant" policies on its employees, each payable to the company. Wal-Mart borrowed money from the insurers, mainly Hartford Life and AIG, to pay for it, listing those premiums as an expense on its Federal taxes, a shocking example of corporate tax evasion. The *Houston Chronicle*, now defunct, exposed this enormous scam. Texas outlaws "dead peasant" insurance on grounds that it provides a clear incentive for employers to murder their employees, the *Chronicle* reported. Wal-Mart got around this by writing the policies in Georgia.

John Antonich, business agent of United Food and Commercial Workers (UFCW) Local 88, a meat cutters' local in St. Louis, told the *World* he had a phone call from a man who told him his wife died after working for Wal-Mart for many years. "He told me he got a check for $10,000 from the life insurance company but Wal-Mart got $40,000," Antonich said.

In a similar case, he said, a man who had worked decades for Wal-Mart and was near retirement was forced by the company to transfer eighteen times from one store to another, a clear attempt to force him to quit. "He died of a heart attack and his widow got $16,000 but Wal-Mart got $50,000.00," said Antonich.

In Plainview, Texas, Jane Sims lost her husband, Doug, a Wal-Mart worker, from a heart attack after twenty-three years of marriage. Wal-Mart collected $64,000 but his widow did not get a penny from the life insurance policy. She has sued Wal-Mart for their ghoulish preying on the dead. The practice is illegal in twenty-nine states.

"Wal-Mart puts out all this crap about how benevolent they are. But this dead peasants insurance shows us how heartless they really are," Antonich said. The practice of profiteering on the death of their employees was so outrageous that Wal-Mart cancelled all the policies after the *Chronicle* and other media exposed the racket.

"This is not just an issue of union rights. It is an issue of the survival of hundreds of small retailers across the country who are being wiped out by Wal-Mart. This company is literally destroying small towns in the Midwest."

Wal-Mart workers are fighting back with a blizzard of lawsuits as well as a nationwide struggle to unionize the giant. A federal jury in Portland, Oregon, ruled last December 19 in favor of 400 Wal-Mart workers who filed a lawsuit accusing Wal-Mart of forcing them to work overtime without pay or face being fired.

However, it was not a class action lawsuit so only the 400 workers who joined in the lawsuit will be compensated.

Former Wal-Mart workers Carolyn Thiebes and Betty Alderson, both of whom worked in managerial positions at a Wal-Mart in Salem, filed the lawsuit. Wal-Mart managers, they testified, forced employees to clean up the store after they had clocked out. Wal-Mart managers, they said, reprimanded employees who demanded compensation for this overtime.

"I saw associates do work for the benefit of the company that they weren't compensated for," Thiebes testified. Thiebes, who oversaw payroll between 1992 and 1998, said managers instructed her to delete overtime and holiday pay of employees on a weekly basis. When she complained about this wage chiseling, she was transferred from the Salem store to Dallas, about fifteen miles away. She was so fed up she found another job. Another hearing is scheduled to determine the award for the 400 employees.

At least thirty-nine class action lawsuits in thirty states have been filed against Wal-Mart, making it the second biggest target of civil litigation after the federal government. The company reportedly paid $50 million two years ago to settle an off-the-clock lawsuit covering 69,000 workers in Colorado, and it recently paid $500,000 to 120 workers in Gallup, New Mexico to settle an overtime lawsuit.

Two former Wal-Mart workers in Michigan sued Wal-Mart. Lindsay Ann Armantrout, one of the plaintiffs, told the *World* by telephone that if the court accepts their plea, current Wal-Mart workers in Michigan could benefit from a favorable class action ruling against the company's bully tactics. Armantrout was hired by the Wal-Mart store in Grandville, Michigan and assigned to the store's snack bar at $6.75 an hour. "I was pregnant, it was a job and they were hiring," Armantrout said in a deposition. Armantrout charged that she often worked straight through her shift because she was not allowed to leave the grill unattended and management regularly brushed aside her requests for someone to spell her.

"Sometimes it would be, 'We don't have anyone to cover for you' or 'I'll find somebody,' but they didn't." Sometimes she was so tired she would sit at a booth when there were no customers, she said in her deposition. Management reprimanded her for taking these breaks even though they are promised by law.

Armantrout said her wages were shorted in other ways. After she punched out at night, managers demanded that she clean up the store. Even if they didn't want to stay late, employees were stuck in the store because the doors were locked and they had to wait for a manager to agree to let them leave, she charged.

Armantrout said she demanded to be paid overtime and her bosses promised to "take care of it." But when she checked her pay stub, the money was not there. "I'd just get tired of asking," she said.

Martha Lair, the lead attorney in the Michigan lawsuit, told the *World* in a phone interview from her office in Denver, that if the Michigan court accepts their lawsuit as a class action, it would cover not only former but also 92,000 current employees of Wal-Mart in Michigan. "Our case is similar to the Oregon lawsuit in that Wal-Mart workers in Michigan were also required to work off the clock," said Lair. "Wal-Mart is reporting billions in income each year and four of the ten richest people in the world are Wal-Mart heirs. They are getting that way because their employees are earning minimal wages and working off the clock. This is a company that has ridden the backs of their hourly employees to extreme profitability."

Last November 21, tens of thousands joined in a "People'sJustice@Wal-Mart" at 125 Wal-Marts in forty-nine states. The slogan was, "America Can't Live on a Wal-Mart Paycheck." It was co-sponsored by the UFCW, the AFL-CIO, National Organization for Women (NOW) and more than 300 other grassroots organizations. "This Day of Action is not about protesting Wal-Mart," said UFCW President Doug Dority. "We're here to demonstrate our support for the Wal-Mart workers, our communities and American values."

On an average, Wal-Mart workers earn $8.50 an hour for twenty-eight to thirty-two-hour workweeks. Over 700,000 Wal-Mart workers are without health insurance and 500,000 walk away from Wal-Mart jobs every year.

Dority pointed out that Wal-Mart faces dozens of lawsuits including the "largest sex discrimination lawsuit in history" and has been found guilty by the National Labor Relations Board (NLRB) of "illegal surveillance, threats and intimidation" at stores in Denver, Orlando and Paris, Texas, where the UFCW is trying to organize the workers.

"Wal-Mart's claims that its 'associates' don't want union representation rings hollow as the NLRB issues three new complaints against the retail giant," charged a press release by the UFCW. "Workers in Denver are organizing with the United Food and Commercial Workers Local 7 and have suffered from Wal-Mart's big bully tactics." Wal-Mart goes on trial February 10 for illegal surveillance of union supporters.

Antonich faxed to the *World* an internal Wal-Mart manual titled "Wal-Mart: A Manager's Tool Box to Remaining Union Free." It is marked "confidential" and lays out in painstaking detail the dirty tricks Wal-Mart managers are expected to use to deny their workers the right of union representation.

"As a member of Wal-Mart's management team, you are our first line of defense against unionization," it states. "It is important you be . . . constantly alert for efforts by a union to organize your associates and constantly alert to any signs your associates are interested in a union."

The manual proclaims that Wal-Mart's "open door" policy makes "third party representation" unnecessary. "It is our position every associate can speak for him/herself without having to pay his/her hard-earned money to a union . . . ."

Managers are instructed to instantly telephone the Wal-Mart "union hotline," at the first sign of union activity. The booklet also warns them to be on the alert for danger signs of worker discontent.

One chapter, "Union Authorization Cards" declares, "In the event you find a union authorization card in your facility or hear associates are attending union meetings and signing authorization cards, it is imperative you contact the Union Hotline at (501) 273-8300 immediately. Wal-Mart must respond to this type of union activity immediately in an effort to stop card signing before the required thirty percent signature have been obtained."

Several chapters are devoted to ferreting out "salts," union organizers who are sent into a Wal-Mart store to organize from the inside.

One Wal-Mart program featured in the booklet is "TIPS" for "Threaten, Interrogate, Promise, Spy." It states, "Know your TIPS. As long as you do not threaten, interrogate, promise or spy on your associates, Wal-Mart, through your efforts, will be able to share its views on unionization in an open, honest and legal manner." Yet all the practices exposed by the lawsuits and by the NLRB reveal that threats, interrogation, spying and broken promises are Wal-Mart's stock-in-trade and the way it keeps its employees powerless wage slaves.

Wal-Mart is one of the biggest contributors to the campaign coffers of George W. Bush and the Republican ultra-right, which helps explain why the Bush administration has been so slow to enforce labor rights and anti-discrimination laws against the Arkansas-based firm.

Two years ago, Wal-Mart poured $100,000 into the successful campaign to railroad a "Right-to-Work (for less)" union-busting referendum, in Oklahoma. They hope to put similar anti-union laws on the books in Colorado, Indiana, Kentucky, Montana, New Hampshire and New Mexico.

"Union members across the country should take note of Wal-Mart's support of measures like 'right-to-work' before they spend any of their union wages at Wal-Mart stores," said Edwin Hill, president of the International Brotherhood of Electrical Workers.

Abramoff Pleads Guilty, Tom Delay Throws in Towel
People's World

January 6, 2006
WASHIINGTON—Jack Abramoff pleaded guilty to influence peddling and his crony, Representative Tom DeLay, Republican of Texas, gave up his drive to win back his post as House Majority Leader last weekend.

Both were signs that the sewer of corporate corruption engulfing Washington has broken wide open, implicating dozens of lawmakers, mostly Republicans, in a crucial election year. DeLay gave up his drive when White House Republicans started circulating a petition urging that he be barred from leadership.

"This is the most corrupt Congress in U.S. history," said Toby Chaudhuri, communications director of the Campaign for America's Future (CAF,) which is running television and newspaper ads in Texas and Ohio calling on voters to "clean the stables." Targeted in the ad is DeLay, who is seeking re-election from his district that includes rt of Houston, and Bob Ney, Republican of Ohio.

In his guilty plea, Abramoff admitted that he showered Ney with lavish gifts and contributions in exchange for Ney's agreement to use his office to aid Abramoff's clients. "Abramoff is fingering Representatives Bob Ney and Tom DeLay as central figures in this scandal," Chaudhuri told the *World*. "There's a cancer growing on this Congress."

The Bush Administration and lawmakers on Capitol Hill are rushing to give to charity contributions they received from Abramoff doled out from the $66 million he swindled from six Native American tribal casinos. White House Spokesman, Scott McClellan, announced that the Bush-Cheney Campaign would turn over $6,000 in Abramoff cash to the American Heart Association, but not the $100,000 Abramoff contributed as a "Bush Pioneer." Abramoff's ties to Bush run much deeper than money. Bush named Abramoff to his "presidential transition team" advising the administration on policy toward Native American Indian tribes. Abramoff's former top aide, Susan Ralston, is now the top aide to Bush's chief strategist, Karl Rove. Abramoff was a frequent guest at White House holiday parties and reportedly met Bush at a fundraising event.

The scandal lifted the lid on a much broader crisis of corporate influence peddling, the lobbying "industry" centered on "K-Street" in downtown Washington. It is crowded with more than 70,000 registered lobbyists, most of them representing banks, corporations, or ultraright action committees promoting the Bush-Cheney agenda.

After Bush seized office in the stolen 2000 election, DeLay, together with Senator Rick Santorum (R-PA) and Republican strategist Grover Norquist, spearheaded what they called the "K-Street Project." *Washington Monthly* featured an article in its July/August 2003 edition, "Welcome to the Machine: How the GOP Disciplined K Street and made Bush Supreme." Corporate lobbyists, once bipartisan in nature and "loyal only to the parochial interests of their employers . . . are being replaced by (Republican) Party activists who are loyal first and foremost to the GOP," the article charged.

Through them, Republicans can now marshal armies of lobbyists divided into "friendly" and "unfriendly" columns. Those in the "unfriendly" column were simply frozen out, refused access to the corridors of power. DeLay even met with the CEOs of the largest corporations and told them that they were to fire any lobbyists who were Democrats or independents and replace them with Republicans. —*Washington Monthly*

Ohio GOP Caught in "Grannygate"
The People's World

October 31, 2011

CLEVELAND—Ohio voters are calling it "Grannygate," and it has blown away Ohio Governor John Kasich's credibility in his desperate drive to block the repeal of his union-busting law, SB 5, in the November 8 election.

The Ohio labor movement and its allies collected 1.3 million signatures to place an initiative on the ballot to repeal the law. A "No" vote on Issue 2 is a vote to repeal SB 5.

The granny in "Grannygate" is Marlene Quinn, a seventy-eight-year-old Cincinnati woman whose grandson Jan and great granddaughter Zoey and Zoey's grandad were saved by firefighters in a house fire a year ago. Quinn was so outraged by Governor Kasich's drive to ram through SB 5, stripping firefighters and other public employees of collective bargaining rights that she volunteered to make a TV ad for "We Are Ohio," urging voters to vote "No on Issue 2."

"Cincinnati firefighters risked their lives to save Zoey and her grandfather and I trust them to know what y need to protect our communities," Quinn said in the original TV ad broadcast across the Buckeye State. "I'm voting 'no' on Issue 2 to stop Senate Bill 5 because I don't want the politicians in Columbus making decisions for the safety of my family and the firefighters who saved Zoey."

But then, to the consternation of people of this state, the so-called "Building a Better Ohio," Republican backers of SB 5, stole footage of Marlene Quinn and used it to produce a TV ad urging voters to vote exactly the opposite of what Quinn said. The altered ad uses the footage of Quinn thanking the firefighters but deleted her line urging voters to "vote No on Issue 2." They substituted a line read by a woman with a voice similar to Quinn's saying, "vote Yes on Issue 2."

The scam TV ad touched off a firestorm, not least from Quinn herself. "I want an apology," she told Cincinnati reporters. "I did not say that. I said 'No.' How dare they! I didn't give them permission to do this . . . They just stole it and said, 'well, she's just an old lady; she won't know any better.' They don't know this old lady."

Later she said, "I think it's dishonest and downright deceitful that they would use footage of me to try to play tricks and fool voters. It's insulting to the brave firefighters who saved the lives of my grandson and my great granddaughter Zoey."

She demanded that TV stations pull the ad and that "Building a Better Ohio" and Governor Kasich apologize to her. So far, thirty stations have complied with the demand and stopped airing the ad. But Kasich has not apologized. In fact, he endorsed the ad. "I think we've been pretty factual," he said. "They've been emotional and we've been factual." Kasich said he does not "run the campaign" but did not mention that his chief of staff, Beth Hansen, is on leave to head up the effort to save the vicious union-busting law.

Quinn then appeared in a new TV ad sponsored by We Are Ohio. "Ohio firefighters risked their lives to save my great granddaughter so I know how important response time is," she says. "That's why I'm voting No on Issue 2."

She adds, "But the organizations behind Issue 2, stole my words to make it seem like I support Issue 2. They must be desperate to twist the words of a grandma to get their way. Don't let the politicians put our communities at risk. Vote 'No' on Issue 2."

It appears that "Grannygate" may have backfired disastrously for Kasich and his fellow corporate right-wing supporters of SB 5.

Polls show fifty-seven percent of likely voters favoring repeal of SB 5 compared to thirty-two percent who support the law.

The labor movement in Ohio is taking nothing for granted. An army of volunteers is going door to door and phone banking to voters across the state to get out a massive "No on Issue 2" vote.

"Grannygate" is doubtless a precursor of the dirty tricks the Republicans will resort to in the 2012 election to suppress the vote, win majority control on Capitol Hill and oust President Obama from office. A victory by labor and its allies here November 8 will be a sure sign that the ninety-nine percent are fed up with the GOP dirty tricks and determined to retire them from office in 2012.

Chapter *8*

Heroes

Soldiers and the Wars They Fought

War veterans have marched in the vanguard of peace demonstrations for as long as I have been reporting on the activities of the anti-war movement. Especially dramatic were the veterans of the Abraham Lincoln Brigade marching with their banners. They put their lives on the line volunteering to fight in defense of Spain's elected government against Francisco Franco and his fascist legions in 1937. They were the "premature anti-fascists" and their presence was a warning that wars of aggression—imperialist wars—are a breeding ground for dictatorship.

I have known many Lincoln Brigade veterans and interviewed them over the decades. Several were on the staff of the *Worker* and the *Daily World*: Jerry Cook, Dave Gordon, and Joe Brandt. Among the writers who influenced me most were Joe North, who covered the war in Spain for the *Daily Worker* and Art Shields, who barely escaped with his life while covering the anti-fascist struggle in Spain.

Moe Fishman visited the offices of the *Worker* perhaps twice or three times each month, limping in to deliver press releases from the nearby offices of the Veterans of the Abraham Lincoln Brigade in New York City. I include in this book my remembrance of Fishman.

Among my friends during my college years was Danny Watt and through him I met his father, George Watt, a hero of the Spanish Civil War.

I stayed with Lincoln vet, Mike Klonsky, in South Miami Beach when I made a speaking trip to Florida in the late 1970s.

Felix Kusman, a machine gunner in Spain, served as CPUSA Chairman, Gus Hall's chauffeur when Gus was denied his driver license so I got to know him well while I was on the *Worker* staff in New York.

The Lincoln vets were of varied background. Yet they shared some admirable qualities. They were quiet spoken, modest, unpretentious, staunch in defense of workers and their right to organize, strong defenders of racial and gender equality. They were always first to stand up and speak out against war.

In my childhood and as a young adult I knew Oiva Halonen, a union machinist in Seattle who had volunteered to fight in Spain and served as a machine gunner. My tribute to Oiva is in my first book, "News From Rain Shadow Country."

Vietnam Veterans Against the War (VVAW) inherited many of the qualities of the Lincoln Vets. A deep friendship grew up between the Spanish Civil War volunteers and these veterans of a younger generation marching against the Vietnam War.

When VVAW marched into Washington, D.C. in April, 1971 in a protest called "Dewey Canyon II" it transformed the struggle to end the Vietnam War. Many had suffered grievous wounds, their chests laden with battle ribbons and medals for combat valor. Their witness presented incontrovertible proof that the U.S. government was guilty of armed aggression against Vietnam. The war was atrocious, and morally depraved.

Veterans joining the movement set the stage for opposition to become a majority sentiment, an enormous shift in mass public opinion that culminated in forcing the U.S. withdrawal from Vietnam and the resignation of Nixon.

Ever since that fateful day in 1971 when veterans flung their medals on the West Steps of the Capitol, antipposition within the U.S. military has been a major acle to Pentagon schemes of global domination.

Soldiers—and veterans—have been a force for emancipation whether they be Harriet Tubman, Lincoln Brigade vets, my great grandfather, a sharpshooter who marched from Atlanta to the Sea, Ludmila Pavlichenko who fought to defeat Hitler fascism, or Vietnam Veteran, David Cline, president of Veterans for Peace.

Moe Fishman Never Gave Up
By Tim Wheeler
People's Weekly World

August 18, 2007
NEW YORK—Moe Fishman sat on a folding chair along Broadway surrounded by other Veterans of the Abraham Lincoln Brigade (VALB) in New York City the morning of April 29, 2006. The Lincoln vets held a banner greeting the tens of thousands of anti-Iraq war protesters who marched past. When contingents caught sight of the VALB banner, they would break into cheers for the famed "premature anti-fascists."

Fishman's leg hurt from the severe wound he received in combat during the Spanish Civil War, but he was still jaunty in his blue beret, his eyes sparkling with joy at the march's enormous size.

"We are here to show our respect for the peace movement and to join in the call for an end to this atrocious Iraq war," Fishman told the *World*. "We have stood against war and fascism for seventy years. We want a foreign policy based on peace and mutual respect, not war and global domination."

Fishman, who served for decades as executive secretary-treasurer of VALB and who led the Lincoln vets in hundreds of antiwar marches over the past seven decades, died of pancreatic cancer in New York City August 6. He was ninety-two.

Peter Carroll, chair of the board of governors of the Abraham Lincoln Brigade Archive, said in an obituary that Fishman remained active to the end, attending meetings in the United States and Spain to prepare for the 70th anniversary of the outbreak of the Spanish Civil War in 1937.

Moe Fishman was born in New York City on September 28, 1915. He left school during the Great Depression and became a laundry worker and truck driver. He helped unionize his fellow workers and joined the Young Communist League. He remained a convinced socialist the rest of his life.

When the war in Spain began, Fishman volunteered to help defend the Spanish Republic, but was rejected. He applied again and was accepted because of his truck driving skills. Arriving in Spain in April 1937, he trained as an infantryman with the George Washington Battalion. During the battle of Brunete in July 1937, he was wounded in action, resulting in a lifelong limp.

On returning home, Fishman worked for the Joint Anti-Fascist Refugee Committee while studying to become a licensed radio operator. His proficiency with the wireless enabled him to serve with the Merchant Marine during World War II.

ing the Cold War, Fishman and his comrades summoned as hostile witnesses before the House merican Activities Committee and the Subversive

Activities Control Board (SACB). VALB was put on the U.S. attorney general's infamous "list of subversive organizations. The entire executive board resigned rather than register with SACB.

Fishman and Milt Wolff stepped forward to keep VALB together as an organization. Wolff became national commander and Fishman executive secretary-treasurer, a post he held the rest of his life. In the 1970s, the federal courts ruled the attorney general's list and SACB rulings were unconstitutional.

But the VALB treasury was empty, and in 1957, the two even considered disbanding the group, an idea the membership resoundingly rejected. About this time, Fishman received an appeal from a Spaniard interned in a Franco prison. At Fishman's insistence, VALB plunged into defense of the victims of Franco repression, a focus until Franco's death in 1975.

Fishman continued to lead VALB in its wide-ranging progressive activism including staunch opposition to the Vietnam War. During the 1980s, VALB raised funds to send an ambulance to Nicaragua in solidarity with the Sandinista revolution.

The Lincoln vets are honored today as heroes of the struggle for democracy, peace and justice, especially by groups like Vietnam Veterans Against the War and Veterans for Peace. Not so many years ago, Moe Fishman often visited this paper's offices, hand-delivering press releases and VALB newsletters, stopping to greet Jerry Cook, Dave Gordon, Joe Brandt and other Lincoln vets on our staff. We will miss him.

The Courage of David Cline
Daily Online

October 25, 2009

NEW YORK—The Death of Veterans for Peace leader David Cline on September 15 in Jersey City, New Jersey, touched off an outpouring of tributes from his fellow veterans that continues to this day.

Veterans for Peace President, David Cline, of VFP tripled photo courtesy of Veterans for Peace

Cline was one of the antiwar movement's clearest thinkers and certainly among its most inspirational mass leaders. The membership of VFP tripled while he was president.

He spoke often of the special role of veterans, military families and active-duty soldiers in countering President George W. Bush's exploitation of the September 11, 2001, terrorist attacks to justify "preventive war."

A foot soldier with the 25th Infantry Division during the Vietnam War, Cline was wounded three times. He came to understand that the decade-long quagmire was a "rich man's war and a poor man's fight."

On his return to the U.S., Cline plunged into the GI antiwar movement at Fort Hood, Texas. He edited the underground *Fatigue Press* and co-founded the Oleo Strut Coffee House in Killeen, Texas, where GIs learned the truth about the war.

The refusal of three Fort Hood soldiers, Black, Latino and white, to go to Vietnam inspired a nationwide movement with the demand "Defend the Fort Hood Three" led by the Young Workers' Liberation League.

Cline co-founded Vietnam Veterans Against the War (VVAW) with its "Dewey Canyon III" march, in which hundreds of war veterans threw their combat medals on the U.S. Capitol steps. The whole story is told in the remarkable film *Sir! No Sir!*

I first met Cline March 29, 2003, while covering VFP's "Operation Dire Distress" just as the invasion of Iraq began. Veterans in combat fatigues marched near the White House, singing, "Hey, hey, Uncle Sam, we remem-
:nam. War will mean that soldiers die. War will
ıat mothers cry . . . Bring our troops back to our
ey shouldn't die for Bush's oil."

Cline, a tall, thin, gravel-voiced man was singing out the lines. The vets sang them back. Those "karma cadences" became the voice of the entire antiwar movement. Cline was leading from the ranks.

I interviewed Cline many times after that.

When VFP and military families marched to Dover Air Force Base on March 20, 2004, I walked with Dave for forty-five minutes. An interview turned into a conversation. "I read Sam Webb's piece on socialism," he said at one point, referring to a pamphlet by the chairman of the Communist Party USA. "I liked it a lot. There's a lot in it I agree with."

A few weeks later, after a VFP rally at Faneuil Hall in Boston, Cline spoke of the Democratic National Convention that was just opening. "We have to remove the neo-conservatives from the White House and Congress," he told me. "We have to have a movement with longevity to push for progressive change in foreign and domestic policy."

In Fayetteville, North Carolina, near Fort Bragg, on the second anniversary of the war, he told me, "Some upper-class people can ignore this war. Those fighting and dying, mostly people of color, can't ignore it. All across the country, they are saying, 'Support the troops in the only way that is real: bring them home alive now.'"

The VFP convened in Dallas a few months later. Cindy Sheehan got the idea of camping near Bush's ranch outside Crawford, Texas, while addressing the convention. Cline assigned forty vets to help her set up "Camp Casey," named for her son who died in Iraq.

A few days later, the VFP bus was headed east when Hurricane Katrina struck. At Cline's suggestion, the bus detoured to New Orleans where VFP helped establish the first emergency medical center to serve thousands of residents trapped in the flooded city.

A year later, Cline led "Walkin' to New Orleans," a march from Mobile to New Orleans to protest the squandering of tax dollars in Iraq while victims of Katrina along the Gulf were abandoned.

During the scandal at the Pentagon-run Walter Reed Hospital, I telephoned Dave for his comment. He was outraged at the treatment of these veterans. For years, he told me, he wouldn't go to the Department of Veterans Affairs—run VA medical centers—because he was so angry about how veterans were treated. Yet he led a struggle to keep open a VA clinic in lower Manhattan. We put his testimony on keeping that clinic open on our op-ed pages.

David telephoned in March 2006 to ask us to write a feature on a VFP delegation to Hanoi to form a joint U.S.-Vietnamese movement demanding treatment of Agent Orange victims. David led that delegation. He posted our article widely, including on the VFP web site.

A Vietnamese delegation made a return visit to the U.S. a few months later led by Nguyen Van Quy, a Vietnam War vet. Nguyen and Cline showed each other their wounds, joking about how long it was taking them to heal. The next day, during a meeting, Cline presented his Purple Heart to Nguyen, a man he now considered his friend and comrade-in-arms.

"It was a gesture that could only come from David," wrote veteran Billy Kelly, who was there. Soon after returning to Vietnam, Nguyen died of complications from his Agent Orange exposure. "And now David," Kelly concluded. David Cline, presente!

The Real Heroism of Pfc. Jessica Lynch

November 22, 2003
WATCHING DIANE SAWYER'S interview with former Private First Class Jessica Lynch on ABC's *Primetime*, it was easy to see why the young soldier is a hero to the people of her own hometown, Palestine, West Virginia, and the rest of the Mountaineer State.

Lynch is a truck driver's daughter, a wisp of a girl, dreaming of a bright and happy future. She plans soon to marry a fellow soldier, Sergeant Ruben Contreras. Like so many in the economically stricken heartland of our country, she joined the military seeking opportunity and a more secure future for herself.

The Humvee she was riding in crashed during an ambush in the town of Nasiriya, Iraq, March 23, with the death of eleven of her comrades. Poised in answering even the hardest questions about her twenty-two day captivity and her struggle to recover from her terrible injuries, Lynch showed she has iron in her soul. The bones in one leg were so badly smashed that the Iraqi doctors caring for her planned to amputate.

Pfc. Jessica Lynch at Walter Reed Hospital. Public domain photo

Despite excruciating pain, she turned her face when they attempted to anesthetize her. She also suffered such serious back injuries that they apparently caused neurological damage. Normal bowel function has not returned. She takes heavy doses of painkillers, including morphine.

It is also understandable why George W. Bush wanted to turn her into a "poster child" of the Iraq war. There is ample precedent for using the devout, plain folk of Appalachia to promote a needless and unpopular war. Sergeant Alvin York, born in a log cabin in Pall Mall, Tennessee, was transformed into the "poster boy" of World War I, a sharpshooter who knocked out dozens of machine guns and captured 132 German soldiers single-handed, according to the myths.

Similarly, the *Washington Post* swallowed the whole Pentagon fiction that Lynch kept firing her M-16 until the ammunition was gone as her comrades lay dead beside her. Then came the rescue by a U.S. commando team, all videotaped for consumption back home. It could not have escaped Bush's political operative, Karl Rove, that footage of that rescue would play well on the 2004 campaign trail alongside footage of Bush landing on the deck of the aircraft carrier Abraham Lincoln and strutting in front of a huge "Mission Accomplished" banner.

Jessica Lynch's real courage, her real heroism, is that she refused to play the role scripted for her by the Pentagon. In fact, she said, her rifle jammed. "I'm not about to take credit for something I didn't do," she said. "I did not shoot. Not a round. Nothing. I don't look at myself as a hero. My heroes are Lori (Private First Class Lori Piestewa,) the soldiers that are over there . . . "

Piestewa is a Hopi Indian woman, a single mother of two, who was Lynch's best friend and roommate at boot camp. She died in the ambush.

Lynch thanked the Iraqi doctors and nurses for saving her life, and denied they mistreated her. She praised the Iraqi nurse who stroked her hair and sang lullabies to her.

Sawyer asked Lynch if the videotaping of her rescue bothered her.

"Yeah, it does, that they used me as a way to symbolize all this stuff," she replied. "It's wrong. I don't know why they filmed it."

Repeatedly she castigated those who tried to transform her into a female Rambo. "It hurt," she said. She criticized the administration and the media for rarely mentioning her comrades who died. Lynch remembers and is still grieving.

Lynch has also criticized the media for failing to focus on her sister POW Shoshana Johnson, who is African American. Lynch has backed Johnson's demand that she receive comparable medical care and disability benefits. We should be angry that "chicken-hawks" George W. Bush and Dick Cheney, who supported sending other people to fight and die in the Vietnam war while arranging not to go themselves, put these young women and 130,000 other soldiers in harm's way to satisfy their greed for oil and world domination.

Now Bush shuns the dead—refusing to attend funerals and barring the media from filming the returning caskets. In refusing to become a tool of Bush-Cheney war propaganda, Jessica Lynch stood up for all the dead and wounded of this unilateral, preemptive war—Iraqi, American, British, Italian.

"Fabricating that story is an extension of the big lie," Reverend Jesse Jackson told the *Chicago Defender*. "She [Lynch] needs to be honored for her integrity, for telling the truth," he said.

Perhaps the most poignant moment in the *Primetime* interview was when an Iraqi man who had guarded Lynch's hospital room told her, "I wish you the best, a happy, normal life." Jessica Lynch's face fell. She murmured words too soft to hear. But the deep sadness in her eyes seemed to ask: "How can my life be normal?"

The Woman Who Defended Sevastopol
RedNet; April 7, 2001 edition of the Peoples Weekly World

I REMEMBER MY PARENTS praising the heroism of the Soviet people in defending their country from the Hitlerite horde when I was a child during the Second World War. They told me the Soviets were fighting and dying to save themselves— and humanity—from fascist enslavement and mass extermination. One story they told me made a deep impression: the U.S. visit of a female Soviet sniper. Her story came back suddenly when I overheard my co-workers discussing the

Ludmila Pavlichenko 1942. Taken from courtesy of: http://borneobulletin.com

new movie, *Enemy at the Gates*, about the duel between Soviet sharpshooter Vassily Zaitsev and Nazi sniper Major Konig during the battle of Stalingrad.

I couldn't remember the name of this woman sniper but a few minutes on the Internet brought her whole story up. Her name was Ludmila Pavlichenko and she was credited with terminating 309 Nazi soldiers. A search of the *World's* archives produced a treasure trove of photos of her visit to the U.S. and numerous articles about her.

Pavlichenko was born in 1916 in Belaya-Tserkov, Ukraine. As a young woman, she worked as a machinist at the Arsenal Works in Kiev. She was a history student at Kiev University, and she took up sharp-shooting as a team sport.

She was on vacation with her husband at a spa in Odessa on June 22, 1941, when the Nazis invaded with 150 divisions—more than three million German troops, reinforced by another two million Rumanian and Italian fascist soldiers—armed with thousands of tanks, artillery and warplanes. It was the biggest military invasion in human history.

Pavlichenko first learned of the attack when Luftwaffe planes bombed beautiful seaside Odessa. She and her husband immediately joined the Red Army. Both were assigned to sniper duty in the famed Order of Lenin 25th Chapayev Infantry Division, named for a hero of the Bolshevik Revolution.

The Soviet people were struggling to save themselves from Nazi enslavement and mass extermination. Conventional "femininity" was a luxury that had to be put aside. Pavlichenko was a disciplined and extremely brave soldier who understood that only by inflicting casualties on the invading army could her country and its socialist revolution be saved. Still, the photos of Pavlichenko reveal a smiling, gentle-looking young woman.

Pavlichenko served with units defending Odessa in 1941. The Nazis captured Odessa and forced the Red Army to retreat down the Crimean Peninsula to Sevastopol, the naval base of the Soviet Union's Black Sea fleet. Pavlichenko and her husband were in Sevastopol during the eight-month Nazi siege of 1942 when Black Sea marines and Red Army soldiers fought desperately to hold on to this last Soviet bastion of the Crimea.

The Nazis sent fourteen divisions—240,000 troops, including the criminal Waffen SS—against Sevastopol, which was key to Hitler's hopes of conquest of the Caucasus and the huge offshore oilfields of the Caspian Sea. Sevastopol was cut off and could only be supplied and reinforced by ships and submarines that ran a gauntlet of Nazi dive-bombers, torpedoes and mines. It was here that Pavlichenko caused such mayhem among the Nazi invaders with her ordinary army rifle equipped with a telescopic sight.

Like Zaitsev, she had a duel with a Nazi sniper who was inflicting heavy casualties on the Red Army. She engaged the sniper for eight hours in a cat-and-mouse game in no-man's-land before she dispatched him. She then crawled across the battlefield to his body, retrieved his rifle and a diary in which he had recorded the time and place of more than 400 "kills" he had inflicted on Allied soldiers on the Western Front.

In his gripping book, *Last Days of Sevastopol*, *Pravda* correspondent, Boris Voyetekhov, who was there for three weeks and witnessed the evacuation, reports that at least 90,000 Nazis died storming Sevastopol. The Soviets evacuated the last defenders by sea in the third week of July, 1942.

Pavlichenko was summoned from the front to receive the Order of Lenin from Mikhail Kalinin, President of the USSR Supreme Soviet. She was later decorated as a "Hero of the Soviet Union" and was promoted to the rank of Major. She was wounded four times and saw her husband fall in combat in the defense of Sevastopol, one of 22 million Soviet men, women, and children who died defending their country.

First Lady Eleanor Roosevelt invited her to tour the U.S. in 1942 on behalf of Soviet War Relief. Pavlichenko was greeted in New York by Mayor Fiorello LaGuardia, Furriers Union President Ben Gold, National Maritime Union President Joseph Curran and other Congress of Industrial Organizations (CIO) leaders at a rally at Cooper Union Auditorium.

She spoke at a rally sponsored by the CIO and Ukrainian-American groups in Chicago. She was the guest of honor at the International Student Assembly in Washington, D.C., August 31, 1942. She visited the White House, the first Soviet citizen to receive such an invitation. She then toured Canada, speaking to similar rallies.

After the war, she returned to her profession as a historian, writing a book, *Heroic Truth*, about the Chapayev Division's role in the defense of Sevastopol. Pavlichenko was a leader of the Soviet Women's Committee, the Soviet Union of Journalists and the Central Committee of the Komsomol (Communist Youth League).

She died of a heart attack October 26, 1974. She was fifty-eight.

In an interview with *Soviet Military Review* in March 1971, she described her feelings on the day of the Nazi attack. "Everything was boiling hot within me. It was so vile to attack us. We young people loved our country dearly. Every one of us felt that Soviet power had given us everything—education and political freedom, the right to a job and leisure," she said. "Soviet power had eliminated exploitation of man by man, it had emancipated our people, it had taken our people on the highway of social, scientific, technical and cultural progress . . . I could think of nothing else but to enlist in the Red Army as a volunteer to fight the Nazis."

Seeing Guernica With Clear Eyes

People's World

NEW YORK—Danny Watt took me to see Guernica when it was on display at the Museum of Modern Art in New York in the spring of 1959. It was a natural for Danny because his father was George Watt, a hero of the Abraham Lincoln Brigade who had fought as a volunteer against Franco fascism in Spain. When I met George Watt, he was a beloved "Lincoln vet" idolized by his son, Danny.

Danny, who had grown up in a cramped apartment on Tremont Ave. in the Bronx had come to visit us on our dairy farm in Sequim, Washington. Breathing the clean, fresh air of Clallam County, gazing at the snowcapped Olympic Mountains, had been a marvelous experience for Danny and now he was returning the favor, showing off his home town to me.

I had come down to New York City from Amherst College where I was a freshman suffering agonies of homesickness, failing the required Math-Science course.

The two hours I spent sitting on that museum bench looking at Guernica was the most instructive moment of that visit. It is a very large painting, a very black and white canvas, a very stark and unforgiving image of murderous Nazi mutilation.

It is also a highly symbolic painting and the symbols are mystifying. There is the bull standing at the far left of the canvas, his mouth open, his tongue out, as if frozen by the horror that surrounds him. Just beneath him is a mother, her head thrown back, holding the remains of her dismembered child. There is a long corpse lying flat along the bottom of the canvas. A horse, also disemboweled, has his head thrown straight up, screaming. The canvas is covered with a confused mass of body parts— as if a bomb, or more than one, has torn life itself into shreds.

Flying in the open door, her eyes full of anguish, her arm outstretched toward the bull, is a woman holding a lamp.

This is Pablo Picasso's rendering of the genocidal crimes of Hitler's Condor Legion in its carpet bombing of the Basque city of Guernica, April 26, 1937. The Basque government reported that 1,564 women, children and men died in this totally unprovoked attack on an undefended city.

Picasso's painting became a symbol of the struggle against fascism and imperialist war.

The mural-sized painting was first exhibited in Paris, then taken on a brief world-wide tour before ending up at the Museum of Modern Art. Picasso had made clear the painting was not to be delivered to Spain until after democracy was restored to that tortured nation. When Franco died and the fascist dictatorship was abolished, Guernica was sent to Spain. It is now exhibited at the Museo Reina Sofia in Madrid.

In the autumn of 1963, I returned to Amherst College with my wife Joyce and our infant son, Morgan. A classmate, Dick Stein, lived upstairs from our off-campus apartment. He and his partner, Carole, became close friends.

As I was trying to decide what courses to take, Dick suggested Dr. Frank Trapp's Art History course. He had high praise for Trapp. He had taken one of Trapp's courses and was signing up for another one. I took his advice.

Trapp's method was to project slides of paintings, drawings, statues, and architectural masterpieces on a giant screen and then talk about them. He was a marvelous teacher with deep insights into the meaning of the art he lectured about.

Trapp was lecturing on great art of the 20th Century offering insights into the genius of the French Impressionists, the post-Impressionists, the Expressionists, up to the period of modern, non-objective art.

Then one day, he flashed on the screen Guernica, full size.

He began to speak about the painting: the chaos, the disemboweled body parts flung on the canvas, the grim black, white, and gray color scheme, Picasso's refusal to give us any refuge in a well-ordered, easily understood reality.

Trapp argued that the bull symbolized the vicious brutality of the bombing attack, the face of fascism. The bull had charged into the room wreaking havoc, goring men, women and children left and right, leaving the dead and dying all around him.

I raised my hand. "No, no," I said. "That can't be right. There is no way Picasso would surrender the bull, a symbol of Spain, to the fascists. No. The bull is standing in the midst of the carnage, frozen, unable to act. He is a symbol of the Spanish people, confused by the mass destruction around him but also enraged, his tongue out, bellowing with anger. And see to the right, flying in the window, is a woman holding a lamp, the spirit of enlightenment. She is trying to reach the bull to bring understanding. It is Picasso's message that once the woman with the lamp reaches the masses of the people—represented by the bull—then you have an invincible force that will defeat the fascists."

As I spoke, I heard Trapp in the darkened auditorium exclaiming, "Yes! Yes! You are right. I see it now!"

When the class was over, Dick and I walked back to our apartments together. "That was great, Tim. Your interpretation of Guernica was a real eye opener."

That was a high point of my years at Amherst College. Learning to see Guernica through clear eyes, understanding what the great Pablo Picasso was telling us about the struggle to defeat fascism. I have carried that lesson with me my entire life

Homage to Medgar Evers
February 11, 1994

Behold the Mississippi flowing
with the waters
of a continent and still stained
with the blood of Medgar Evers.

Deep flows the river with the evil
of stolen lives,
the floodcrest of trouble in the land.
Jackals slinked
around his home in 1963.

Surely there came a cry
from his heart, "run, run,"
when the telephone rang
and death was on the line.

North through Tupelo was the path
of escape to Detroit,
the option of life.

What necessity, strong as the river
made him stay?
Did he love his people more
than life itself?

"Jim Crow has got to go."
The words burned in his brain
the night the shot rang out.

Myrilie cradles him.
The children cry in the dark,
"Daddy, get up!"
Thirty-one-years for the wheel
of justice to grind. The widow
takes her lonely stand.

We are not deceived. De la Beckwith
did not fire the fatal shot alone.
Still hidden under the
cowards hood
of absentee ownership are those
who gave the order.

They lynch Black men
in Mississippi jail cells.
They drive Black women
with high-tech whips
in delta catfish plants.

You stood rooted like a tree in the
delta earth, Medgar Evers.
You would not run.
You did not speak flattering lies
about the America that is
knowing what America can be.
Patriot in the land of cotton,
our burning cause is the
Mississippi you died for

Obama Honors a Freedom Fighter, Rev. C. T. Vivian

WASHINGTON—At a White House ceremony November 20, President Obama conferred the Presidential Medal of Freedom on the Reverend C. T. Vivian, one of the nation's staunchest fighters for racial equality and voting rights.

Vivian was one of sixteen recipients of the award this past Wednesday, including former President Bill Clinton, and television personality Oprah Winfrey. Obama hailed Vivian for serving as one of the Reverend Martin Luther King Jr.'s closest advisers and for putting his life on the line in the struggle to end segregation.

Ironically, Obama himself, the first African American president, is living proof of Vivian's success.

I got to know Reverend Vivian in March 2005 when I was assigned by this publication's predecessor, the *People's Weekly World*, to cover the Edmund Pettus Bridge Crossing Jubilee in Selma, Alabama. This was a march commemorating the 40th anniversary of the brutal attack on voting rights marchers crossing that bridge on their way to the state capitol in Montgomery, Alabama, to demand equal voting rights. Alabama state troopers brutally attacked the marchers on March 7, 1965, nearly clubbing to death John Lewis, D-Ga., then the national chairman of the Student Nonviolent Coordinating Committee.

That attack backfired badly on Alabama Governor George Wallace. Scenes of the vicious attack were aired on network television, touching off nationwide outrage. A few months later, Congress approved and President

Photo above, Rev. C.T. Vivian (right) with author at
Democratic National Convention in Denver, Aug. 2012

Lyndon Johnson signed the Voting Rights Act of 1965,
clearing the way, ultimately, for thousands of African
Americans to win election to public office, most notably
President Obama.

Reverend Vivian was present at the opening shot of
that struggle, leading a march February 16, 1965, to the
courthouse in the nearby town of Marion, seat of Perry
County, to protest the arrest of Reverend James Orange,
a leader of the Southern Christian Leadership Conference (SCLC). The police had been instructed to target
Reverend Vivian, also an SCLC leader. After the police
assault, the marchers scattered. Marcher Jimmie Lee
Jackson hid with his mother in a closed and darkened
café. State Trooper James Fowler tracked Jackson down
and shot him to death as Jackson attempted to cover his
mother with his own body.

Outrage over the police murder of Jimmie Lee Jackson
triggered the first attempt to march across the Edmund
Pettus Bridge.

Forty years later, March 5, 2005, I joined thousands of marchers peacefully marching across the

bridge. The main demand of the march was renewal, without weakening amendments, of the Voting Rights Act. Specifically, the march demanded renewal of the "pre-clearance" clause. This was a section of the law that requires states with a history of voter discrimination to submit any changes in its voting procedures for review by the U.S. Justice Department. President George W. Bush and the Republican leadership on Capitol Hill had unleashed a "charm offensive" even as they maneuvered to undermine the Voting Rights Act. They had assigned a delegation led by Senator Bill Frist, R-Tennessee, to join the Bridge Crossing Jubilee. But the marchers were not fooled.

When we reached the east end of the bridge, there was Reverend Vivian standing in the midst of the crowd, a look of joy on his face. I asked him for an interview. "Don't take voting rights for granted," he told me, referring to the theft in Florida of the 2000 presidential election. "We took it for granted that if we had the right to register and vote, our votes would be counted. We never imagined that forty years later we would have to launch a whole new struggle. But we now know that many poor people never had their votes counted in the 2000 election or in the 2004 election. Given the character of the people now in power, we can have no confidence that our votes are being counted."

That interview echoed Reverend Vivian's speech a few hours earlier to the congregation in the Selma church that had served as the headquarters of the voting rights movement in 1965. Senator Frist and other Republicans were in the standing room crowd as Vivian blasted Bush's war in Iraq and the nationwide attack on voting rights by the ultra-right Republicans. Vivian received a standing ovation.

I interviewed Vivian by phone several times after that. In the summer of 2008, I was in Denver covering the Democratic National Convention that nominated Barack Obama for president. I was standing outside the Colorado Convention Center passing out copies of the

People's Weekly World when who walked up but C. T. Vivian. We greeted each other warmly and I handed him a copy of the *PWW*. Someone with a camera was about to click our picture. "Wait a minute," he said, shifting the paper so it was plainly visible under his arm. That's my fondest memory of the Reverend C. T. Vivian, a real hero of the people's movement.

He is still in the thick of the fight for voting rights and for full equality even as the Republicans do all in their power to strip people of that vital tool of democracy. As he told me in 2005, "We have to march all over again."

Invisible Giants Honored in Selma
People's World

March 11, 2005
SELMA, ALABAMA—They were "invisible giants," women and men who served as foot-soldiers of the struggle for voting rights.

They returned here for the fortieth anniversary celebration of the passage of the Voting Rights Act, many graying but most combative as ever.

Some had never left. Amelia Boynton Robinson and Marie Foster, both lifelong residents of Selma, were honored, the latter posthumously, as "Mothers of the Voting Rights Movement" with the unveiling of a black granite monument during this Bridge Crossing Jubilee.

Both women were clubbed by state troopers on "Bloody Sunday," March 7, 1965, as they marched across the Edmund Pettus Bridge on their way to Montgomery to demand voting rights. Foster passed away a few years

ago, but Robinson, now in her nineties, is still delivering speeches on the theme, "You can kill the dreamer but not the dream."

John Rankin, another native of Selma, was elated by the big turnout, including thousands who came from across the country. Rankin told this reporter that he was only seventeen when a trooper clubbed him during the march across the Alabama River in 1965.

This year, he was wearing the bright orange vest distributed to each participant in a follow-up march to Montgomery on March 21, 1965. That march, Rankin said, was under federal protection ordered by President Lyndon B. Johnson.

Later Rankin found a job at a Selma plant that manufactures door and trunk locks for Ford and GM. "It was organized by the International Union of Electrical Workers Local 793, and I served as president of the local for eight of the sixteen years I worked there," he said. "My wife worked there for twenty-seven years. Then, in 1999, they picked up and moved to Mexico. It was a heavy blow to Selma. We lost 406 jobs. For a while, I was scrambling just to feed the kids. I was collecting scrap metal, anything, just to survive. It was especially hard because my wife lost her job at the same time."

The lock company had moved to Selma from New Jersey, where it paid workers a wage of fourteen dollars an hour. In Selma, Rankin said, "they paid us $7.50 an hour, but now they are paying Mexican workers 85¢ an hour. This millionaire owner didn't care about us. All he cared about is profits. We need a law to protect us from that kind of greed just as much as we needed the Voting Rights Act."

Mississippi Circuit Judge Margaret McCray told the *World* she was elected as the direct result of the struggles in Selma as well as the struggles of the Mississippi Freedom Democratic Party. She was one of forty-two members of the Fannie Lou Hamer Sister Roundtable who came to Selma for the jubilee.

McCray had worked in Selma as a young lawyer in the late 1980s to help fight a racist political machine headed by the mayor of that time, Joe Smitherman, who used every trick to deny African Americans voting rights. Smitherman was mayor for thirty-three years, even as the town became majority Black.

"My life was tremendously enriched by standing shoulder-to-shoulder with people like Albert and Evelyn Turner, Rose and Hank Sanders, who put out the call for us to come in," McCray said. "Now Selma has a Black mayor, James Perkins, who was just re-elected to a second term."

Another veteran of Bloody Sunday was the Reverend J. H. Davis. Now eighty-six, he crossed the bridge last Sunday on an old buckboard pulled by a team of horses. He was an Alabama A&M student in 1944 when he joined a delegation that took petitions to President Harry Truman demanding protection of Black voters from Klan terror. Ultimately, Truman signed Executive Order 9981 ending segregation in the military. "We laid the foundation then for the civil rights movement," he said. "Bush is removing people from the voting rolls to neutralize the power of the Black vote. So many people were fooled that the Iraq war is a war of liberation. But we aren't even liberated here. The Black people aren't free; the Native American people aren't free."

He scorned Social Security privatization. "You privatize Social Security and its dead. It's gone!" he said. "Bush says Black people die too soon to collect Social Security. Without Social Security, we'd die off like flies from starvation.

Rev. Vivian Hails Bridge Jubilee Crowd
10,000 March in Selma 40 Years Later
By Tim Wheeler & Joyce Wheeler

March 11, 2005
SELMA, ALABAMA—Singing *Ain't going to let nobody turn me round,* 10,000 marchers crossed the Edmund Pettus Bridge here March 6 to protest Bush-Cheney voter suppression tactics and to demand renewal of the 1965 Voting Rights Act set to expire in 2007.

The multiracial throng, men and women, young and old, retraced the steps of voting rights marchers who were clubbed and tear-gassed by Alabama troopers on "Bloody Sunday," March 7, 1965. That brutal attack galvanized the nation to enact the Voting Rights Act a few months later.

Representative John Lewis (D-Ga.), then a Student Nonviolent Coordinating Committee (SNCC) organizer, was clubbed nearly to death that long-ago day. He led forty of his U.S. House and Senate colleagues at this 40th anniversary "Bridge Crossing Jubilee."

Lewis was engulfed by admiring youth. "It is good to see young people out here making some noise," he told the World as he marched. "A lot of people are too quiet. If you don't like the direction the country is going, you have the responsibility to stand up, to protest nonviolently."

Representative Kendrick Meek (D-Fla.), who led Florida's "count-every-vote" fightback after the 2000 elections, told the World the strategy now "is to get renewal of the Voting Rights Act early."

"We shouldn't wait," Meek said, warning that "the Bush administration has not given us any signal of support."

Senate Majority Leader Bill Frist (R-Tenn.) and other Republican lawmakers joined the march. "They are welcome to join us. But we have to be clear that their agenda is not our agenda," said Ron Daniels, president of the Center for Constitutional Rights, which has defended victims of Bush administration torture in Iraq, Afghanistan, and Guantanamo, Cuba.

"Our agenda is wider democracy," Daniels said. "The reactionary forces talk of 'democracy' and 'freedom' but they condone torture."

A big crowd gathered in front of Brown's Chapel AME Church for a pre-march rally. Coretta Scott King, widow of Dr. Martin Luther King Jr., reminded the crowd that only 216 African Americans held elective office in 1965. Today, 9,300 African Americans are in office. "It was the Voting Rights Act that produced this growth in our political empowerment," she said.

Yet thirty-one percent of African American males in Alabama are denied the right to vote, mostly due to disenfranchisement of former felons. "It is a form of taxation without representation and we need to mobilize to put an end to it," King declared. "This last election showed us once again all forms of devious tricks were used to keep us from voting."

An hour earlier, inside the historic chapel, headquarters of the civil rights movement in the 1960s, Frist sweated as the Reverend C.T. Vivian called on the people to march "all over again," because "our needs are not being met."

Vivian, a close aide to Dr. King during the Selma struggle, flayed Bush for dragging the nation into war. "It is not possible to achieve peace through war," Vivian said. "Just because you have more guns than all the rest of the world, they'll still hate you. I thought we had learned in Vietnam. That war destroyed the anti-poverty program and hurt the poor. The rich were not hurt."

Vivian received a standing ovation.

The Reverend Jesse Jackson echoed that message. "The fight for the right to vote continues," he said. He noted that the recent elections in Iraq used proportional representation, which protects minority voting rights. But in the U.S., he said, millions, disproportionately African American, are denied voting rights.

Meanwhile, Jackson said, "Alabama cannot meet its Medicaid matching formula . . . . Alabama sends thousands of inmates out of state at a cost of $46,000 each. But Alabama spends only $5,000 per pupil on education."

The Bush budget, he added, will slash funding for Pell Grants, Section 8 housing, and food stamps, all devastating cutbacks for working people and the poor.

Jackson called for the collection of 1 million petition signatures to extend the Voting Rights Act. He announced that thousands will march in Atlanta on August 6 to demand the right to vote.

Jackson led the crowd in a chant, "To win the right to vote, organize! End the war!"

Marching in the middle of the crowd were Lutheran pastors Robert and Jeannie Graetz of Dayton, Ohio. "We worked closely with Dr. King during the Montgomery Bus Boycott," the Reverend Bob Graetz said. "I was the only white preacher of a Black congregation in Montgomery. Three bombs were thrown at our house and two went off. If the third had exploded, I would not be here now. It was eleven sticks of dynamite tied to a can of TNT. We had four little children in our house at the time."

Asked to measure the changes since then, he chuckled. "We have a Black mayor of Selma, James Perkins. There have been some economic breakthroughs too. But I think the economic status of the African American community is worse now than in 1965."

His wife of fifty-four years broke in, "They are fighting this war in Iraq on the backs of the people. They want $80 billion more for the war.

My Day on Capitol Hill with Gladys Marin

The death of Chilean Communist Party leader Gladys Marin at age sixty-three brought back memories of a day in 1974 that I spent with her and her interpreter on Capitol Hill visiting the offices of senators and representatives.

It was one of the few times in my nearly forty years as a Washington correspondent that I crossed the line barring reporters from direct involvement in "lobbying" or "partisan politics." When the Young Workers' Liberation League asked me to make the arrangements for Gladys' visit, I asked myself, "How can I refuse, knowing what she has gone through?" So I did it and kept my fingers crossed that I wouldn't end up losing my congressional press credential.

It was very hard to arrange appointments on short notice. Most of the meetings were impromptu encounters in House and Senate corridors. Gladys and I cornered Senator Daniel Inouye (D-Hawaii) at the conclusion of a hearing in the Dirksen Senate Office Building. I told Inouye that Gladys was a "colleague" since she was a member of the Chilean Parliament until forced out by the 1973 fascist coup d'état led by General Augusto Pinochet.

That was enough. Inouye stopped in his tracks to listen. A combat war hero who lost an arm fighting Hitler during World War II, Inouye knew something about fascism. He sat down with her and listened to her recount the ordeal of her people, the murder by the fascists of thousands, with her husband, Jorge Muñoz, then among hundreds of "disappeared."

Inouye told Marin he was doing what he could, including arguing against increased U.S. military assistance to the Chilean dictatorship.

We walked across the hall to the office of Senator James Abourezk (D-S.D.). I was trying to maintain a low profile but Abourezk insisted that I join Gladys, the interpreter and him in his office. He looked me up and down. "I remember you. You're a reporter."

I replied, "Yes, but I'm off-duty." I promised him that if he wished, everything he said would be off-the-record.

A lively exchange followed, with Abourezk, one of only two or three Arab Americans in Congress, questioning Gladys closely about conditions in Chile. She explained that she was living in exile and traveling around the world to build a solidarity movement in hopes of restoring democracy in her country. Abourezk promised to do all he could to promote that cause in Congress.

On the other side of the Capitol, we walked into the office of Representative Bella Abzug (D-N.Y.). We nearly ran over "Battling Bella" in the reception area. Wearing her big floppy hat, she was on her way to the House floor. I pleaded with her to give Gladys a few minutes.

"I haven't got time, " she snapped. "Why didn't you call for an appointment?" She made a move toward the door. "Mrs. Abzug," I exclaimed, "Gladys Marin is your colleague, a duly elected member of the Chilean Parliament. You owe it to her to listen to her story."

To my amazement, Bella turned back. She led us into her office and sat down with a grumpy expression.

Softly, Gladys said, "After the coup in September of last year, I was forced to flee for my life. I am living in exile like many others from the Popular Unity government. We are working to build a movement of solidarity against the dictatorship. We need your help."

The moment Gladys began to speak, Bella fell silent, listening raptly. "Do you have a family?" she asked.

"Yes. My husband Jorge Muñoz is missing. I was forced to leave him and my two children behind. I don't know if my husband is alive."

Gladys went on to recount the terror unleashed upon the Chilean people, her voice trembling.

Tears welled in Bella's eyes. "You are a very brave young woman," she said.

Bella, too, vowed to speak out more forcefully against Washington's connivance with the fascist regime. As we parted, Bella threw her arms around Gladys in a warm embrace.

By the time that day was over, we had visited fifteen or more offices, meeting with lawmakers and their aides. Gladys was elated. She told me that we in the U.S. were underestimating what we could accomplish in exposing Pinochet and forcing an end to U.S. support of the regime.

Over the years, I followed Gladys's career—her return to Chile, her becoming the leader of the Communist Party of Chile. She filed the first lawsuit against Pinochet and his fellow butchers, seeking justice in the murder of her husband and ten other Communist leaders.

But the Gladys I remember is the beautiful woman I spent a day with on Capitol Hill, her dark eyes full of sorrow, her clenched jaw and firm mouth a portrait of grace under fire. She is Chile's "La Pasionaria." She is "Mother Courage.

Mandela Visits Washington D.C.

WASHINGTON—When Nelson Mandela delivered a speech to a joint session of Congress on June 26, 1990, I was one of a hundred or more reporters in the House Press Gallery. I had been assigned by *peoplesworld.org*'s predecessor, the *People's Daily World*, to cover the momentous event.

Mandela was greeted by a standing ovation. Members of the Congressional Black Caucus erupted in cheers to welcome this great freedom fighter.

Rarely is a non-head-of-state invited to speak to a joint session of Congress. In Mandela's case, it was especially improbable since he had just been released from twenty-seven years imprisonment on Robben Island. He was still being denounced by the ultra-right in Washington as a "terrorist" and a "Moscow-line Communist" who deserved to be in jail. I myself had written a full-page article to coincide with Mandela's visit, exposing the role of the CIA and other such circles in the nation's capital in helping keep Mandela in prison.

Mandela was escorted to the speaker's dais by a big delegation of senators and representatives. Standing head and shoulder above them, literally, was Representative Ron Dellums, D-Calif., who had toiled since 1972 to push through an anti-apartheid sanctions bill. In 1986, the Senate, then controlled by the Republicans, unexpectedly overrode Reagan's veto of the bill, which banned most trade with South Africa and cleared the way for billions of dollars in divestment from South Africa. It was crucial in bringing down the racist apartheid regime.

Mandela told the lawmakers that day in 1990, "We should take this opportunity to thank you all for the principled struggle you waged which resulted in the adoption of the historic Comprehensive Anti-Apartheid Act which made a decisive contribution to the process of moving our country forward towards negotiations."

Mandela added, "The stand you took established the understanding among the millions of our people that here we have friends, here we have fighters against racism who feel the hurt because we are hurt, who seek our success because they too seek the victory of democracy over tyranny."

He said he was speaking not only about the lawmakers, themselves, "but also of the millions of people throughout this great land who stood up and engaged the apartheid system in struggle, the masses who have given us such strength and joy by the manner in which they have received us since we arrived in this country."

That welcome included a ticker-tape parade in New York; a huge rally in Detroit where he was greeted by leaders of the United Auto Workers and by civil rights heroine Rosa Parks; a victory celebration in Oakland; a celebration in Los Angeles and similar outpourings in other cities across the nation.

"To deny people their human rights is to challenge their very humanity," Mandela said that day. "To impose on them a wretched life of hunger and deprivation is to dehumanize them. But such has been the fate of all black persons in our country under the system of apartheid . . . The injury is made that much more intolerable by the opulence of our white compatriots and the deliberate distortion of the economy to feed that opulence."

The democratic reconstruction of South Africa, he added, requires an economy that "can provide food, houses, education, health care, social security and everything that makes human life human that makes life joyful and not a protracted encounter with hopelessness and despair."

The U.S. senators and representatives put in office by transnational banks and corporations nodded as Mandela said the "private sector is an engine of growth and development." But then Mandela warned, "It should never be that the anger of the poor should be the finger of accusation pointed at all of us because we failed to respond to the cries of the people for food and shelter, for the dignity of the individual."

The struggle against apartheid had been building for years. There were sit-down protests and hundreds of arrests in front of the South African Embassy in Washington sponsored by Randall Robinson and the TransAfrica organization.

When Reagan vetoed the Dellum's anti-apartheid bill while spouting clichés about "constructive engagement," the anti-apartheid movement responded with angry streets demonstrations. April 25 through the April 27 of 1987, more than 100,000 protesters marched in Washington for peace and justice in Central America and in South Africa. On campuses across the nation, the demand for divestment grew so loud it could not be ignored. Many universities withdrew many billions of dollars in investments in South Africa. The labor movement also responded. The International Longshore and Warehouse Union refused to load cargo coming from or heading toward South Africa. I helped report on all these struggles.

Mandela's speech still rings true twenty-three years after he delivered it. Huge progress has been won in South Africa in overcoming racist apartheid. Yet the gap between rich and poor yawns wide. Mandela struck a responsive chord when he said working people in South Africa and working people of the U.S. are fighting the same battle against tyranny. The OUR Walmart protesters, the fast food workers across the nation demanding a $15 an hour minimum wage; those who march for immigration reform; those who march for voting rights threatened by Republican vote suppression tactics. They all march in the spirit of Nelson Mandela.

George A. Meyers: With A Song In His Heart

Whenever it was George A. Meyers' turn to speak at meetings of the Communist Party National Committee in New York City, the room fell silent and people sat up and listened.

That certainly included me. I listened to every word. When he spoke, you were hearing the voices of the grassroots. He also sang with a pure tenor voice. Sometimes at the end of a contentious meeting, someone would call out, "George, give us a song."

And with a chuckle he would stand and sing, "I'll Take You Home Again Kathleen."

That song reflected his Irish roots. His mother was Irish, his father, a union coal miner of German extraction. He loved both his parents but had a special love of his mother for her staunchness. She was the "fighting Irish" and George inherited his spirit of fightback from her.

George A. Meyers (left), my granddaughter and Fred Gaboury on our front porch in Baltimore—photo courtesy of Margaret Baldridge

He was a big, genial man and restless. He spent weeks at a time on the road. He kept his ear to the ground wherever he went.

A couple of years after his release from a four year Smith Act prison term, George was assigned by the Party as a kind of roving ambassador traveling throughout the South, Appalachia and the industrial Midwest and into the Rocky Mountain west where he visited Utah steelworker, Wayne Holley and his family, or down to Arizona where he communed with Lorenzo and Anita Torrez. Lorenzo was a legendary copper miner who won immortality by having a speaking role in the great film, *Salt of the Earth*.

George was a close personal friend of Florence Reece of Harlan, Kentucky, composer of *Which Side are You On*. He was also a close friend of Don West, the Mountaineer poet of Pipestem, West Virginia.

When he was visiting New York, he stayed with other dear friends, Art and Esther Shields. Art is now revered as the nation's greatest labor reporter who had reported live: the *Battle of Blair Mountain* and barely escaped with his life from fascist Spain during the last days of Madrid during the Spanish Civil War.

If George was in Ohio, he stayed with steelworker, George Edwards. Unlike George Meyers, George Edwards was a man of small stature. They were so close, that people referred to them as "Big George" and "Little George."

Everywhere George went, he met with local and state trade union leaders, civil rights and peace movement leaders, discussing with them every burning issue, whether it was racist job discrimination, the drive by the corporations to bust unions and shut down the factories, or the struggle against imperialist war. So when George spoke, he was reporting what he had learned by listening to people where they lived.

Sometime in the 1970s he and coalminer Anton Krchmarek, better known as Kerch, who served as the Ohio District CP Organizer, had met with leaders of Miners for Democracy in West Virginia. George and Kerch urged the miners to consider a one-day mine stoppage to protest President Nixon's schemes to gut the coal miner's Black Lung law. The miners listened with interest. After all, Kerch was a miner, and George was a former textile worker who suffered from Brown Lung disease. A few days after that meeting, the coal miners walked out on strike and kept the Virginia mines closed for a month. They too were listening when George spoke.

In 1973, when OPEC stopped delivery of crude oil to the U.S. and the nation was hit by an energy crisis, I was assigned to cover a meeting on the subject in Washington organized by the AFL-CIO Industrial Union Department.

The keynote speaker was Machinist Union President, William Winpisinger. "Wimpy" delivered a stemwinder against the energy hold-up. But unlike others who were aiming at OPEC and the oil-producing nations, Winpisinger directed his fire at Exxon, Mobil, Texaco, and other U.S. oil corporations who were using the crisis to jack gasoline and home heating oil prices to ruinous levels. Winpisinger branded them as thieves and called for their nationalization.

The next day the CPUSA National Committee was meeting in New York. I hustled up to the meeting with Winpisinger's speech in my briefcase. When it came time for my five minutes at the microphone, I read aloud a five-minute excerpt from Winpisinger's angry blast at the oil corporations and his call for nationalization. I got a very warm response from the crowd.

When I stepped back to my seat, there was George Meyers, beaming. He grasped my hand and thanked me. The Party was then in the midst of a struggle against those who said the U.S. labor movement were "labor aristocrats." George understood perfectly that Winpisinger's stemwinder was the best possible answer to this error.

I didn't know it at the time, but George was already meeting Winpisinger on a regular basis, developing a warm, trusting relationship with the President of the 900,000 member International Association of Machinists.

George adopted as his own, Wimpie's admonition that in the movement "we can disagree but we should never be disagreeable."

Years later, President Ronald Reagan smashed the Professional Air Traffic Controllers Organization (PATCO.) In the months that followed, George told Party meetings of the growing anger in the labor movement, the spreading calls for a nationwide general strike or some other mighty fightback against this ruthless unionbusting.

George and the Party were not just observers of that movement, they were helping organize it. One AFL-CIO Central Labor Council after another endorsed a giant solidarity action. The Teamsters, Machinists, Steelworkers, United Mine Workers and others endorsed the call. It culminated in a meeting in Buffalo where plans were set in motion for a huge march and rally.

AFL-CIO President, Lane Kirkland, fearful that he and the AFL-CIO Executive Council would be left in the dust, endorsed the idea. The result was Solidarity Day, September 19, 1981, with well over half a million workers marching on Pennsylvania Avenue in solidarity with PATCO and against unionbusting. George was overjoyed.

Years before anyone else detected it; George Meyers wrote a report *Fresh Winds* arguing that a profound mood of anger was blowing in the ranks of labor, a fightback attitude strongly embraced by many local, state and national leaders. (Actually, Fred Gaboury, a logger from Washington State who worked closely with George for many years, coined the phrase Fresh Winds. George seized on the phrase as expressing perfectly what was happening in the labor ranks.)

George was a bear in denouncing those who engaged in bashing labor leaders. He saw this as the crudest kind of leftwing opportunism, propagated by what he called the "Phony Left" who slandered union leaders.

George insisted that in every part of the country, in every industry, there were leaders, African American, Latino, and white, who were committed to class struggle trade unionism, struggling to rebuild the labor movement from the ground up, fighting the open class warfare waged by the corporate ultra-right.

He was a strong proponent of the movement to organize rank and file caucuses, Black caucuses, women caucuses, and other forms of grassroots democracy to instill fightback against the corporate ultra-right. Yet when the labor movement came alive, George argued that it was time to shift the emphasis away from the caucus movement and focus on mobilizing the unions as a whole. He had a keen sense of timing.

There is another crucial issue on which George was ahead of his time. He rejected "gay bashing." He influenced me deeply on this question on which the Party had been slow to change. He befriended Gay and Lesbian trade unionists and activities for equality and spoke out against those who attacked or belittled them.

In 1969, George and his wife, Allie, were moving to New York City. George had been assigned as Labor Secretary of the CPUSA. I was then Washington correspondent for the *Daily World*. Our daughter, Susan, had just been born. Joyce and I now had three children. Joyce's mother, Leatha Provost, had joined us. We needed a roomy house to accommodate three adults and three children.

George urged us to move into his house in Baltimore. We accepted the invitation and rented Meyer's commodious house for nearly five years, paying their eighty-nine dollar monthly mortgage. When the Meyers decided to move back to Baltimore, we found a house about three blocks away on the same street.

I commuted to Washington five days—and sometimes six days each week. Joyce got a teaching job in the Baltimore City Public Schools. We were active members of the Communist Party of Maryland, befriending wonderful comrades like Joe Henderson, an African American steelworker, Jake Green, a founding member of the National Maritime Union, Howie Silverberg, a steelworker, and Jim Baldridge, a shipyard worker (later a hospital worker active in Local 1199B,) his wife Margaret Baldridge, a school teacher, and many others.

One day in the mid-1970s, George knocked on our door. He asked me if I would come with him to a Labor Studies panel discussion at Federal City College in Washington D.C. "There might be a good story in it for you," he said.

George had been invited by David Selden, former President of the American Federation of Teachers, now teaching a labor studies course at Federal City College. Just a year or so earlier, Albert Shanker, a hardline Cold Warrior, had defeated Selden's bid for re-election as AFT President.

The topic for the panel discussion was: "What was the Secret of Success for the Congress of Industrial Organization?" How had the CIO been able to organize millions of workers in the mass production industries? How had the CIO won reforms like the National Labor Relations Act, the Fair Labor Standards Act? Social Security? Unemployment Compensation? The job-creating WPA and Civilian Conservation Corps?

George was to share the platform with Roy Hudson Wells, a former organizer for the United Electrical Radio and Machine Workers. Hudson Wells and his wife Ruth, residents of Garrett Park, Maryland, were George's close friends.

When we arrived at the meeting room, it was filled with students African American and white. In the course of discussion, Wells argued that the key to victory for the CIO was the unity of the left forces, those committed to socialism, and the center forces who believed that reform was the path to a fair, stable, secure living for all workers.

George nodded in agreement with Well's point and added some points of his own. He rejected the line that the left, by itself, could organize the mass production industries. The left, he said, simply lacked the strength to win that battle on its own. The left needed the center forces and in turn, the center forces needed the left. It had to be a unity based on mutual trust, he said.

The left understood that the labor movement must in the first place overcome racism. At that time George Meyers was the president of the Maryland-D.C. CIO. So in Baltimore, the CIO had focused on this issue, negotiating equal hiring and working conditions, fighting to end the employers' practice of assigning Black workers to the most dangerous, hazardous work places like the coke ovens at Bethlehem Steel's Sparrow's Point Mill.

The corporate owners understood perfectly that their hope for smashing the CIO lay in a "divide and conquer" strategy. Their chance came after WWII, he said. George quoted General Motors CEO, Charles Wilson, appointed Secretary of Defense by President Eisenhower. Wilson once told Congress, "What's good for General Motors is good for America." But he had another quote, George said, "The problems of the United States can be summed up in two words: Russia abroad, labor at home."

That was a declaration of war. The strategy of Wilson and the corporate masters was to unleash a vicious Cold War campaign aimed at driving Communists out of the labor movement. A nightmare followed of witch-hunt hearings by the House UnAmerican Activities Committee, the blacklisting of Communist Party members and sympathizers. The leaders of CPUSA were tried under the anti-communist Smith Act, McCarran Act, and Taft Hartley Act and thrown in jail for as long as eight years. George himself, served four years. His crime was serving as a staunch, selfless, union organizer.

Under the pressure of the onslaught, the center forces collapsed. The left-center coalition, the engine that drove CIO organizing, was smashed. Several left-led unions like UE and the Mine Mill and Smelter Workers Union were expelled from the CIO.

The rightwing in the labor movement, those who advocated collaboration with the corporations, were put in power, like George Meany who bragged that he had "never walked a picketline."

The working people have paid dearly for corporate America's victory in smashing the CIO's left-center coalition, George said.

Throughout this exchange, David Selden had comments of his own. But at the end he nodded, telling the crowd he agreed with George and Hudson's analysis.

George was elated by the meeting as we drove home to Baltimore. The ideas expressed were not new to George. He had decades of struggle to get these ideas down. But the meeting crystallized the ideas. And David Selden's agreement with the analysis was the clincher. George saw it as clear evidence that many center forces were rethinking what had happened to the labor movement during the Cold War. Many had concluded that buying into "Big Lie" anti-communism had been a deadly mistake.

Now, it was imperative to rebuild the left-center unity if they ever hoped to revive the energy and momentum of the CIO.

George Meyers's attitude toward the center forces was more than a tactical maneuver. It reflected his love of the people, his respect for them, his modesty, his readiness to learn from those with views different from his. He was a staunch advocate of grassroots democracy in the ranks of labor and everywhere else.

He even had a nuanced position on the role of the conservative wing in the labor movement. He made a clear distinction between those who were open agents of monopoly capitalism, like Meany and Shanker, and those who embraced conservative ideology. Conservatives could be won. They could be drawn into unity if the left-center coalition was reestablished. "We should not forget that they too are part of the labor movement," George said.

The point is, the movement is alive. It develops. In a dynamic situation, the center can move to the left and pull the conservative forces with them. He often told us that the labor movement's action program should be based on "the most advanced positions of the center forces."

I wrote the story up for the *Daily World*. George was pleased. He said I caught the essence of the discussion. (When I got ready to write this article, I couldn't find that article. So this story is written from my memory of that meeting.)

George loved to drive out to Lonaconing, Maryland. He often invited me to go with him, introducing me to his brothers and sisters, showing me the sights of that lovely little coalmining town on the banks of Georges Creek, the handsome white frame house on Main Street where he had grown up.

Once in a while we drove down the Potomac River toward Cumberland to the site of the Celanese Textile Mill where George had worked in the spinning department. The mill is closed down now, replaced by a prison. George breathed in so much dust working in that mill that he later developed Brown Lung disease that plagued him the rest of his life. He organized the workers in the Celanese mill into the largest union local in the nation, more than 10,000 workers strong, members of the Textile Workers Union of America. It was from that base that George was later elected President of the Maryland-D.C. CIO. He met with United Mine Worker President, John L. Lewis, to chart the CIO's drive to unionize the nation's workers. In 1939, he joined the Communist Party USA.

In the late 1990s, George decided to donate his expansive library. He looked around and decided that Frostburg State University, about six miles up the valley from Lonaconing, would be a good repository for his books and papers. He met and befriended Doctor David Gillespie, the director of the FSU Library.

Gillespie, himself the son of a West Virginia coal miner, suggested creating the George A. Meyers Collection at Frostburg State. It happened. Literally tens of thousands of books, pamphlets, and political memorabilia including lapel buttons, posters of the labor movement, peace, and equality movements and works of art, poured into the library. It was at that library, with the assistance of Gillespie, that I retrieved articles to write this book from their microfilm of the *Daily Worker/Worker/ People's Weekly World* archives.

Our home has photos of George displayed alongside images of my family. We are not alone. Over the years, I have traveled widely, staying at the homes of many comrades. I have lost count of the number of walls adorned with photos of George A. Meyers. He was a man full of love, with a song in his heart. He had an abiding faith that the working class will lead our nation's struggle for democracy and socialism.

Memorial Mass Honors George A. Meyers
People's Weekly World

November 13, 1999

LONACONING, Maryland—George A. Meyers, a native son of this little coal mining town, was remembered as a principled fighter for the rights of working people, the poor, and the oppressed during a memorial mass here November 1.

The sanctuary of St. Mary of the Annunciation Roman Catholic church was crowded with family, friends and co-workers for the service conducted by Father James Hannon. He pointed out that it was All Saints Day and that they had gathered to celebrate the lives of those in the congregation who died in the past year, including Bishop Francis Murphy, "and in a special way, the life of George Meyers."

Sister Marietta Culhane, pastoral life director of the church, told the congregation that she was privileged to know George Meyers. "He lived to the fullest extent of the Christian social principles that our church embraces," she said. "He cared about workers, the poor, and the oppressed. He cared about the rights of Black people. He marched to a different drummer. He was an outstanding Catholic man and we honor him."

As the congregation left the church, the organist commented that in her opinion "George got his commitment to social justice right here in this church." Generations of the Meyers family belonged to the church and George Meyers graduated in 1930 from LaSalle High School, a Roman Catholic school in nearby Cumberland. A few years later, he got a job in the Celanese textile factory, there, and organized the 10,000 workers into Textile Workers Local 1874. Later he was elected president of the Maryland-D.C. CIO. He joined the Communist Party USA in 1939 and at the time of his death, he was chair emeritus of the Party's Labor Commission. He died in Baltimore October 18, after a long illness.

Many in the congregation later gathered for a reception at the home of Mary and Catherine Meyers, sisters of George. Dr. David Gillespie, library director of Frostburg State University just up George's Creek from here, said the thousands of books, pamphlets, and other memorabilia in the library's George A. Meyers collection will stand as a permanent memorial.

F. DeSales Meyers said his brother George, eldest child in a large family, had been like a father to him after their father, a coal miner, died of Black Lung disease. Meyers cut such a broad swath in Allegany County, he said, that there was much talk of his running for Congress. "He knew and befriended people from a very wide political spectrum," he said.

He recalled a story about his brother: During a witch-hunt Senate hearing in the 1950s, a Maryland history professor was being grilled because Meyers had once slept overnight at his home. The charge was "harboring" a Communist. "Republican Senator J. Glenn Beall, who lived up in Frostburg and knew George well, told the hearing, 'George Meyers has slept in every house in western Maryland.' The subject was dropped."

At Meyers' request, his son Douglas and daughter Barbara, accompanied by Gillespie and his assistant, Francine Zembower, scattered Meyer's ashes from the summit of Dan's Mountain, which rises above Lonaconing.

Song of the Georges Creek Miners

We are the miners of Georges Creek
We dig steam coal for the merchant fleet.
We sweat and toil where the sun don't shine,
Our picks break coal in the Broken Heart Mine.
We hammer, drill, blast, and haul
Praying to God that the roof don't fall.
Sixteen tons we shovel per shift
When the sun drops low on the Dan Mountain rift.

We are the miners, united in grime,
We fought Rockefeller on our picketlines.
We starved and lost in '22,
Then rose again, the fight not through.
And we are the miners of Georges Creek,
Sixteen tons before we sleep.
From Lonaconing and Seldom Seen,
We dig together in the eight-foot seam.
So pray to God that our roofs don't fall
Injure one, injure all.

And when the hours of our shift have run
We give our nickels to the college fund
To build a college in Frostburg town,
Where strip operators would strip the ground.
Our sons and daughters soon will learn,
That our headlamps in the darkness burn.
They light the face as we dig the coal.
They light the truth that can free us all.
So listen Rockefeller to a miner's muse
We are many, you are few.

—By Tim Wheeler for George A. Meyers, son of a
Georges Creek miner, Friends of the George A. Meyers
Collection, Lewis J. Ort Library, Frostburg State
University, October 25, 1997.

Two Black Workers Who Made History

People's World

February 6, 2009

BALTIMORE—Helen Evans was turning the pages of an album of photos of her father, Joseph P. Henderson, when her eye fell on a picture of him as a Laborers union organizer in Washington, D.C., during the 1940s.

Joseph P. Henderson

Henderson had been a chauffeur for "Underwear King" P.H. Hanes in Winston-Salem, North Carolina, she told a visiting reporter. "Daddy kept asking him for a raise and Hanes refused," she said. "My father had a friend who got him a construction job in Washington, D.C. Daddy jumped at the opportunity."

When Hanes learned that he was losing the handsome driver of his Cadillac limousine, he was furious. "Hanes told him, 'What do you want? I'll pay anything,'" Helen said, laughing at the memory. "Daddy told him, 'It's too late. I've got another job.'"

So Henderson moved with his family to the nation's capital. He was smart and energetic and soon the Laborers union recruited him as an organizer. He was signing up so many of his fellow workers that he became a target for revenge. Returning home from a meeting one night, shots rang out, barely missing Henderson.

"They were trying to kill or intimidate my father. But they couldn't scare him. He just went right on organizing," Evans recalled.

Coming full circle

It wasn't all terrorism. The labor movement was surging at that time. The Congress of Industrial Organizations

(CIO) was organizing millions in the steel, auto and other basic industries. Labor gave crucial mass support for President Franklin Delano Roosevelt's New Deal and helped elect and reelect Roosevelt Henderson's talents were not overlooked by people in high places.

The phone rang one day and it was the White House inviting Henderson to come for a visit. "Eleanor Roosevelt was requesting his presence," Helen Evans said. "They told my father Mary McLeod Bethune was going to be at the White House that evening. They wanted him to come over."

Helen Evans smiled at that bright memory and its special meaning today. President Barack Obama had just invited labor leaders to come to the White House to see him sign several executive orders to "level the playing field" between labor and management. "Daddy must be smiling. We have come full circle," she said.

Organizing at Bethlehem Steel

By 1945, the CIO had signed Joe Henderson up as an organizer. They sent him to Baltimore where he got a job at ARMCO Steel and later at Bethlehem Steel's Sparrows Point mill. Henderson recruited 1,300 workers to the United Steelworkers of America, mostly African American workers segregated in the coke oven department of the giant mill.

Henderson was a determined and resourceful foe of Bethlehem Steel's racist job practices. During a memorial for Joe Henderson at USWA Local 2609 in Dundalk, May 5, 1996, steel union leader Bernard Parish spoke movingly of Henderson's leadership in that fight.

For many years, Parish told the crowd, his father, Charlie Parish, had struggled to win promotion to millwright at Sparrows Point. Repeatedly, the company rejected him. One excuse was that Charlie Parish lacked the skills and knowledge to become a millwright.

"Joe and a white worker, Bill Wood, taught my father how to read blueprints so he could pass the exam and become a millwright," Parish said. Charlie Parish would go to the Henderson home where the three steelworkers pored over blueprints until Parish could quickly decipher them. Parish went on to make history as the first Black millwright at Sparrows Point.

Both Henderson and Wood were members of the Communist Party of Maryland, an organization then waging a determined struggle to win job equality.

Of witch-hunts and black lists

Henderson, and his close friend George A. Meyers who had been president of the Maryland-D.C. CIO, were hauled before witch-hunt hearings and blacklisted from the steel and other basic industries during the 1950s. Meyers spent four years in federal prison under the infamous Smith Act. Bill Wood's brother, Roy Wood, also went to prison on the same trumped up charges.

Blacklisted, Joe Henderson and George Meyers became partners in installing awnings on houses in and around Maryland. For as long as they lived, both were deeply engaged in the struggles of organized labor, against racism and for world peace. Both continued as leaders of the Communist Party USA until they died.

The witch-hunt had nothing to do with "violent overthrow of the government." It had everything to do with corporate America's vicious drive to decapitate organized labor. Helen scoffed at the Cold War caricature of her father. "If a family in Turner Station was about to be evicted, Daddy would go over and pay their rent," she said. "If they were hungry, he would buy food for them," she said. "He was not a violent man. He was full of love for people."

Ben Careathers, Unsung Hero of Steel

Ben Careathers (pronounced CaRUHthers) was another "unsung hero" of steel labor, also an African American and like Joe Henderson a lifelong member of the

A widely distributed pamphlet exposing the unionbuster's drive to jail Ben Careathers and smash the United Steelworkers

Communist Party USA. Careathers moved to Pittsburgh from his birthplace near Chattanooga, Tennessee in the 1920s. In 1937, he got a job as a laborer at the Jones & Laughlin steel mill in Pittsburgh. He joined the Communist Party, impressed with their consistent fight against racism and their stand in support of industrial unionism in which all workers in a given industry belong to the same union.

Battle of Little Steel

This was the period of the battle to unionize J & L, Republic Steel, Youngstown Sheet & Tube, and other steel companies misleadingly called "Little Steel." United States Steel had agreed to sign a contract with Steel Workers Organizing Committee. But Republic Steel boss, Tom Girdler, had announced that his mills would be unionized over his dead body. On Memorial Day 1937, Chicago police opened fire on striking Republic Steel workers at a peaceful picnic. Ten people were killed in this massacre.

This was the atmosphere when Philip Murray, chairman of the Steel Workers Organizing Committee, recruited Careathers to organize Jones & Laughlin steelworkers in Aliquippa, Pennsylvania. The town was patrolled night and day by Andrew Mellon's private army of gun thugs. SWOC organizers had been arrested, beaten, and driven out of town.

Art Shields, the great labor reporter, tells Careathers' story in his autobiography, *On the Battle Lines*. Said Careathers, "I didn't register at a hotel like the organizers before me. I dressed like a steelworker and went in while the plant was changing shifts and the streets were crowded. I boarded with a Black family that knew me. I met with small groups of workers quietly. And I soon had a high stack of signed membership application cards."

Careathers took the union cards, hundreds signed by African American workers, to CIO headquarters.

"I gave them to Clinton Golden, the regional director," Careathers said. "He rushed into Murray's office. I can still hear him yelling: 'Look at what I've got Phil!'" Careathers had signed up more than 2,000 J&L workers into SWOC, later renamed United Steelworkers of America. It was part of the immense struggle that ended with complete victory for the USWA.

Frame up

But again, corporate America struck back. Careathers tells the story in his own words in a powerful pamphlet, *The Frame-up of Benjamin Lowells Careathers*. It consists of his opening statement at his Smith Act trial May 18, 1953. Again, the phony charges were that he and his fellow defendant, Steve Nelson, a veteran of the Abraham Lincoln Brigade who was wounded while fighting fascism in Spain, were conspiring to teach and advocate the violent overthrow of the government by force and violence. A higher court threw out the charges against Careathers but Nelson spent over two years in prison.

"This charge we deny," Careathers told the jury. "Force and violence is a weapon of reaction, of fascism....The Southern plantation owners use force and violence against the Negro people to keep them and their political machines in power. Communists advocate the bringing about of social change by peaceful means."

Communists on SWOC staff in 1936 and 1937 gave "everything that we had to organize the powerful United Steelworkers of America," Careathers continued. The real conspiracy, he charged, was the drive by the witch-hunters to smash the USWA using anti-communism as a cover.

Careathers conviction was later overturned by the higher courts. But he and other Communist union organizers were driven from the labor movement and some were jailed. The labor movement went into a long downward slide. Only in recent years has it made a dramatic comeback although still it has far, far, to go.

In this new, hopeful atmosphere, Black workers like Joe Henderson and Ben Careathers can be honored during African American history month for the major contribution they made to the freedom struggles of Black people and in truth, all people.

Harold Wade Jr.   Benjamin J. Davis Jr.

Remembering Harold Wade Jr. and Benjamin J. Davis Jr.
People's World

June 4, 2018

SEQUIM, Wash.—I regret that I did not meet Harold Wade Jr., who entered Amherst College as a freshman in 1964, the same year I graduated from that institution. He was one of a handful of African Americans admitted to Amherst, then an all-male liberal arts college. Wade died tragically in a drowning accident in the Bahamas in 1974. Two years later, through the determination of his mother, Thelma Wade, Amherst College Press published a book, *Black Men of Amherst,* which Harold Wade Jr. wrote before he died.

I am grateful to Kathleen Whittemore who wrote a cover story for the Winter-Spring 2018 edition of *Amherst,* dedicated to Harold Wade Jr. Her story, headlined "His Black History: The Unfinished Story of Harold Wade Jr. '68," brings my classmate alive for me. Harold Wade graduated with honors from Amherst and went on to Harvard Law School. After he graduated, Wade moved back to New York City, where he got a job as an assistant to Deputy Mayor Paul Gibson.

But Whittemore is silent on one point: Did Wade make mention of Benjamin J. Davis Jr., who graduated from Amherst in 1925? I devoted a chapter in my book, *News From Rain Shadow Country* to Davis's visit to his alma mater at the invitation of Prof. Tom Yost. I heard Davis speak and went to Yost's home afterward, where I met and spoke at length with Davis about his eventful life as an African-American Communist.

Finally, I found a copy of Wade's book online for $12.64. It arrived, a hardcopy in perfect condition. It is stamped "Withdrawn" from the University of the Pacific library in Stockton, California.

When I opened the slim book, I found many pages devoted to Benjamin J. Davis, Jr. Wade recounts in detail Davis' services as an Atlanta attorney for Angelo Herndon, a Black youth, framed on "insurrection" charges for daring to organize a multiracial march of the unemployed in 1932. Convicted by an all-white jury, Herndon faced the death penalty. Ben Davis vowed to appeal the case to the U.S. Supreme Court.

Wade writes, "After the Herndon trial, liberal blacks and whites formed a coalition to defend Angelo Herndon— in much the same way as similar groups rally to 'Free Huey' or 'Free Angela.'" The Supreme Court threw out Herndon's conviction in a 5-4 decision. In the middle of the legal fight, Wade reports, Davis joined the Communist Party USA.

Wade quotes a 1947 article by Ben Davis entitled "Why I am a Communist." He also quotes Angela Davis' interview in *Ebony* magazine on why she too joined the Communist Party. Racist oppression is central to the system of capitalist exploitation, both argue. The Communist Party USA has played a spearhead role in the struggle against racism and for the unity of African-American and white people throughout its history. "Black, Brown, and White Unite. Same Class, Same Fight," has long been one of the party's main slogans. And like the CPUSA, Ben and Angela Davis, though not related, both argue that socialism is central to winning full equality.

Ben Davis moved to New York where he became a *Daily Worker* reporter assigned to Harlem. In 1941, Adam Clayton Powell, then a member of the New York City Council, announced he would not seek re-election because he was running for a seat in the U.S. Congress. Ben Davis announced he was a candidate to fill the City Council vacancy. Wade reports that Davis won under New York's progressive system of "proportional representation."

Writes Wade, "Benjamin Davis has the distinction of being the highest elected avowed Communist in the history of the United States...and in 1943 he was the only elected black in New York City government. Throughout the 1940s, he and Powell were the most dynamic politicians in black politics in America."

Ben Davis, Wade adds, "was so popular that in 1945 he ran virtually unopposed." Together with fellow Communist Pete Cacchione of Brooklyn, Davis "became responsible for the passage of rent control regulations in New York City."

Cold War witch-hunters targeted Ben Davis and other top leaders of the Communist Party, Wade continues.

"The Red Baiting Era of Joe McCarthy had begun.... Judge Medina sentenced Davis to five years and a $10,000 fine. Davis became the first person expelled from the New York City Council.... While serving time in the Federal Penitentiary at Terre Haute, Indiana, Davis filed a case to desegregate federal prisons."

After his release from prison in 1955, Davis returned to the *Daily Worker*. In 1959, he was elected National Secretary of the CPUSA.

"In 1960 Davis visited Amherst at the invitation of undergraduates to speak about the Communist Party and related topics," writes Wade. "Observers report that Davis recalled fond memories of his student days at Amherst, despite the fact that, as an outstanding violinist, he was denied admission to the orchestra."

Wade writes that "Ben Davis's autobiographical notes were released from prison one year after his death and ten years after his release from prison. Since they were not published until 1969, his story is just being re-told." Wade is referring to *Communist Councilman From Harlem* published by International Publishers in 1969.

Wade reports that Amherst became a college of the wealthy elite in the 1890s. During those years, he adds, an estimated 1,700 Negroes were lynched in America. "This period of capital accumulation was precisely the period in which blacks were being deprived of all their rights," he writes.

He dwells on one of the most dramatic incidents in African-American history: Dr. W.E.B. DuBois' debate with Booker T. Washington in which DuBois debunked Washington's line that African Americans should strive only to be skilled tradesmen, not seek higher education at places like Harvard.

Harold Wade Jr. makes no secret which side he is on: Dr. DuBois all the way. Wade's book helped push open the doors of places like Amherst for African-American applicants. And women too, since during these same years, Amherst decided to become a co-educational school.

Whittemore reports that Frost Library may republish *Black Men of Amherst*. I hope so. The book reads as fresh, clear, and strongly argued as the day Harold Wade Jr. wrote it.

Benjamin Davis, Jr.'s 1969 autobiographical book, "Communist Councilman from Harlem," is available from International Publishers.

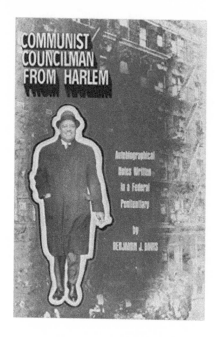

Epilogue

People's World Nov. 13, 2018

Give Thanks to Grassroots and Their Candidates for Winning "Blue Wave" Election
By Tim Wheeler

SEQUIM—On Thanksgiving, give thanks to the grassroots movements and all their candidates who barnstormed across the nation, rallied the voters to oust rightwing Republicans and stop Donald Trump.

Some grouchy pundits, Trump "yes men," deny there was a "Blue Wave." As my dad used to say, "There are none so blind as those who will not see."

A medal should be struck for "Combat Valor" and pinned on the tunics of all these brave women and men who led this "Blue Wave", who won this battle. The battle, not the war. The war continues without let up. Two days after the election, thousands of demonstrators in 1,000 cities and towns protested Trumps moves to sabotage or even shut down the Mueller investigation of his Administration's criminality.

This is a grassroots movement that will not be fooled by Trump lies, nor intimidated by his threats even when domestic terrorists acted on his hatemongering.

In the days before the vote, a Trump fanatic mailed out pipe bombs to anti-Trump leaders. Another neo-Nazi invaded the Tree of Life Synagogue in Pittsburgh and murdered 11 Jewish worshippers. The families of the slain were so enraged they told the White House Trump is not welcome at the funerals.

Instead of retreating, the "Blue Wave" redoubled, grew larger, fired by alarm that Trump has placed our nation in grave danger.

Striking in this upsurge is the boldness of the candidates and the grassroots movement in campaigning deep in "Red" states. Rep. Beto O'Rourke of El Paso, barn-stormed in every city and village in the Lone Star state, seeking to oust the scowling Republican Ted Cruz from the U.S. Senate. He came within 3 percentage points and helped the Democrats pick up more than a dozen seats in the Texas legislature and two seats in the U.S. Congress.

An estimated 113 million voted Nov. 6 despite Republican dirty tricks like closing that polling place in Dodge, Kansas, where 13,000 people vote.

None of the vote suppression tactics stopped the "Blue Wave," not even in Georgia where Stacey Abrams, is seeking election as the first African American woman governor of Georgia. At this writing, she has not conceded.

Her opponent is Republican Brian Kemp who also happens to be Georgia Secretary of State, overseeing his own theft of the governor's mansion.

So many Democratic candidates won that they flipped the House from majority Republican to majority Democrat by at least 31 seats. Ballots are still being counted and some elections were so close they are headed for a recount. Andrew Gillum, seeking election as Florida's first African American governor, just retracted his concession to Republican, Ron DeSantis, because DeSantis' lead is less than half a percent, triggering an automatic recount.. The Blue Wave also flipped five governorships from Red to Blue even in bright red Kansas where Democrat Laura Kelly is now governor elect.

Pollster, Peter Hart, told NBC's Chuck Todd, that the most dramatic Democratic gain is their victories in "Rustbelt" states, Pennsylvania, Michigan, and Wisconsin. Democrat, Tony Evers, Wisconsin Superintendent of Public Education, ousted union buster, Republican Gov. Scott Walker. Democrats also picked up the governorship of Michigan, Gretchen Whitmer. Pennsylvamia Gov. Tom Wolf, a Democrat, was reelected. Illinois Democrats also regained the State House with election of J.B. Pritzker.

The midterms made history: the first two Native American women in history elected to the U.S. House, Sharice Davids of Kansas, a member of the Ho Chunk Nation of Wisconsin, and Deb Haaland of New Mexico, a member of the Laguna Pueblo Tribe., the first two Native American Indian women elected to the House of Representatives. This election sends two Muslim women to Congress, Rashida Tlaib in Michigan and Ilhan Omar of Minnesota, who is also the first Somalia-American elected to Congress.

Alexandria Ocasio Cortez, running in the Bronx, NY, is the youngest women ever elected to the House. She is a member of Democratic Socialists of America.

Black women also made history. In Illinois, Lauren Underwood, defeated her Republican opponent in a district that is predominantly white and solidly Republican. Underwood is the first Black woman elected to the House from Illinois. Ayanna Presley of Massachusetts is the first Black woman elected to Congress from her state. Jahana Hayes a National Teacher of the Year, is the first African American woman elected to Congress from Connecticut. Lucy McBath, a gun control advocate whose son was murdered in 2012, flipped a seat in Georgia's 6th CD held by Republicans for four decades. All are Democrats. More than 20 African American women will be sworn in to the U.S. House of Representatives in January.

The victories also included progressive ballot measures. In Florida, a stunning 64 percent of voters approved Amendment 4 which restores voting rights for ex-felons who number 1.2 million in the Sunshine State. Disproportionately Black and working class, they are expected to swell the Democratic vote.

I stood on a street corner a few weeks ago holding a sign that proclaimed, "Vote YES on I-1639." It is a ballot measure to raise to 21 the age for purchasing semi-automatic firearms. The driver of a pickup leaned out of his cab, shook his fist and shouted, "You STUPID son of a b----!!!"

Yet I-1639 was approved in a landslide along with I-940 aimed at reducing the police shooting of unarmed Black, Latino and Native American Indian people. I just now checked the Clallam County Auditor's web-site. A solid majority of Clallam County voters voted "YES" for I-1639 and yes on I-940. I said to myself: "Don't write off rural voters!"

I-1639 and I-940 are two steps to end gun violence, not enough to save the people who died in the massacre in the Tree of Life Synagogue or in Thousands Oaks, CA.

Building a base for anti-Trump candidates in rural regions long dominated by the Republican right is a major challenge. I look at those maps showing islands of blue, the major cities and urban centers surrounded by a sea of Republican red. Just think of Montana farmer, Jon Tester, a Democrat who won reelection to the U.S. Senate despite all those Trump rallies. We need more "Farmer Jons" to represent rural America.

About the Author

Tim Wheeler has been a news reporter since 1966 working for the *Worker*, *Daily World*, *People's Daily World*, and now the online *People's World*. He served as Washington Bureau Chief of the *Daily World* and its successors for twenty-five years and as Editor of the paper in New York City for eleven years. He joined the Communist Party USA in 1959 and is active in the Party today. Most of those years he, and his wife, Joyce, and their three children, lived in Baltimore, Maryland. He and Joyce now live on the family farm in Sequim, Washington, where he grew up. He is politically active in all the progressive causes he can find time for. He still writes for the *People's World*.

Tim and Joyce Wheeler at Dungeness Spit photo courtesy of John Streater

CPSIA information can be obtained
at www.ICGtesting.com
Printed in the USA
FFHW021440131019
55527837-61350FF

9 780717 807550